George Braun

PUBLISHER'S NOTES

This book is a Reprint

Disclaimer

This publication is intended to provide helpful and informative material. The author and publisher specifically disclaim all responsibility for any liability, loss or risk, personal or otherwise, which is incurred as a consequence, directly or indirectly, from the use or application of any contents of this book.

Any and all product names referenced within this book are the trademarks of their respective owners. None of these owners have sponsored, authorized, endorsed, or approved this book.

Always read all information provided by the manufacturers' product labels before using their products. The author and publisher are not responsible for claims made by manufacturers.

Paperback Edition
Speedy Publishing, LLC
40 E. Main Street, #1156
Newark, DE 19711
This book is a reprint.

DEDICATION

This book is dedicated to all those how wants to learn the secret recipes of the world's best beer and to brew these gifts from the gods in the comfort of home. You Adventuous beer makers will be rewarded for your efforts by having the experience of tasting some of the world's unique, delicious beer available to only an elite few...of course, you can share the experience with special friends!

(If you are a beginner beer brewer, I recommend that you grab a copy of Charlie Papazian's The Complete Joy of Home Brewing; he is my "go to guy" for basic instructions) .

P.S. If you would like to have ALL of my secret recipe collection, go ahead and pick-up my other book:

189 Best Beer Brewing Recipes:
Brewing the World's Best Beer at Home
Book 2

Chapter 1- Wheat Beer

#8 Weizen II

Category Wheat Beer
Recipe Type Extract

Fermentables
5 lb Wheat Dry Malt Extract (from GFSR)
1 lb Bulk Pale Dry Malt Extract

Hops
. 25 oz Hallertau - Northern Brewer Plug Hops (leaf) 7. 5 %AA (30 minutes)
. 75 oz Hallertau - Northern Brewer Plug Hops (leaf) 7. 5 %AA (60 minutes)
. 125 oz Saaz Leaf Hops 2.9%AA (15 minutes)
. 125 oz Saaz Leaf Hops 2.9%AA (finish)

Yeast Wyeast 3056 Bavarian Wheat

100% Wheat

Category Wheat Beer
Recipe Type Extract

Fermentables
1 lb honey (completely optional)
1 ea 6lb can of Irek's Unhopped (orange print on labels)
1 lb Crystal barley Malt 20 Low (for steeping until boil)
1 lb Wheat malt (also for steeping)

Hops
1. 5 oz Hallertauer Hops - I'm not a big hop fan, and this comes

George Braun
Yeast Wyeast Bavarian wheat or German wheat yeast

Procedure For one, I also added 5. 5 # frozen raspberries, though that started out almost like raspberry soda, it mellowed well, though a bit tart. I also use honey for priming instead of afterburner corn sugar. Steep the grains in a couple gallons of water over high temp. Strain out just before it starts to boil. Add the Ireks and boil hops (and honey) boil for an hour, add finishing hops last <10 minutes. I also use the Wyeast Barvarian Wheat (don't recall the #). It adds the clove/banana flavor, but not too much, since it's a mix of 2 strains. There's a couple other Wyeast wheat strains, that vary in strength of clove/banana flavor, the German (#3333) leaning away from the clove and banana. With the above recipe, and using the Barvarian Wheat, my first batch was compared favorably by a friend to Spaten Hefeweisen, though I was a bit more critical of it ;). Also, if you use the Wyeast, make a starter.

American Wheat

Category Wheat Beer
Recipe Type All Grain

Fermentables
8 lbs pale 6-row
3 lbs wheat

Hops
1 oz Northern. Brewer (1 hour)
. 5 oz Hallertauer (1 hour)
. 5 oz Hallertauer (10 minutes)

Yeast Nottingham Dry Ale Yeast.

Australian RedBack

Category Wheat Beer
Recipe Type All Grain

7.75 lbs, mix of 66% malted wheat extract and 33% barley
1 lbs crystal malt (steeped, removed before boil)
1 lbs amber unhopped dry malt extract

Hops
1. 5 oz Kent Goldings hops (5.6% alpha) (60 minute
. 5 oz Kent Goldings (10 minute boil)
. 5 oz Kent Goldings (5 minute boil)
. 5 oz Kent Goldings (in strainer, pour the wort through)

Other
. 5 oz Irish moss (15 minute boil)
. 75 oz Burton water salts

Yeast 2 packs Doric ale yeast (started 2 hours prior to brew)

Procedure My primary ferment started in 1 hour and was surprisingly vigorous for 36 hours. It finished in 48 hours. It has been fermenting slowly for 5 days and now has stopped blowing CO2 through the airlock at any noticeable rate (less than 1 bubble every 3--4 minutes) I took a hydrometer reading last night and it read 1.018. This seems high for a F.G. in comparison to my other beers of the same approximate S.G.
The last 1/2 ounce of hops was put in a strainer in a funnel and wort strained through it on its way to the carboy, as described in Papazian. A blow-off tube was used.

Alcatraz Wheat Beer

Category Wheat Beer
Recipe Type Extract

George Braun

Fermentables

3 lbs dried wheat extract
2 lbs Wheat malt
1 lbs Barley malt
1 lbs dried malt extract

Hops

2. 5 oz Mt. Hood hops

Yeast Wyeast Wheat beer yeast

Procedure one finds *in The Complete Joy of Home Brewing by Charlie Papazian* for an extract brew by adding the Irish Moss in the last 10 minutes of boil.

Al's Amber Wheat Beer

Category Wheat Beer
Recipe Type Extract

Fermentables

2.0 lb bag of Unhopped Wheat Dry malt
1 Ea 3.3lb Can Mutton and Fisson Light Unhopped Extract

Hops

0.25 oz. Cascade Leaf Hops (Flavor)
1.0 oz. Cascade Leaf Hops (Boil)
0.25 oz. Cascade Leaf Hops (Aroma)

Other

1 tsp. Irish moss

Yeast 2 Packages Mutton and Fisson Ale Yeast

Procedure Remove 1 1/4 cup of wheat malt and save in zip-lock bag for priming.

Bring 1. 5 Gallons water and Malts to a boil. When boil starts to fully set your stove timer (watch, hourglass, whatever) for 45 mins. For leaf hops I don't use a hop bag, you can if it makes you feel good.

45 Mins: Add Boil Hops - 1.0 oz.
15 Mins: Add Irish moss - 1 tsp.
10 Mins: Add Flavor Hops- .25 oz.
2 Mins: Add Aroma Hops- .25 oz.
0 Mins: Pour through strainer and funnel (with strainer) directly into o carboy with 2+ gallons of cold water as quickly as possible. Fill to top with cold tap water. Swirl carboy to mix hot and cold evenly. Pitch yeast.

Bavarian Weiss

Category Wheat Beer
Recipe Type Extract

Fermentables
2 ea 3.3 pound cans, M&F wheat malt extract
. 75 cup dry malt extract for bottling (turned out to be too

Hops
1. 5 oz Hallertauer hops (boiling)
. 5 oz Hallertauer hops (Finishing)

Other
. 25 tsp Irish moss

Yeast Wyeast Bavarian wheat liquid yeast

Procedure one finds in The Complete Joy of Home Brewing by Charlie Papazian for an extract brew by adding the Irish Moss in the last 10 minutes of boil.

Berliner Weisse

George Braun
Category Wheat Beer
Recipe Type All Grain

Fermentables
5 lbs pale malt
1 lbs Munich malt
1 lbs barley flakes
2 lbs wheat malt

Hops
1 oz Hallertauer hops (boil)

Yeast

Procedure This was a beer soured a la Papazian, except that I added some acidophilus capsules to the souring mash. I believe that most of the souring was due to the bacteria in the capsules. Submitted by: Aaron Birenboim,

Blackberry Wheat

Category Wheat Beer
Recipe Type Extract

Fermentables
6.6 lbs Irks Wheat extract
. 5 lbs Amber Dry Malt Extract
2 cups Carapils
3. 5 quarts FROZEN blackberries added to help cool wort
1 cup corn sugar for priming

Hops
1. 5 oz Hallatter hops (bittering)
. 5 Saaz hops (finishing)

Other
1 tsp Irish moss

Yeast Wyeast #3056 and 1 quart starter

Procedure Put cracked Carapils in cold water and leave in until just before boil. Add Wheat extract and DME and boil. Added Bittering hops, boil 25min. Add Irish moss, boil 30min. Add finish hops, boil 2 min, Remove from heat. Put pot in a sink of cool/cold water and add Blackberries. As they thaw crush berries with your spoon. Remove hop bag (a lot easier than straining them out). Put everything in 6 1/2 gal bucket or carboy fill to 6 gal mark with water and pitch yeast.
Start at 70 degrees F, after ferm starts to move to 60 F, xfer to 2ndary after 5-7 days. Leave in secondary 7-14 days (I go 14) you may want to use gelatin or polyclar to help settle things out (5-7 days before bottling). Bottle with 1 cup corn sugar. Wait 2 weeks and enjoy so good homebrew.

Blow Me Away Holiday Ale

Category Wheat Beer
Recipe Type Extract

Fermentables
6 lbs William's Weizenmalt syrup
2 lbs dark DME
2-3/4 lbs buckwheat honey
1 lbs crushed crystal malt
. 25 lbs crushed chocolate malt
2/3 cup corn sugar (priming)

Hops
2. 5 oz Cascade hops (boil)
1. 5 oz Hallertauer hops 3.6 alpha (boil)
. 75 oz Hallertauer hops (finish)

George Braun

Other

4 tsp whole allspice
1 tsp Irish moss

Yeast yeast

Procedure Steep grains in 2 gallons water while heating to boil. Remove grains. Add extracts and honey. Boil 1 hour with boiling hops, add 1 teaspoon Irish moss at 30 minutes. Simmer allspice in water for 3 minutes, remove allspice and add water to primary. After fermenting, prime with corn sugar and bottle.

Casual Dunkelweizen

Category Wheat Beer
Recipe Type Extract

Fermentables

3.3 lbs Northwestern Weizen extract
3.3 lbs Northwestern amber extract
. 5 lbs crystal malt (crushed)
. 5 cup black patent malt (lightly crushed)

Hops

2 oz Mt. Hood hops (8.6 AAU)

Other

1 tsp gypsum
. 5 tsp Irish moss

Yeast Wyeast Bavarian Wheat liquid yeast

Procedure The black patent was *VERY* lightly crushed because I just wanted a light brown beer---not a black beer. The grains were steeped to just before boil and strained out. Add extract and all of the hops. Boil 60 minutes. Add to cold water in fermenter and pitch yeast.

Cherry Wheat

Category Wheat Beer
Recipe Type Extract

Fermentables
1 ea 3.3-lb can of light malt extract syrup
3 ea 1-lb cans of wheat malt extract syrup
. 5 lb crushed crystal malt

Hops
2 oz Hallertauer hop pellets (boiling

Other
8 lbs. Crushed sour cherries

Yeast Wyeast weizenbeer yeast

Procedure Bring three gallons of water to 160-deg F. Steep the crushed crystal malt for 45 min. Strain out. Bring to boil. Add the malt extract syrups and boiling hops. Boil 1 hour. Remove from heat. Add the crushed cherries to the hot wort and steep for 10 minutes. Pour the lot (cherries and all) into a primary fermenter and cool to yeast pitching temperatures. Add the yeast culture and ferment 5-7 days in primary. Siphon the beer off the cherries into the secondary fermenter and let go another seven days or until fermentation is complete. Bottle with 3/4 cup of corn sugar.

Corrales Blanco

Category Wheat Beer
Recipe Type All Grain

George Braun

Fermentables

5 lb Belgian Pils malt
4 lb red winter wheat berries
1 lb steel cut oats

Hops

1 oz Saaz hops (60 min)
0. 5 oz Hallertauer Hersbrucker hops (45 min)

Other

1 oz coriander (steep)
10 ml 88% Lactic Acid at bottling
1 cup Curacao liquor at bottling

Yeast, Yeast Labs Belgian White yeast

Procedure Add 2. 5 gal 130F water to grains.
Mash malts 30 min @ 122F.
Add 1 gal boiling water to grains.
Mash 30 min @ 140F.
Add 1 gal boiling water to grains.
Heat and mash at 158F to conversion.
Mashout at 175F for 5 minutes.
Sparge at 170F.
Boil for 90 min.
Cool and pitch yeast.

Day After 1040A Wheat

Category Wheat Beer
Recipe Type Extract

Fermentables

1 lbs malted wheat
4 lbs Weizen extract
2 lbs pale malt extract

Hops
1 oz Mt. Hood hops (boil)
1 oz Hallertauer hops (finish)

Yeast Wyeast Bavarian wheat yeast

Procedure Put 2. 5 gallons of cold, filtered water into pot. Added malted wheat (in muslin bag) to pot and brought the water to 180 degrees. Steeped the wheat for 30 minutes. Removed bag of wheat and brought the water to boil. Added malts and boiling hops to pot and let boil for 60 minutes. Turned off the heat and added finishing hops. Force cooled the wort in an ice bath and put into primary fermenter. Added cold water to fermenter to bring the water level to 5 gallon mark. Pitched yeast.

Dog Gone Bad Cherry Wheat Ale

Category Wheat Beer
Recipe Type Extract

Fermentables
3 kg Ireks Weizenbier extract (hopped)
. 5 lbs. Ireks wheat malt (grain)
. 5 lbs. Munich malt (grain)
5 lb cherries (I think I used Bing)
2 oz. Ocean Spray Cranberry Juice Cocktail
. 75 cup corn sugar for bottling

Hops
1 oz. Hallertau - alpha 2.4%
1 oz. Cascade - alpha 4.9%

Yeast 1 pkg #3056 Wyeast Bavarian Wheat yeast

Procedure Crack grains, bring to boil, remove @ boil
Add extract

George Braun
@ 30 min. add 1/2 oz. Cascade
@ 58 minutes, add 1/2 Cascade + 1 oz. Hallertau
@ 60 minutes, remove hops and turn off heat
add cranberry and crushed cherries (I removed pits)
steep for 20 minutes - temperature @ 170 degrees
pour all of wort (including cherries) into 5 gal. fermentation bucket along with cold H20 to fill Note: don't use carboy - cherries will clog blow-off! add yeast when temperature goes below 80 degrees
I let the primary go, left the cherries in for 1 week, and then racked off to carboy.

Drew's Brew Wheat

Category Wheat Beer
Recipe Type Extract

Fermentables
2 ea 4 lb cans Alexanders 60% wheat 40% barley unhopped extract
1 lb 80L crystal malt, crushed

Hops
2 oz 5.3 alpha Styrian Golding hop plugs
2 oz 6.1 alpha Cascade whole hops

Yeast Wyeast #3056 Bavarian Weissen yeast

Procedure 3 days before brewing, pop the Wyeast package. 2 days before brewing, pitch Wyeast package contents into a starter made from 2 cups water, 1 cup light dry malt extract, and 1 Tettnanger pellet. I use this type of starter on all my batches and pitch *after* high krausen. Brew Day: 1) "Teabag" the Crystal malt, and add to 3 gallons cold water. 2) Bring almost to a boil and remove the "teabag". 3) Add malt extract and bring to a boil. 4) Add Styrian Goldings hops and boil for one hour. 5) Add

Cascade hops, return to boil and remove from heat. 6) Steep 15 minutes. 7) Chill with immersion chiller to 80F. 8) pour into clean fermenter and top up to 5. 5 gallons total volume with cold water. 9) shake up starter, pitch and vigorously stir wort. 10) Ferment ~3 days at ~68F. 11) Rack to secondary. 12) bottle when clear (~1 week) with 1.25 cups light dry malt extract.

Dunkelweizen

Category Wheat Beer
Recipe Type All Grain

Fermentables
5 lbs wheat malt
3 lbs light Munich
1.25 lbs Briess 2-row
8 oz light crystal (20L)
2 oz medium crystal (40L)
2 oz chocolate malt (400L)

Hops
1 oz Hallertauer hops (4.9% alpha, boil)

Yeast wheat yeast (Wyeast Bavarian wheat or Yeast Labs W51)

Procedure This, along with a 90-minute boil, gave me the medium-amber color I was looking for. Time will tell if the crystal and chocolate will give the beer an undesirable harshness. I think you'd want a fairly soft finish in any Weizen. I've tried this year's SA Summer Wheat (Dunkelweizen) and I think it's too harsh, as well as under-carbonated. The color's right, though.

Dunkelweizen

Category Wheat Beer

George Braun
Recipe Type All Grain

Fermentables
7 lb Dark Wheat Malt
2. 5 lb Munich Malt
2 lb Caravienna Malt
. 5 lb Carapils Malt

Hops
1 oz Hallertaur Hersb. (2.9 AAU) 60 minutes
1 oz Tettnanger (6.2 AAU) 15 minutes
1 oz Hallertaur Hersb. (2.9 AAU) 1 minute

Yeast Wyeast #3068

Procedure Single Step Infusion (no protein rest) at 158 degrees F.

Franken-Weizen

Category Wheat Beer
Recipe Type All Grain

Fermentables
3 Lb Vienna malt
6. 5 Lb Wheat Malt
2 Lb 2-Row malt

Hops
1 oz Tettnanger, 4.4%AA, 45 min
1 oz Saaz (Domestic), 4.0%AA, 15 min

Yeast Wyeast 3068

Procedure My water is moderately soft; added 2 teaspoons of gypsum to the mash.

Mash schedule: 40 minutes at 50C; added an infusion to raise to 60C, rest for 15 minutes; added heat directly to raise to 70C, rest for 60 minutes; raised temp to mash-out.

Primary ferment 7 days at 21-22C. Secondary ferment at 20C for 12 days. Force carbonated in the keg to 2.7 volumes of CO2.

Franko's Magnificent Eichenweizzen

Category Wheat Beer
Recipe Type Extract

Fermentables
1 lbs light, dry extract
3.3 kg Ireks wheat extract

Hops
1 oz Hallertauer (7. 5 % alpha)
. 25 oz Hallertauer (7. 5 alpha) (finish)

Other
1 tsp Irish moss
1 oz Oak chips

Yeast Wyeast 3056 Bavarian Wheat

Procedure Boil 1--1/2 gallon water. Add Irek's wheat extract, 1 pound dry malt extract, and 1 ounce Hallertauer. Boil 40 minutes. Add 1/2 ounce finishing hops, 1 ounce oak chips, and 1 teaspoon Irish moss. Let cool. Add water to bring volume to 5 gallons. Pitch yeast

George Braun

German Weisen Beer

Category Wheat Beer
Recipe Type Extract

Fermentables

1 can Irek Wheat Malt Extract (unhopped)
1 lb Light DME
1 cup Cara-Pils Malt
1 cup Crystal Malt-10L
. 75 cup Priming Sugar

Hops

1. 5 oz. Hallertauer Hops (bittering)
. 5 0z. Saaz Hops (for finishing)

Other
1 tsp. Irish Moss

Yeast 1 pack Wyeast #3056 Wheat Yeast

Procedure Crack all grains and place in grain bag. Dissolve can of malt and DME in 1-2 gal. of water in the stock pot. Add the gab of grain to the pot and adjust the heat to achieve boiling temperature. The instant the water starts to boil, remove the grains from your stock pot. Add the bittering hops and maintain the boil. After 25 minutes, add the Irish moss and continue to boil. After 20 minutes, add the finishing hops and boil for an additional 2 minutes ONLY. Remove the stockpot from the heat and attach a lid. Place the pot in a sink of ice to cool until it reaches 75-80 degrees. Pour the cooled wort into a sanitized fermenter and top off to 5 gallons. Add the active yeast starter. Once fermentation has started, move the fermenter to an area of 55-65 degrees.

Hefeweizen

Category Wheat Beer
Recipe Type All Grain

Fermentables
5 lbs wheat malt
3 lbs 6 row lager malt

Hops
1 oz Tettnang hops (45 minutes before end of boil - alpha
. 5 oz Saaz (25 minutes - 3.8% alpha)
. 5 oz Saaz (10 minutes - 3.8% alpha)

Yeast Wyeast 1056 ("American Ale")

Procedure Mash in 11 quarts water and protein rest 30 minutes at 130F. Starch conversion 90 minutes at 149F. Mash out and sparge 1 hour at 168F. Boil 1 hour, adding hops as indicated above.

Hefeweizen Dunkel

Category Wheat Beer
Recipe Type Extract

Fermentables
6 lbs. Northwestern wheat (50/50) malt extract
3.3 lbs. Northwestern gold malt extract
. 25 lbs. Roasted barley
. 25 lbs. chocolate malt
. 25 lbs. black patent
. 75 cup corn sugar for priming

Hops
. 75 oz. Hallertauer hops (4.6%) (@60 minutes)
. 25 oz. Hallertauer hops (4.6%) (@2 minutes)

Other
. 5 tsp. Irish Moss (@10 minutes)

Yeast Wyeast #3056 Bavarian wheat lager yeast

Honey Wheat

Category Wheat Beer
Recipe Type Extract

Fermentables
1 can Munton & Fison's Premiere Weizen
2 lbs Light honey (strawberry clover)
. 75 cup sugar or equivalent malt extract

Other
1 lb Dextrose

Yeast A suitable Weizen yeast (preferably liquid)

Procedure Boil honey, Weizen extract and dextrose for 15 minutes in 1. 5 gal water. Tip into fermenter, and add water to make up 5 gal. Allow to cool and add yeast. Fermentation should be complete in around 3-4 days. Bottle with priming sugar.

Honey Wheat Beer

Category Wheat Beer
Recipe Type Partial Mash

Fermentables
1 3kg can Ireks wheat/barley extract
1. 5 lb clover honey

Hops
1 oz Tetnang hops (3.4%AA??) During the boil for 45 min
1 oz Hallertauer hops (German) (4. 5 %AA??) for last 10 min

Yeast 1 pkg Wyeast Weihenstephan Wheat variety

Hoppy Amber Wheat

Category Wheat Beer
Recipe Type Extract

Fermentables
6.6 lbs wheat malt extract
1. 5 lbs dark, dry malt
1. 5 lbs crystal malt
1 lbs wheat malt

George Braun
. 25 lbs chocolate malt

Hops
2 oz of Hallertauer hops (Alpha 4.2) for full boil
. 5 oz Saaz hops (Alpha??) For 20 minutes
. 5 oz Saaz hops to finish

Other
. 5 lbs wheat flakes

Yeast yeast

Procedure Mash the crystal malt, wheat malt and flaked wheat with 2 1/2 gallons of water using your favorite mash method. I used a step mash, holding for 20 minutes at 130 degrees, 30 minutes at 150 degrees and 155 for 20 minutes. Steep the specialty malts while bringing the rest of the water to a boil. Remove specialty grains and add extracts and wort from the mash as boil begins. Add Hallertau hops at beginning of boil. Add 1/2 ounce of Saaz at 40 minutes. Turn off heat after 60 minutes, and add last 1/2 ounce of hops.

JazzBerry Juice

Category Wheat Beer
Recipe Type Extract

Fermentables
6.6 lbs Alexanders Unhopped Wheat LME (60/40)
1 lbs Malted Wheat
4. 5 # Raspberries, frozen, thawed, strained (48 oz of juice)
5/8 c. Bottling Sugar to prime

Hops
1 oz. Mt. Hood Hop Pellets (boil) 5. 5 AA

1 oz. Hallertauer Hersbrucker Plugs (at 45 min) 4.6 AA

Other
. 5 tsp Gypsum (rehydrated 20 min.) in the boil
. 5 tsp Irish Moss (rehydrated 20 min.) last 20 min. of boil

Yeast 1 pkg Wyeast Bavarian Wheat Liquid Yeast (in starter)

Procedure Place wheat malt in a bag, in cold 2. 5 g water in pot, bring to 160 deg. and hold 1 hour. Remove grain bag. Pour 2 cups or so of water over the bag to rinse good stuff back into the pot. Add LME, bring to boil. Add boiling hops and gypsum. at 40 min add Irish moss, at 45 min add HH hops. At 1 hour, cool pot in water bath (tub) till 70 deg., about 40 min. Strain into carboy holding 2 gal preboiled, cooled, filtered water. Aerate Fully. Pitch yeast starter, aerate again. My ferment started at 6 hours. Rack to secondary after 5 days on top of the juice from the raspberries. I bottled at 23 days.

Mad Monk Oatmeal Honey Wheat

Category Wheat Beer
Recipe Type Extract

Fermentables
6 lbs Williams dark Oatmeal Extract Syrup
3 lbs Dry Weizen Extract
1 lbs Honey

Hops
1/2-1 oz of Cascade hops for bittering
1/2-1 oz of Cascade for Flavoring at the end of Boil or Dry Hopped

George Braun

Maple Wheat Ale

Category Wheat Beer
Recipe Type Extract

Fermentables
6 lbs malt/wheat extract
1 qt. VT grade A maple syrup

Hops
. 5 oz Northern Brewers hops 60m = 9.8 IBU
1 oz H'Taur hops 40m = 4.0 IBU

Yeast Wyeast 1056 Chico SN

Procedure Ferment at 68-70 for 3-4 days. X-fer to secondary for at least 2 weeks. Keg or bottle anytime after that.

Old Bavarian Dunkles Weissbier

Category Wheat Beer
Recipe Type Extract

Fermentables
4 lbs Dark malt extract
4 lbs wheat malt extract

Hops
. 8 g alpha acid (Tettnanger or Hallertauer (2.8 HBU))

Yeast Liquid Weissbier yeast

Procedure Boil 70 minutes, adding 1/2 hops at start, 1/2 at 40 minutes, and small quantity of aroma hops at 55 minutes. Allow to complete fermenting (the book says 3-4 days) Add 1 1/2 quarts of unhopped wort and some lager yeast, bottle.

Pumpkel Weizen

Category Wheat Beer
Recipe Type Extract

Fermentables
6.6 lbs NW Weizen LME
1.4 lbs Alexander's Kicker Pale Malt
1.0 lb Crystal (lovi 60)
1 small roasted pumpkin (4 lbs for about 4. 5 cups)

Hops
1.0 oz Perle 7.4 aau (boiling)
. 5 oz Tettnang 4.4 aau (finishing)

Yeast Wyeast 3068 Weihenstephan Wheat

Procedure Cut pumpkin in half, seed, and roast in oven at 375 for 1 1/2 hours. Peel away skin and food process to a pulp. Add grains to 3 quarts water and bring to a boil. Strain grains, add 5 quarts water and bring to a boil. Add LME, pumpkin mush, and Perle in the hop - bag. Boil for 20 minutes and add Tettnang to hop-bag. Boil another 15 minutes. Remove hop bags and strain wort. Add strained pumpkin material to 2 quarts of water and bring to boil. Strain this back into the wort. Allow to cool and pitch yeast. Secondary in 4 days and bottle when fermentation ceases.

Raspberry Wheat

Category Wheat Beer
Recipe Type Extract

Fermentables

George Braun
5 lbs Frozen Raspberries
3.3 Kg, Ireks Weizen
1.25 lbs Bavarian Wheat

Hops
1 oz. Tettinger Hops for 20 min boil

Yeast 1 Pkg WYeast Saaz Ale

Procedure The OG was 36, and the carboy just finished a rather vigorous 3 day fermentation with the first blow-by out of my 7 Gal Carboy.
After 5 days, rack and add raspberries.

To prepare the raspberries blend them frozen and then nuke them until room temperature (which should sterilize them). Place into secondary carboy and rack into the carboy. One week in secondary, then into the bottles.

RazzWheat#1

Category Wheat Beer
Recipe Type Extract

Fermentables
6 lbs Breiss Weizen Wheat Extract
40 oz Honey
60 oz raspberries, added to cooling wort.

Hops
1 oz Mt. Hood (60 min)
. 75 oz Hallertua (10-15 mins)

Yeast 3068 Wyeast

Procedure Leave in through primary, remove going into secondary. Bottled with 1-cup dextrose boiled in 3 quarts water, cooled. Primary: 5-7 days; secondary 3-5 days.

Red Wheat Ale

Category Wheat Beer
Recipe Type All Grain

Fermentables
3 lbs pale malt
3 lbs wheat malt
4 oz medium crystal (~40L)
1 oz chocolate malt

Hops
1/3 oz Chinook Pellets for 45 minutes (4 HBU)
. 5 oz Cascade Pellets for 20 (2. 5 HBU)
. 5 oz Tettnanger Pellets for 10 minutes

Yeast Whitbread ale yeast

Procedure Treat 7 gallons water with 1/4 ounce gypsum. Mash in 8 quarts at 170F for a target of 156F. When beer is fermented, prime with 1/2 cup sugar, fine with 1/2 teaspoon of gelatin, keg or bottle.

Rocket J. Squirrel Honey Wheat Ale

Category Wheat Beer
Recipe Type Extract

Fermentables
3 lbs Bavarian dry wheat extract
2 lbs Clover honey
. 5 lbs Buckwheat honey
. 5 lbs light Crystal malt (20 lovibond?)

Hops
1 oz Centennial hops 11.1% AAU's

Yeast 24 ounces Wyeast 1056 slurry (from previous batch)

Procedure Bring 1 and a half quarts water to 170 degrees and turn off heat. Add crystal malt and steep for 40 min. The temperature was 155 degrees after adding malt and stirring. In another pot, start 3 gallons water boiling. When it comes to a boil, strain in liquid from crystal malt and also pour another quart of hot water through the grains. Add the wheat extract and honey. Bring to a boil. Skim the scum off and then add 3/4 ounce hops for 1 hour. Turn off heat and add the last 1/4 ounce hops. Whirlpool and let stand to let the trub collect. Siphon into carboy and top to 5 gallons. Add yeast and shake vigorously. Bottle with 4 oz. corn sugar.

Rye Wit

Category Wheat Beer
Recipe Type All Grain

Fermentables
3 lbs 6--row pale malt
1. 5 lbs rye malt
1. 5 lbs wheat malt
3 lbs honey
2 lbs dry malt extract

Hops
1 oz Hallertauer (boil)
. 5 oz Hallertauer (15 minute boil)
. 5 oz Hallertauer (2 minute boil)

Other

1 oz whole cardamom
1 oz coriander seed
. 5 oz orange peel

Yeast Belgian ale yeast

Procedure Protein rest 120+F for 30 minutes, Mash 150F for 90 minutes. Boil for 60 minutes, adding 3 pounds honey, 2 pounds DME (enough to raise gravity to 1.050) and 1 ounce Hallertauer. In last 15 minutes of boil, add half of cardamom and half of coriander, and another 1/2 ounce of Hallertauer. In last 5 minutes of boil, add remaining cardamom and coriander and orange peel. In last 2 minutes of boil, add 1/2 ounce Hallertauer. Chill and pitch a Belgian ale yeast, such as the one newly offered by Wyeast, or culture some yeast from a fresh bottle of Chimay.
Note: Crack the cardamom shell and lightly crush the coriander seed. Strain them out before moving wort to the fermenter. The cardamom is not a traditional spice for this beer, so leave it out if you prefer.

Scotto's Rapier-Like Wit

Category Wheat Beer
Recipe Type Partial Mash

Fermentables
3 lb Dutch extra-light DME
12 oz N. Western light DME
1 lb clover honey
3.3 lb N. Western Weizen extract

Hops
1. 5 oz Hallertauer leaf hops

Other

George Braun
2 oz coriander
0. 5 oz orange peel

Yeast Wyeast Belgian white pitched from 32 oz of 1.050 starter

Procedure The yeast was pitched when VERY active, and visible signs of fermentation were within 6 hours. O.G. was 1.060. Racked to secondary after 8 days, gravity only 1.040. After a week in secondary, gravity is 1.032. Fermentation has taken place at an average temp of 65 degrees.

Simple Wheat Beer

Category Wheat Beer
Recipe Type Extract

Fermentables
2 cans Alexander's wheat malt extract

Hops
1 oz Hallertauer hops (boil 60 minutes)
. 25 oz Hallertauer (10 minute boil)

Other
. 5 tsp Irish moss (15 minute boil)
. 75 cup corn sugar to prime

Yeast Wyeast #3056 Bavarian wheat yeast

Procedure Boil extract and hops. Add hops and Irish moss as noted in the ingredients section above. Dump in fermenter with enough cold water to make 5 gallons. Pitch yeast.

Simple Wheat Beer

Category Wheat Beer
Recipe Type Extract

Fermentables
6.6 lbs wheat malt extract

Hops
1 oz Hallertauer hops (boil 60 minutes)

Yeast Wyeast Bavarian wheat yeast

Procedure Boil extract and hops. Dump in fermenter with enough cold water to make 5 gallons. Pitch yeast.

Strawberry Wheat

Category Wheat Beer
Recipe Type Extract

Fermentables
1. 5 lbs honey
1 can Morgan's Wheat
1. 5 lbs light dried malt
2 lbs fresh or frozen berries

Hops
2 oz Tettnangers (reduce if you don't like hoppy beers)

Yeast ale yeast

Procedure Boil the honey, an ounce of the hops, & the Irish moss in some water 15 minutes. Add Morgan's kit malt and bring back to a boil. Add fruit. Lower heat. Steep at 150 degrees 20 minutes with the second half of the hops.
That's it! Toss in some cold water & yeast and let 'er go.

After 4 days, rack off into a secondary fermenter, leaving the fruit behind the primary.

Summer Lemon Wheat

Category Wheat Beer
Recipe Type Extract

Fermentables
6.6 lbs Northwestern Weizen extract
3 lbs light dry malt extract
2 lbs honey
2 oz pure lemon extract
1 cup corn sugar for priming

Hops
2 oz Hallertauer hops

Other
4 whole lemons

Yeast, dry ale yeast

Procedure Boil 2 gallons of water, remove from heat and add the malt extracts and honey. Add 1-1/2 ounces of the hops at this time. Return to heat and boil for 50 minutes. After removing from heat, add the remaining 1/2 ounce of hops, the lemon extract, and the juice from the 4 lemons. Chill wort to 72 degrees, transfer to primary fermenter and pitch yeast. Ferment for 7 days at 72 degrees. Rack to secondary fermenter and let sit another 7 days. Bottle and let sit for 4 weeks.

SunWeiss

Category Wheat Beer
Recipe Type Extract

Fermentables
1 lbs Klages malt
1 lbs malted wheat
1 can John Bull unhopped light extract syrup

Hops
1 oz Saaz hops pellets

Other
. 5 tsp Irish moss

Yeast lager yeast

Procedure Microwave mash the Klages and wheat. Sparge with 1 gallon of water at 170.
Add extracts and 2/3 of the Saaz hops.

I used hot water to get to the protein rest temperature, and then from there used the microwave temperature probe and its hold temp feature for the two conversions rests, and mash out to 170F. I used Med High power, and stirred every 10 minutes or so. The emphasis in mashing was on the body, not fermentable sugar. It worked. The beer has considerably more malt flavor, body, and the dry hopping gave it a bit more tang than it usually has. Old recipe just used 1/2 pound of malted wheat, cold to boil, to add a bit of flavor.

Tamalpais Wit

Category Wheat Beer
Recipe Type Extract

Fermentables
4-1/2 lbs light, dry wheat malt extract
2 lbs orange honey

George Braun

Hops
1 oz Hallertauer or Northern Brewer (7. 5 HBU, boil)
1 oz Hallertauer or Hersbrucker (3 HBU finish)

Other
1. 5 oz crushed coriander
. 5 oz dried orange peel

Yeast Belgian Ale yeast (Wyeast 1214)

Procedure Bring 5 gallons of water to a boil, then add the first three ingredients. Boil 45 minutes, then add 3/4 oz. coriander. Boil 10 minutes, then add the remaining coriander and orange peel. Boil 5 minutes, and add the finishing hops for a final 2 minutes. Chill immediately to 75 F, aerate into 5 gallon carboy, and add yeast. Ferment using a blow-off method, then prime with 3/4 cup corn sugar and bottle.

WTO Wheat

Category Wheat Beer
Recipe Type Extract

Fermentables
3.3 Lbs Light Malt Extract
3.3 Oz Wheat Malt Extract

Hops
1.0 Oz Willamette Hops
1.0 Oz Fuggles Hops
0. 5 Oz Hallertau Hops

Other
0.25 Tsp Irish Moss

Yeast Windsor Ale, English Ale Yeast 11 Grams

Procedure Total Brew Time: 90 minutes All Hops Pellets Willamette Hops at Start Fuggles with 30 Minutes left Hallertau with 15 Minutes left Irish Moss with 15 Minutes Left 2 Packages Windsor Windsor Ale Yeast, Not Rehydrated

Wacky Weizenbock

Category Wheat Beer
Recipe Type Extract

Fermentables
6 lbs Brew master Dried Wheat Extract
3 lbs Brew master Dried Amber Malt Extract
. 5 lb chocolate malt

Hops
2 oz Hallertauer fresh hops (boiling - 1 hour)
. 5 oz Hallertauer fresh hops (flavor - last 20 minutes)
. 5 oz Hallertauer fresh hops (aroma - last 2 minutes)

Yeast Wyeast Liquid Wheat Beer Yeast

Procedure Prepare according to the standard Papazian method for extract beers. Starting gravity: 1.61 Starting Potential alcohol: 9% Ending gravity: 1.16 Ending Potential alcohol: 2% Primary and Secondary fermentation took 1 month. I believe that the high alcohol content (7%) pickled the yeast and stopped fermentation in its tracks. Bottled with 1 1/4 cup DME

Weissbier

Category Wheat Beer
Recipe Type Extract

George Braun

Fermentables
1 ea 6 lb. can of Ireks wheat extract (100% wheat, BTW)
0. 5 lbs. malted wheat
1 ea 4 lb. can of Alexander's "Kicker" barley extract
0. 5 lbs. light crystal malt

Hops
1. 5 oz. Hersbrucker hop pellets

Yeast Brewtek German Wheat Yeast #1

Procedure Make a 500 ml starter several days ahead. Give yourself a week to get the slant stepped up to this level.
Steep the malts in 1 gal water @ 170 F for 20 min. Remove grains and add extracts. Stir until dissolved, then bring to a boil. Add 1oz hops. Boil 30 minutes, add remaining hops (0. 5 oz). Remove from heat. Chill and pitch yeast. Ferment - NOW HEAR THIS - at 75 to 80 F. At this point (8 days in the primary; just had racked to the secondary) my air conditioner broke. We had just packed up to leave for a week in Florida, so I left it. Middle of July in GA - no AC. It stayed in the primary for 12 days. It bubbled furiously for most of the 20 day fermentation. I bottled it and started drinking it in 2 weeks. Delicious!

Weizen Heimer

Category Wheat Beer
Recipe Type Extract

Fermentables
2/3 cup Honey or DME (priming)

Hops
1. 5 oz. Cascades or Hallertauer hops (60 minute boil)

. 5 oz. Cascades or Hallertauer hops (15 minute finish)

Other
. 25 tsp Irish Moss
6.6 lb Wheat LME
1 lb crystal malt 40L (cracked)

Yeast 1 pkg. Wyeast 3068 Wheinstephen Wheat Yeast

Procedure Primary ferment: 3-5 days Secondary ferment: 5-8 days

Weizen Schmeizen

Category Wheat Beer
Recipe Type Extract

Fermentables
6.6 lbs IREKS wheat malt extract
6.6 lbs IREKS light malt extract

Hops
2 oz Hallertauer leaf hops (4.4% alpha) (60 minute boil)
1. 5 oz Cascade hops (alpha 5.7%) (30 minute boil)
. 5 oz Hallertauer plug

Yeast Wyeast #3056

Procedure Bring 3 gallons water to boil, remove from heat and add malt extract syrup (yes, all of it). Bring mixture to boil, add Hallertauer bittering hops. After 30 minutes, add the Cascade bittering hops, 15 minutes later add Hallertauer plug (I used hop bags for all 3 additions). Cool wort (about 3. 5 gallons) to about 100F, siphon onto another 3--1/2 gallons of cold tap water, aerating vigorously. This produced 7 gallons of wort with an S. G. =1. 065 (I get great extract efficiency from my extracts!).

Rack to two carboys with about another 1--1/2 gallon water (total yield to 10 gallons). Pitch yeast at about 75.

Weizenbock

Category Wheat Beer
Recipe Type Extract

Fermentables
1. 5 light DME
1 can (3lb 10oz) of Glenbrew Brew Mart Australian Dunkelbock
3 lbs of wheat DME

Hops
1 oz Hallerteau hops (3.7 alpha)

Yeast Glenbrew kit yeast

Procedure Boiled DME and hops for 15 mins in 1 1/2 gals of water. Added liquid malt and continued boil for 10 mins. Added to 3 1/2 gals of cold water and used yeast from Glenbrew kit. After 5 days I racked to the secondary and added the findings from the Glenbrew kit. Leave in secondary for 10 days, then primed and bottled.

Weizen? Why Not?

Category Wheat Beer
Recipe Type Extract

Fermentables
6 lb Williams wheat extract
1 lb crystal malt
. 5 lb toasted barley
1 lb honey

Hops
2 oz Cascades hops (boil)
. 5 oz Cascades hops (finish)

Yeast 1 package Wyeast wheat yeast

Procedure Make a 2-quart starter before brewing. Steep crystal and toasted barley in 4 gallons water for 40 minutes (use grain bags to make this easier). Add extract, honey and bittering hops. Boil wort for 1 hour. Remove from heat. Add finishing hops and steep 2 minutes. Chill and pitch yeast. After 3 days, rack to secondary. Bottle after 8 days.

Wheat Ale

Category Wheat Beer
Recipe Type All Grain

Fermentables
4 lbs Harrington
3 lbs Belgian Wheat
. 25 lbs Crystal (60L)

Hops
. 5 oz Chinook (12aa) boiling
1 oz Mt Hood (5 mins before end of boil)

Yeast WY1056

Procedure 40-60-70 Mash Schedule / 90 min boil

Wheat Beer #1

Category Wheat Beer
Recipe Type Extract

George Braun

Fermentables

6 lbs Wheat/Malt extract
1 lbs honey
3 cups crystal malt
1 lbs DME

Hops

2 oz Hallertauer (boil 60 minutes)
. 5 oz Hallertauer (finish 2 mins)

Yeast Wyeast Bavarian wheat yeast

Procedure Cooled overnight outside. Rack to new carboy next day and pitch WYeast Bavarian Wheat.

Wheat Beer #2

Category Wheat Beer
Recipe Type Extract

Fermentables

6 lbs Wheat/Malt extract
1 lbs honey
3 cups, crystal

Hops

2 oz Tetnanger (alpha 3.6) boil 1 hour
. 5 oz Tetnanger to finish 2 min

Yeast WYeast Bavarian Wheat (from a previous batch)

Procedure Cooled overnight outside, rack and repitch slurry from previous batch.

Wheat Amber

Category Wheat Beer
Recipe Type Extract

Fermentables
3 lbs light dry malt extract
1 can Kwoffit Bitter kit (hopped extract)
1 lb crystal malt
. 5 lbs wheat malt

Hops
? oz Fuggles Leaf Hops

Yeast Kwoffit yeast

Procedure Steep the crystal and wheat malts. Boil the resulting mixture with the Kwoffit kit and the light extract. Add a small amount (up to 1/2 ounce) of the Fuggles hops in the last minute of the boil.

Wit Christmas

Category Wheat Beer
Recipe Type All Grain

Fermentables
11 lbs German 2-row pils
1. 5 lbs flaked oats

Hops
. 5 oz Cascade 45 minutes
. 5 oz Cascade 30 minutes
1 oz Saaz 15 minutes
1 oz Saaz steep

Other
9-1/2 lbs flaked wheat
. 75 oz Centennial 90 minutes
10 grams coriander in boil
70 grams Curacao in boil

George Braun
2. 5 grams coriander in secondary

Yeast Belgian White Wyeast #3944

Procedure Mash in 110F (43.3C) 10 min. Boost to 128F (53.3C) 30 mins. Boost to 158F (70C) 50 mins.
Add spice 10 minutes before knockout..

Chapter 2- Stout Beer

All-Grain Stout

Category Stout
Recipe Type All Grain

Fermentables
3 lbs Klages
3 lbs pale malt (dark)
2 lbs pale malt (very light)
2 lbs Vienna malt
2 lbs barley flakes
1 lbs untyped malted barley
8 oz roasted barley
8 oz black patent

Hops
24 grams Buillion hops
30 grams Cascade hops
4 grams Hallertauer hops

Other
8 oz chocolate

Yeast Wyeast German ale

Procedure The flaked barley has no husk, so I saw no reason not to grind it finely. Mash in at 130 degrees. Let rest 20 minutes or so. Mash at 150 degrees for 115 minutes. Sparge. Let the spargings settle. What seemed to be 3 or 4" of hot break settled out of the initial spargings! Boil for 2 hours. Add hops as follows: 14 grams bullion and 16 grams cascade (very fresh) for 1:45. 10 g bullion and 14 g cascade for 1:05. 4 grams hallertauer finish. Chill with an immersion chiller, and strain the wort through the hops. Makes about 5. 5 gallons of 1.068

Al's Medium-dry Stout

Category Stout
Recipe Type Extract

Fermentables
6.6 lbs John Bull Unhopped Dark Malt Extract
0. 5 lb Roasted Unmalted Barley
0. 5 lb Black Patent Malt
. 5 cup Corn Sugar for priming

Hops
3 oz Cluster Pellets (60 min boil)

Other
1/3 oz Wines Inc. Burton Water Salts
6 gal al Soft Tap water in the brew kettle

Yeast 1 pkg Wyeast #1084 Irish Ale yeast

Procedure I just strongly suggest using the blow off method, because if you don't I feel this beer will be much too astringent.

Amy's Stout

Category Stout
Recipe Type All Grain

Fermentables
5. 5 lb Hugh Baird Pale Ale malt
0. 5 lb Carapils malt (Hugh Baird)
0. 5 lb Hugh Baird 50L crystal
1.0 lb flaked oats (McCann's Irish Quick Oats)
0.7 lb roasted barley

Hops
30 Gram BC Kent Goldings flowers (5%) (60 min)
15 Gram Kent Goldings (15 min)
15 Gram Kent Goldings (5 min)

Yeast, Yeast Lab Irish Ale yeast

Procedure Step mash all grains together @61C for 30 min (3 gal strike), 65C for 30 min. (infuse 2qts boiling water). Sparged 5.8 gallons at 1.038.

George Braun

Yield: 4.7 gallons @ 1.046 (I did add some top-up water during the boil).

Fermented 1 week in glass at 19-22C with a pint starter of Yeast Lab Irish Ale. FG 1.012.

Bottled with 1/3c corn sugar into 2 5l mini-kegs and 18 bottles.

Baer's Stout

Category Stout
Recipe Type Extract

Fermentables
. 25 lbs flaked barley
. 25 lbs medium crystal malt
6 lbs dark Australian malt extract
. 5 lbs dark Australian dry malt
.25 lbs black patent malt
. 5 cup molasses

Hops
2 oz Cascade hops (boil)
2/3 oz Northern Brewer hops (finish)

Yeast Wyeast British ale yeast

Procedure Steep flaked barley and crystal malt for 50 minutes at 153 degrees. Strain and boil 90 minutes. Add 1/3 of boiling hops after 30 minutes. Add black patent and molasses at 45 minutes.

After 60 minutes, add 1/3 of boiling hops. At end of boil add remaining hops. Steep. Strain, cool, and ferment.

Barney Flats Oatmeal Stout

Category Stout
Recipe Type Partial Mash

Fermentables
5 lbs 2--row pale malt
1. 5 lbs steel cut oats
. 5 lbs malted wheat
1. 5 lbs 80 L. crystal malt
1 lbs, black patent malt
1 lbs chocolate malt
1 lbs roasted barley
. 5 lbs Cara-pils malt
3 lbs dark Australian DME

Hops
1 oz Chinook pellets (13.6% alpha) (boil 60 minutes)
. 5 oz Perle pellets (8% alpha) (boil 35 minutes)
.25 oz Hallertauer pellets (3% alpha) (boil 35 minutes)
. 25 oz Tettnanger pellets (3.4% alpha) (boil 35 minutes)
.75 oz Hallertauer (steep for aroma)
. 75 oz Tettnanger (steep for aroma)

Other

George Braun
. 5 lbs lactose
1 tsp Irish moss

Basic Stout

Category Stout
Recipe Type Extract

Fermentables
6-8 lbs dark malt extract
1/2-1 lbs roasted barley
1/2-1 lbs, black patent malt

Hops
. 75 oz bittering hops (e.g., Bullion)
small amount aromatic hops (optional)

Yeast ale yeast

Procedure To these skeleton ingredients I add other adjuncts, or remove things if the wind blows from the south. A nice beer is made by using only dark malt and black patent malt. A good strong bittering hops is key; Bullion is lovely, as is Nugget or Chinook.
There are no appreciable differences between making stouts and other ales, save the larger quantities of grain. Beware of 9-pound batches as these can blow the lids off fermenters.

Bitch's Brew Oatmeal Stout

Category Stout

Recipe Type Extract

Fermentables
6 lbs dark, dry malt extract
2 lbs amber dry malt extract
1 lbs crystal malt
. 75 lbs roasted barley
. 5 lbs black patent malt
2 cups Quaker Oats

Hops
2 oz Bullions hop (boiling)
. 5 oz Willamette hope (finishing)

Yeast 2 packages Whitbread Ale Yeast

Procedure Steep the Oats, and the cracked grains for 1/2 hour in cold water. Heat mixture and remove grains as a boil is reached. Throw in malts and make your wort. Boil Bullions for 45 minutes, Willammette for 5-7 minutes. Have fun.

Black Betty

Category Stout
Recipe Type All Grain

Fermentables
13.0 Lbs 2-row barley
2.0 Lbs white wheat
1.0 Lbs crystal 20L
1.0 Lbs black patent

Hops
2.0 Oz magnum ~ 15%

Yeast Nottingham Dry Yeast

Procedure This is a single step infusion. Allocate the correct amount of water into the pot and dissolve the gypsum into it. I then heat the water to approximately 150 F and add the grains, stirring to achieve a mixture. Then I place the pot (make sure it will fit) into a preheated oven set at about 165 F. Mash for about 1 hour. Note that the times are approximate and that you are controlling it, checking and stirring every 20 minutes or so. Sparge using hot water in the correct amount so that husk tannins are not extracted. Boil with all hops for about 45 minutes. Cool slightly, and split between primary fermenters. Top off with good drinking water. Once the wort cools to yeast friendly temperature, pitch the yeast and ferment. Only primary ferment for at least two weeks, to allow the high gravity to render into alcohol. Bottle as usual and try to keep your sweaty paws off until it matures. Enjoy.

Black Cat Stout #1

Category Stout
Recipe Type Extract

Fermentables

6.6 lbs Munton & Fison dark extract syrup
1 lbs Munton & Fison dark, dry extract
. 5 lbs, black patent malt
.75 lbs crystal malt
. 5 lbs roasted barley
. 5 cup dark molasses

Hops
. 75 oz Willamette hops (boil)
. 75 oz Cascade hops (boil)

Other
1 tsp vanilla
. 5 cup French roast coffee

Yeast 2 packs Edme ale yeast

Procedure Brew a pot of coffee with 1/2 cup of French roast coffee. Steep specialty grains in water, as it boils. Remove grains. Boil malts, hops, and vanilla 60 minutes. Strain wort into fermenter. Pour in pot of coffee. Add ice water to make 5 gallons. Pitch yeast. Rack to secondary after 3 days. Bottle 23 days later.

Black Gold Stout

Category Stout
Recipe Type Extract

Fermentables

George Braun

6 lb M&F Dark Extract Syrup
1 lb M&F Dark DME
8 oz. Black Patent Malt
12 oz. Chocolate Malt
12 oz. Crystal Malt
. 75 C. corn sugar for priming

Hops

1 oz. Chinook Hop Pellets (60 min)
. 5 oz. Northern Brewer Hop Pellets (60 min)
. 5 oz. Northern Brewer Hop Pellets (20 min)

Other

1. 5 tsp. Single Fold Pure Vanilla Extract
. 75 C. Freshly Brewed Espresso

Yeast EDME dry ale yeast

Procedure For this I used distilled water with 1 Tbsp. water crystals added. Steep specialty grains, then remove. Add vanilla, espresso and extracts. Boil for an hour and cool. Rack to primary and pitch yeast. Within minutes activity was observed. Within 12 hours active fermentation, *WARNING* after this stage you WILL need to use a blow off rig. The activity subsided after 2 1/2 days, then racked to secondary for 12 days to ensure no bottle bombs! Bottled with corn sugar and aged @room temp for 8 days. It is now 3 weeks in the basement and better than ever.

Blackstrap Stout

Category Stout
Recipe Type Extract

Fermentables
7.4 lbs. Dark malt extract syrup
1 lbs. Black Patent malt
1 lbs. Chocolate malt
. 5 lbs. Crystal malt
. 5 lbs. Flaked barley
. 5 cup Blackstrap molasses
3 oz Blackstrap molasses to prime

Hops
3 oz Cascade hops (bittering)
1 oz Fuggles hops (finish)

Yeast Edme dry yeast

Procedure Standard

Procedures (with the exception of forgetting the Irish Moss -- but I don't think that's going to be a real big deal).

Blackberry Stout

Category Stout
Recipe Type Extract

Fermentables
6 lbs dark DME

George Braun
6-8 cups roasted barley
3 lbs blackberries

Hops
1 oz Kent Goldings 60 minute boil
. 5 oz Fuggles 30 minute boil
. 5 oz Fuggles

Yeast Wyeast Irish Ale

Procedure I used frozen blackberries and put them in the bottom of a plastic primary, and poured the hot wort onto them to partially sterilize. No need to crush them up or anything; they were a faint pink by the time I racked to the secondary 5 days later.

Blackstrap Stout

Category Stout
Recipe Type Extract

Fermentables
7.4 lbs. Dark malt extract syrup
1 lbs. Black Patent malt
1 lbs. Chocolate malt
. 5 lbs. Crystal malt
. 5 lbs. Flaked barley
. 5 cup Blackstrap molasses
3 oz Blackstrap molasses to prime

Hops

3 oz Cascade hops (bittering)
1 oz Fuggles hops (finish)

Yeast Edme dry yeast

Procedure Standard procedures (with the exception of forgetting the Irish Moss -- but I don't think that's going to be a real big deal).

Broglio's Quaker Stout

Category Stout
Recipe Type Extract

Fermentables
6 lbs dry amber extract
1 lbs crystal malt
. 5 lbs roasted barley
1 lbs Quaker oats

Hops
1 oz Eroica hops (boil)
1 oz Kent Goldings hops(finish)

Yeast 2 packs Edme ale yeast

Procedure In two gallons of cold water, add crystal, barley, and oatmeal. Steep until water comes to boil. Sparge with about 1 gallon of hot water. Add dry extract. Bring to boil. Add Eroica hops. Boil 45 minutes. In last 5 minutes of boil, add Kent Goldings hops. Cool to about 75 degrees.

Transfer to primary and pitch yeast. Have a homebrew and wait.

Chocolate Mint Coffee Stout

Category Stout
Recipe Type Extract

Fermentables
1 cup black patent
1 cup roasted barley
3 lbs. dark DME (Telford)
. 25 cup Hershey's Mint Chocolate Syrup

Hops
1 oz. Perle (8%) half in boil, half at 30 minutes
1 oz. Hersbrucker (1. 5 %) finishing

Other
1 cup chocolate
1 can Telford Shamrock Stout (4 lbs.)
2 oz. Hershey's unsweetened baking chocolate
. 5 cup Hershey's cocoa
.25 cup Chocolate Mint coffee (ground)

Yeast 2 packs Nottingham ale yeast

Procedure Leave grains in for 10 minutes of the boil.

Cherry Fever Stout

Category Stout
Recipe Type Extract

Here is a great fruit beer recipe! This recipe is designed for the intermediate brewer.

Fermentables
3.3 lbs. John Bull plain dark malt extract syrup
2. 5 lbs Premier Malt hopped flavored light malt extract syrup
1. 5 lbs plain dark dried malt extract
1 lbs. crystal malt
. 5 lbs. roasted barley
. 75 c. corn sugar or 1 1/4 c. dried malt extract (for bottling)
. 5 lbs. black patent malt
3 lbs. sour cherries

Hops
1. 5 oz Northern Brewer hops (boiling): 13 HBU
. 5 oz. Willamette hops (finishing)

Other
2 lbs. choke cherries or substitute with 2 lbs. Most sour cherries
8 tsp. gypsum

Yeast 1-2 pkgs. ale yeast

Procedure Add the crushed roasted barley, crystal and black patent malts to 1 1/2 gallons of cold water and bring to a boil. When boiling commences, remove the spent grains and add the malt extracts, gypsum and boiling hops and continue to boil for 60 minutes. Add the 5 lbs. of crushed cherries (pits and all) to the hot boiling wort. Turn off heat and let the wort steep for 15 minutes (at temperatures between 160-180 degrees F {71-88 C} in order to pasteurize the cherries. Do not boil. Add the finishing hops 2 minutes before you pour the entire contents into a plastic primary fermenter and cold water. Pitch yeast when cool. After 4-5 days of primary fermentation, rack the fermenting beer into a secondary fermenter. Secondary fermentation should last about 10-14 days longer. Bottle when fermentation is complete.

Chocolate Stout

Category Stout
Recipe Type Partial Mash

Fermentables
2 lb Pale Ale malt
1 lb Munich malt
. 5 lb 80L Crystal
.25 lb Chocolate malt
. 25 lb Black Patent malt
3.3 lb American Classic Amber extract syrup
3 lb Dutch DME (I don't know the brand, but it is high in dextrins)
. 5 lb brown sugar
. 5 inch brewers licorice

Hops

1 oz Brewers gold (8. 5 %alpha) hops - bittering

Other
2 oz fresh grated ginger
3 oz unsweetened bakers chocolate
1 tsp Irish moss

Yeast 2 package dry Whitbread yeast

Procedure 5Q mash water, 2 1/2 (?) G Sparge water, mash in at 138F, brought to 155F for 1 hour., mash out at 168F
Added extracts and sugar and brought to boil. Added the ginger, licorice, chocolate, and hops after boil started. I was afraid that the chocolate would burn on the bottom of the boiler, so I set each 1 oz piece on my stirring spoon and dipped gently in the wort until they melted.

The real interesting thing about the brew was that after pitching, a thick bubbly layer of stuff formed on the surface of the beer in the carboy almost immediately after fermentation started, and never left, even after I expected the Kraeusen to fall. There was the usual amount of activity in the beer, but never more than an inch of Kraeusen.

The good thing was that after racking to my secondary carboy, I left most of the stuff that was sitting on the surface in my primary, and almost all of the rest in my secondary when I racked to my bottling bucket.

I primed with amber DME, and the results even after only two weeks are wonderful, however, there is still a small layer of this sediment even in the bottle at the surface of the beer.

Christmas in Ireland

Category Stout
Recipe Type Extract

Fermentables
4 lbs Mountmellick Irish Stout Extract
3 lbs Munton & Fison Amber DME
. 5 lbs Crystal Malt (60 Lovibond)
.25 lbs Black Patent Malt
1 lbs Clover Honey

Hops
1 oz Bullion hops (bittering)
. 5 oz Hallertau hops (finishing)

Other
12 inches Cinnamon sticks (or 6 teaspoons ground cinnamon)
4 oz Ginger Root
2 tsp Allspice
1 tsp Cloves

Yeast 1 package WYeast #1084 Irish Stout Yeast

Procedure Simmer honey and spices in covered pot for 45 minutes. Add cracked grains to 2 gallons cold water and bring to a boil. As soon as boiling starts, remove grains with a strainer. Add malt extracts and bittering hops and boil for 55 minutes. Add finishing hops and boil for 5 more minutes. Remove from heat. Stir in honey and spice mixture and cool. Strain into fermenter containing 3 gallons cold (previously boiled) water and pitch yeast (when cool). After vigorous primary fermentation subsides, rack into secondary. Bottle with 7 ounces corn sugar or 1-1/4 cups DME when fermentation completes.

Citadelle White

Category Belgian Ale
Recipe Type All Grain

Fermentables
5 lbs 2-row pale malt
3 lbs Belgian wheat malt
110 grams corn sugar in 4.75 gallons for priming

Hops
. 5 oz Styrian Goldings (6.8% AA), boiled for 60 minutes

Other

George Braun

. 75 lbs hard red winter wheat
10 grams ground coriander (boiled 10 minutes)
zest of 4 oranges and one lime (added after end of boil)
12. 5 ml 88% lactic acid (added at bottling)

Yeast Hoegaarden white yeast cultured from brewery sample

Procedure Strike with 8 quarts @ 135F for 20 minute protein rest at 122- 124F; Add 1 gallon boiling water to raise to 145F, then heat to 158F for 30 minute scarification; add 2 gallons boiling water for 10-minute mash out at 170F; transfer to lauter tun and let sit 20 mins, then sparge with 6 gallons water @ 180F. I stopped sparging at 1.008, collecting 6.25 gallons at 1.037. Boiled for 90 minutes and cooled with immersion chiller.

Clydesdale Stout

Category Stout
Recipe Type All Grain

Fermentables
300 g Roasted Barley
300 g Chocolate Malt
600 g Crystal Malt (I've been using a fairly low lovibond crystal)
500 g Rolled Oats
2 kg pale malt

Hops
50 g Northern Brewer (boil 60min)
15 g Northern Brewer (boil 15min)
10 g Northern Brewer (end of boil)

Other
. 5 teaspoon Irish moss

Yeast Wyeast Irish ale yeast

Procedure Infusion mash this stuff for about 45min., initial strike temp. is 156 F. Do decoctions as necessary to maintain temp. and then to mash out.
After sparging, etc. add about 2kg dark malt extract powder and 250g demerarra sugar, plus the hops (all pellets).

No hops strained out or racking off trub. That's right, everybody into the pool. Top up to about 22 L or so. Pitch with Wyeast Irish Ale yeast starter.

Coffee Stout

Category Stout
Recipe Type Extract

Fermentables
6 lb Stone Mountain Brewery amber malt syrup
3 lb Geordie light DME
1 lb crystal malt 10L

George Braun
8 oz. chocolate malt
2 oz. roasted barley

Hops
6 oz. Cascade hops (5.2% AA), bittering
1 oz. Cascade hops, flavoring and aroma

Other
8 oz. Italian espresso beans

Yeast 15 g. Windsor dried ale yeast

Procedure Ground specialty malts and steeped in 1 1/2 gal. cold water. Brought water up to temp and held at 150 - 160 deg F for 1/2 hour. Added extracts, brought to boil and added bittering hops. Boiled for 1 hour. Added 1/2 oz. hops and ground coffee 10 minutes before end of boil, added 1/2 oz hops at end of boil. OG 1.070. Kegged 18 January 1996; FG 1.034 (estimated alcohol, 5.9% abv). Tapped keg 25 February 1996.

Coffee Stout

Category Stout
Recipe Type Extract

Fermentables
1 can Stout extract
6 lbs dark Dutch bulk extract
1 lbs chocolate malt

1 lbs crystal malt
. 75 cup brown sugar (priming)

Hops
1 oz Fuggles hops (bittering)
1 oz Fuggles hops (flavoring)

Other
12 cups coffee

Yeast 1 package of Wyeast #1084

Procedure Heat water to 160 degrees and steep grains. Remove grains and heat to boiling. Add extracts and coffee and heat to boil. Add bittering hops and boil for 40 minutes. Add flavoring hops and boil for 20 minutes. Cool and pitch yeast (I used a starter). Rack to secondary when active fermentation subsides. Leave in secondary 3-4 weeks. When ready to bottle boils the brown sugar with a pint of water for priming. This came out with the coffee a bit strong. Next time I try this I'll probably cut back to 6 to 8 cups of coffee.

Colorado Crankcase Stout

Category Stout
Recipe Type Extract

Fermentables
3.3 lbs Edme SFX dark malt extract
3.3 lbs John Bull dark malt extract

George Braun

2 lbs amber dry malt extract
1 lbs crystal malt
1 lbs roasted barley
1 lbs chocolate malt
. 75 lbs, black patent malt
. 5 stick brewers licorice

Hops

2 oz Brewers Gold hops
2 oz Fuggles hops

Other

. 5 lbs French roast coffee beans

Yeast Wyeast #1028: British ale

Procedure Steep grains in water while heating. Remove grains just before boiling. During the boil, add licorice and extract. Add 1 ounce of Brewer's Gold for 60 minutes, 1 ounce for 45 minutes, and 1 ounce of Fuggles for 30 minutes. Cool wort and pitch yeast. Add ungrounded coffee beans and remaining ounce of Fuggles. The next day skim off all crud, including coffee beans and hops. One day later, rack to secondary. Ferment three weeks and bottle.

Coopers Clone

Category Stout
Recipe Type All Grain

Fermentables

9. 5 lbs 2-row lager malt
. 25 lbs chocolate malt
.75 lbs crystal malt (60L)
1.25 lbs roast barley

Hops

1 oz Pride of Ringwood hops (9. 5 % alpha, 60 minute boil)

Other

1 lbs dextrose

Yeast, Yeast labs Australian ale yeast (or Wyeast London)

Procedure Single step infusion mash or step mash. Culturing yeast from a bottle of Coopers if available, otherwise use yeasts mentioned in the ingredients list.

Cottage Coffee Stout

Category Stout
Recipe Type Extract
Sweet stout with a chocolate aroma and a well balanced, low hopped smooth coffee taste.

Fermentables

3.0 kg Dark Malt Extract (2 cans x 3.3 lbs)
1.0 Lbs Crystal Malt
0. 5 Lbs Chocolate Malt

0. 5 Lbs Black Patent Malt
1.25 Cup Light DME (priming)

Hops

1.0 Oz Kent Golding 5. 5 % AA (bittering)
0. 5 Oz Fuggles 4.7% AA (bittering)
0. 5 Oz Fuggles (flavoring)

Other

0. 5 Lbs Lactose
0. 5 Lbs Hawaiian Chocolate Coffee Beans crushed not ground (or your favorite Java blend)

Yeast Wyeast #1084 Irish Ale

Procedure Steep grains in 1 1/2 gal water at 155 F for 15-20 min. Remove and sparge grains with 1/2 gal water, bringing brew to 2 gal total. Stir in malt extract and bittering hops, boil 1 hour. Dissolve lactose in 1 quart water. Add flavor hops and lactose last 15 min of boil. After full boil, remove from heat and steep coffee beans for 15-20 min. Cool wort and pitch yeast. Ferment in primary 5 days, secondary 15 days. Bottle using DME and condition 4-6 weeks. Enjoy.

Crankcase Stout

Category Stout
Recipe Type Extract

Fermentables
1 lbs crushed crystal malt
1 lbs crushed roasted barley
1. 5 lbs crushed black patent malt
9 lbs Munton & Fison dark, dry malt extract
1 can John Bull dark hopped malt extract
2 inches brewers licorice

Hops
2 oz Nugget leaf hops
2 oz Galena leaf hops
1 oz Cascade hops

Other
1 oz amylase enzyme

Yeast 2 packs Doric ale yeast

Procedure Put grains into two gallons water and boil. When a pot reaches boil, remove grains. Add dry extract and stir. Add hopped extract and licorice. Add Nugget, and Galena hops. Boil 70 minutes. This was a big thick mess and needs a big pot---mine boiled over. Add Cascade for finishing. Cool and pitch yeast and amylase. Put in a big fermenter with a blow tube---my batch blew the cover creating a marvelous mess all over the wall- Eventually rack to secondary and ferment a long time (at least 3 weeks).

Cream of Oats Stout

Category Stout
Recipe Type All Grain

Fermentables
6 lbs Klages 2-row pale malt
. 5 lbs Dextrin malt
1-1/8 lbs rolled oats
. 5 lbs crystal malt
. 5 lbs chocolate malt
. 25 lbs roasted barley

Hops
1 oz Clusters boiling hops (7.4 alpha)
. 5 oz Cascade hops

Other
10 oz lactose
. 5 tsp Irish moss

Yeast Wyeast #1007: German ale

Procedure Mash in 3 quarts cold water. Raise temperature to 153 degrees and hold until iodine test indicates complete conversion. Transfer to lauter tun and sparge to yield 7 gallons. Boil 1 hour, adding boiling hops. Add finishing hops and Irish moss in last 10 minutes. Sparge, cool and pitch yeast.

Dark of the Moon Cream Stout

Category Stout
Recipe Type Extract

Fermentables
5 lbs dry, dark malt extract
2 lbs crystal malt 40L
1. 5 lbs crystal malt 20L
12 oz chocolate malt
4 oz roasted barley

Hops
. 5 oz Eroica hops (20 BU)
. 25 oz Chinook hops (12 BU)
.75 oz Nugget hops (12 BU) (subst. N. Brewer (? BU))
1 oz Cascade hops (5 BU)
1 oz Eroica hops (4 BU)

Other
6 oz dextrin powder
. 5 tsp calcium carbonate

Yeast Wyeast #1098 British Ale yeast

Procedure Made a yeast starter 3 days before pitching. Used 2 tablespoons DME and 1 cup water. Next time use 2 cups water. Crack all grains and steep for 30 minutes at about 160 degrees along with the calcium carbonate. Strain out grains and sparge into about 2-1/2 gallons pre-boiled water. Total boil about 5 gallons. Add dry malt and dextrin and bring to a boil. Add 1/2 ounce of Eroica and 1/4 ounce of Chinook when boil starts. 30 minutes later add 3/4 ounce Nugget hops. Chill with an immersion chiller. Rack to a carboy, fill to 5 gallons and let sit overnight to allow the trub to settle out. The next morning rack it to a plastic primary, pitched the yeast starter, and add the 1 ounce of Cascades and Eroica hops

Double Party Chocolate Stout

Category Stout
Recipe Type Extract
A double chocolate stout with a strong cocoa flavor. Color is dark brown, and the aroma is that of cocoa.

Fermentables
6.0 Lbs Light Dry Malt Extract
0.333 Lbs Roasted Barley
0.667 Lbs Chocolate Malt
0.333 Lbs 60 L Crystal Malt
0. 5 Lbs Carapils Malt

Hops
3.0 Oz East Kent Goldings (4.0% AA) 60 minutes
1.0 Oz UK Fuggles (4.0% AA) 30 minutes
1.0 Oz UK Fuggles (4.0% AA) 1 minute

Other
1.0 Lbs Baker's Chocolate
1.0 Tbsp Irish Moss

Yeast White Labs' Irish Ale (WLP 004)

Procedure 1) Steep crushed grains in 5 gallons of 150 F water for 30 minutes. Remove grains and bring water to a boil. 2) Melt chocolate in a double boiler and add to boiling water stirring constantly. 3) Dissolve DME in boiling water, let boil for 15 minutes. 4) Add boiling hops for 60 minutes of the boil. 5) Add flavor hops for 30 minutes of the boil. 6) Add Irish moss for the final 15 minutes of the boil. 7) Steep 1 oz of aroma hops for a minute after turning off the heat on the water. 8) Cool wort and add to fermenter to pitch the yeast. 9) Primary fermentation was 5 days, and secondary fermentation was 10 days. A layer of oil will be present at the top of the fermenting beer, try not to transfer this during any transfer step you have.

Double Stout

Category Stout
Recipe Type Extract

Fermentables
10 lbs dark malt extract
1 lbs, black patent malt

George Braun

2 lbs crystal malt
. 5 lbs flaked barley
.25 lbs roasted barley
. 5 stick licorice

Hops

2 1/2 Bullion hops
1 1/2 Kent Golding hops

Other

3 gallons water
1 tsp ascorbic acid
. 5 tsp citric acid
1 tsp Irish moss

Yeast 3/4 ounce ale yeast (three standard packages)

Procedure Combine water, dark malt extract, and Bullion hop. Boil for 20 minutes. Add black patent malt through Irish moss. Boil for 5 minutes. Remove from heat and add Kent Golding hops. Steep for 5 minutes. Cool and add yeast nutrient and ale yeast. When fermentation has "stopped", add priming sugar and bottle.

Eliminator Stout

Category Stout
Recipe Type Partial Mash

Fermentables

1.0 Lbs Clover Honey
7.0 Lbs Dark Malt
0. 5 Lbs Roasted Barley 1190-13m
0. 5 Lbs crystal barley 120L
0. 5 Lbs flaked oats
0. 5 Lbs flaked barley

Hops
2.0 Oz Fuggles Hops (finish)
1.0 Oz Northern Brewer Hops (boil)

Other
2.0 Tsp gypsum

Yeast Irish Yeast Y108-4

Procedure Add roasted barley & crystal malt to cold water and slowly bring to a boil. After 20 minutes, remove grain. Add honey, malt, flaked oats, barley, gypsum, and boiling hops. Boil for 15 minutes, then removes finishing hops. Cool wort, add to 5 gallon mark on your bucket. When your wort is cool, at 75 degrees, add yeast.

Fat Wanda's Kolsch Klone
Category German Ale
Recipe Type All Grain

Fermentables
7 lbs pale malt
1. 5 lbs Vienna malt

. 75 lbs wheat malt

Hops
1--3/4 oz Hallertauer (5.0%)
. 5 oz Tettnanger (4. 5 %)

Yeast Wyeast European ale

Procedure To keep hopping aroma low, the last addition of hops should come no later than 20 minutes before the end of the boil. The trick to this beer is to cold condition it. After 4 days primary and 4 days secondary fermentation at ale temps (~65F), rack again and cold condition at 40F for 12 days. Then prime and bottle as usual.

Finster's Finest Chocolate Raspberry Stout

Category Stout
Recipe Type Extract

Fermentables
3.3 lbs John Bull plain dark extract syrup
3 lbs plain dry malt extract
1 lbs crystal malt
. 5 lbs roasted barley
. 5 lbs black patent malt
3 lbs frozen raspberries
1-1/4 cups dry malt extract

Hops

1. 5 oz Northern Brewer hops pellets
. 5 oz Willamette hops pellets

Other
Gypsum to create hard water
8 oz baker's chocolate

Yeast 2 packages Edme dry ale yeast

Procedure Heat 1. 5 gal water to 170F. Add grains, cover, and let sit for 30 min. stirring occasionally. Remove grains. Bring to boil. Add gypsum, malt extracts, NB hops, chocolate, and boil for 60 min. Turn off heat. Add raspberries to hot wort (be careful of splashing). Cover, and let sit for 13 min. Add Willamette hops. Cover, and let sit for 2 min. Cool wort. Dump entire mess into primary, aerate, and pitch yeast (I rehydrated it while waiting for the rasp. to steep in wort).
4-5 days in primary. Rack *very carefully* into secondary, to avoid racking fruit particles. 10-14 days in secondary (I went 14).

Generic Stout

Category Stout
Recipe Type All Grain

Fermentables
9 lbs klages
. 5 lbs chocolate malt
. 5 lbs roast barley

George Braun
1 lbs 80L crystal
. 75 stick brewers licorice
1 lbs brown sugar

Hops
2 oz. fuggles

Yeast Wyeast London ale yeast

Procedure I used my standard infusion mash @ 152F, boiled for 90 min. with 3 hops additions, force-chilled and pitched. The yeast (a 1-quart starter) took 36 hours to take off, then pumped up to a nice cruising.

Guinness Pub Draught Clone

Category Stout
Recipe Type Extract

Fermentables
6 lbs John Bull Pale Malt Extract
1 lb Flaked Barley
. 5 lb Roasted Barley
.25 lb Black Patent
1. 5 cups Pale Dry Malt Extract for priming

Hops
1 oz Northern Brewer whole hops (7.7% alpha)

Other
1 tsp gypsum

Yeast Wyeast #1084 (Irish Ale)

Procedure To 2 gal cold water, add grains in a bag, and gypsum. Bring to boil, boil 5 min., and remove grains. Add hops, boil 45 min. Sparge into cold water to make 5 gal of wort. Rack cooled wort off of cold break, pitch yeast.

Grapefruit Taste

Category Stout
Recipe Type Extract

Fermentables
9 lb "Dutch" amber dry malt extract
1 lb Medium Brown Sugar
. 5 lb roasted barley
. 5 lb chocolate barley

Hops
4 oz Northern Brewer hop pellets AA, 8.8%
2 oz Cascade hop pellets AA, 5.4%

Other
1 inch of brewers liquorish
1 tsp Irish moss

Yeast Wyeast #1084 Irish Ale yeast

Procedure I steeped roasted/chocolate barley in 1 gal 160 deg F water for 30 min, strained into

kettle, and sparged with 1/2 gal 170 deg F water. Added an additional gal of water and brought to a boil. Removed from heat and dissolved extract and sugar, returned to burner and brought to boil. Added liquorish and Northern Brewer hops. Added Irish moss at 45 min. Boiled for 55 min and then added Cascade hops. Boiled for additional 5 min and cooled in ice water bath. (total boil 60 minutes).
Strained cooled wort into 2. 5 gal of previously boiled and cooled water in primary fermenter (6.7 gal plastic, closed fermentation). O.G. 1.078. Pitched yeast directly from a smack pack at 78 deg F. Active fermentation noticeable after 12 hours. Primary fermentation was at approx 72 deg for five days. Racked to secondary (5 gal glass) S.G 1.042, tasted fruity but not overpowering. After 13 days total, all fermentation activity ceased. Bottled with 3/4 cup honey. F.G. 1.030.

Guinness Pub Draught Clone

Category Stout
Recipe Type Extract

Fermentables

6 lbs John Bull Pale Malt Extract
1 lb Flaked Barley
. 5 lb Roasted Barley
.25 lb Black Patent
1. 5 cups Pale Dry Malt Extract for priming

Hops
1 oz Northern Brewer whole hops (7.7% alpha)

Other
1 tsp gypsum

Yeast Wyeast #1084 (Irish Ale)

Procedure To 2 gal cold water, add grains in a bag, and gypsum. Bring to boil, boil 5 min., and remove grains. Add hops, boil 45 min. Sparge into cold water to make 5 gal of wort. Rack cooled wort off of cold break, pitch yeast.

Halloween Stout

Category Stout
Recipe Type Partial Mash

Fermentables
5 lbs pale malt
1 lbs crystal malt
1 lbs chocolate malt
3.3 lbs John Bull unhopped dark malt extract

Hops
1 oz Clusters hops pellets
1 oz Hallertauer leaf hops
. 5 oz Willamette hops pellets

Other

1 tbsp Irish moss

Yeast 2 packs Red Star ale yeast

Procedure Mash malts in 2-1/2 gallons of 170 degree water; 154 degrees, pH 5.2, maintain at 140-150 degrees for 90 minutes. (Ending pH was 4.8.). Sparge and bring to boil. Add dark extract. Add Clusters and Hallertauer hops 20 minutes into boil. Add Irish moss after another 10 minutes. Add Willamette hops in last 15 minutes. Cool wort and add to carboy. Pitch yeast. Set the carboy in cool basement with blow tube. On the second day, replace the blow tube with airlock. Bottled after 29 days.

Imperial Stout

Category Stout
Recipe Type All Grain

Fermentables
1 lbs Wheat malt
1 lbs Crystal malt (60L)
1 lbs Belgian Biscuit
. 75 lbs Chocolate malt
.75 lbs Black Patent
. 5 lbs Roasted Barley
2 lbs dark brown sugar
5--1/2 lbs Belgian Pale malt
3 lbs Dextrine malt
3 lbs Belgian Carapils

2 lbs Belgian Special-B

Hops
1 oz Bullion hops (10%)
1 oz Cascade hops (5.9%)
1 oz Kent Goldings (4.9%)
1 oz Fuggles (3.1%)
1 oz Mt. Hood (3. 5 %)

Other
2 Licorice

Yeast Wyeast Chico ale yeast

Procedure Mashed 1 hour at 160 F. Collected 7 gallons, boiled down to 5--1/2 gallons.
Submitted by: Chris Campanelli

Irish Christmas Stout

Category Stout
Recipe Type Extract

Fermentables
4 lbs Mountmellick Irish Stout Extract
3 lbs Munton and Fison Amber DME
. 5 lbs (2 cups) Crystal Malt (60 Lovibond)
.25 lbs (1 cup) Black Patent Malt
1 lbs Clover honey

Hops
1 oz Bullion hops (bittering)

. 5 oz Hallertau hops (finishing)

Other

12 inches Cinnamon sticks or 6 teaspoons ground cinnamon
4 oz Ginger root, freshly peeled and grated
2 tsp of Allspice
1 tsp Cloves
4 grated rinds from medium size oranges

Yeast 1 package WYeast #1084 Irish Stout Yeast

Procedure Simmer honey and spices in covered pot for 45 minutes. Add cracked grains to 2 gallons cold water and bring to a boil. As soon as boiling starts, remove grains with a strainer. Add malt extracts and bittering hops and boil for 55 minutes. Add finishing hops and boil for 5 more minutes. Remove from heat. Stir in honey and spice mixture and cool. Strain into fermenter containing 3 gallons cold (previously boiled) water and pitch yeast (when cool). After vigorous primary fermentation subsides, rack into secondary. Bottle with 7 ounces corn sugar or 1-1/4 cups DME when fermentation completes.

Irish Stout

Category Stout
Recipe Type Extract

Fermentables

6 lbs dark malt extract
. 5 lbs 80L crystal malt
. 5 lbs 120L crystal malt
. 5 lbs roasted barley
.25 lbs chocolate malt
. 25 lbs, black patent

Hops
1 oz Bullion hops (Boil)
1 oz Fuggles hops (Finish)

Yeast WYeast #1084

Procedure 1. Bring 1--1/2 gallons water to boil while steeping the crystal malts. Boil for 5 minutes, remove the grains.
2. Add the boiling hops and gypsum, boil for 50 minutes.
3. Add the Fuggles, turn off the heat, and put the lid on the brew pot.
4. Sparge the wort into enough water to make 5 gallons.

Joan's Potholder Oatmeal Stout

Category Stout
Recipe Type All Grain

Fermentables
5 lbs 2--row pale malt
1. 5 lbs steel cut oats
. 5 lbs malted wheat

George Braun

1. 5 lbs 80 L. crystal malt
1 lbs, black patent malt
1 lbs chocolate malt
1 lbs roasted barley
. 5 lbs Cara-pils malt
3 lbs dark Australian DME

Hops

1 oz Chinook pellets (13.6% alpha) (boil 60 minutes)
. 5 oz Perle pellets (8% alpha) (boil 35 minutes)
.25 oz Hallertauer pellets (3% alpha) (boil 35 minutes)
. 25 oz Tettnanger pellets (3.4% alpha) (boil 35 minutes)
.75 oz Hallertauer (steep for aroma)
. 75 oz Tettnanger (steep for aroma)
1 oz Cascade (dry hop)

Other

. 5 lbs lactose
1 tsp Irish moss

Yeast Wyeast Irish ale yeast

Procedure Single-step infusion mash, partial mash recipe.
Strike Temperature 170 into 12 liters of treated water, alla Burton on Trent. Note This was a little too thick, so use a little more water. Mashed for 45 minutes, 170 F. proteolytic step for 10 minutes.

Sparged for almost two hours, while adding runoff to brew kettle to get boiling. Sparge SG ran from 1.09 down to about 1.025 when I had enough wort. Added 3 lbs DME (Dark Australian) to bring wort to 1.06 SG. I added 8 oz. of lactose and a tsp. of dry moss before killing the fire.

I pitched a large starter of the Irish Wyeast strain and got lots of blow off. I had the extra wort in a 4 liter auxiliary. I used this to fill up the secondary after racking off the lees. Dry hopping was done in the secondary with the cascade. After 2 weeks, the SG was only down to 1.03, and fermentation was very slow.

Josh's Better Xingu

Category Stout
Recipe Type Extract

Fermentables
6.6 lbs M&F Dark Extract
1 lbs Crystal Malt
. 5 lbs Chocolate Malt
.25 lbs Black Patent Malt
. 25 lbs Roast Barley

Hops
2 oz Northern Brewer (Boiling only. No finishing hops)

Other

. 5 lbs Lactose
. 75 cup Dextrose (priming)

Yeast Wyeast 1028

Procedure Crack and steep specialty grains at 150 degrees for about an hour in 1/2 gal water. Sparge with 1. 5 gallons of 165 degree water. Add the extract and gypsum. When boiling, add the hops. Boil for one hour. Add the lactose to the boil for the last 15 minutes.

Kahlua Stout

Category Stout
Recipe Type All Grain

Fermentables
5 lbs 2-row barley
2 lbs 120L caramel malt
2 lbs 20L caramel malt
2 lbs British crystal
1 lbs wheat malt
1 lbs roast barley

Hops
2 oz Northern Brewer hops (boil 75 minutes)
. 5 oz Styrian Golding hops (boil 75 minutes)

Other
1 lbs dextrin

Yeast Whitbread ale yeast

Procedure Mash at 160 degrees F. Add Kahlua extract to primary before pitching yeast

Klingon Stout

Category Stout
Recipe Type Extract

Fermentables

George Braun

6.6 lbs dark malt extract syrup
1 lb crushed crystal malt
. 5 lb black patent malt
1/3 lb roasted barley

Hops
1. 5 oz Northern Brewers hops--boil 60 min.
1 oz Tettnanger hops --finishing last 2 min.

Other
2 quarts prune juice WITH NO PRESERVATIVES!!!!
. 75 c. corn sugar to prime

Yeast ale yeast

Procedure Steep grains 30 min at 150F. Strain into brew pot and rinse with one gal hot water. Add extract, boiling hops and additional gal. water and boil 1 hour. Add finishing hops last 2 min. Turn off heat and add prune juice to pasteurize for 10 min (probably not necessary since the juice is already pasteurized). Pour into primary fermenter and top with cold water up to 5 gal. Pitch yeast when cool. Rack to secondary a week later. Bottle when ready. Age at least 4 week.

Krudge

Category Stout

Recipe Type Extract

Fermentables
1 can M&F stout, extract
1 lbs amber dry malt extract
1 lbs dark malt extract
7 oz black patent malt
7 oz chocolate malt
7 oz roast barley
21 oz crystal malt

Hops
2 oz Chinook hops (boil)
1 oz Centennial hops (boil)
1 oz Cascade hops (finish)

Other
. 5 oz gypsum

Yeast ale yeast

Procedure Crush grains; steep at around 150F; sparge with lots of cold water. Add extracts, gypsum, boiling hops. Add finishing hops 5 minutes before the end; total time in copper around 45 minutes. Chill brew pot with ice; bring to about 3--1/2 - 4 gallons. Primed with corn sugar.

Mach Guinness

Category Stout

George Braun

Recipe Type All Grain

Fermentables

5 lbs pale 2 row British malt
1 lbs rolled barley
1 lbs roasted barley
2 lbs light dry malt extract
2 cups corn sugar

Hops

2 oz bullion Hops (1. 5 boiling

Yeast 1 package Whitbread Ale Yeast

Procedure Mash 5 pounds 2-row, rolled barley in at 132 degrees. Protein rest 30 minutes. Starch conversion 2 hours at 153 degrees. Mashed out 15 minutes at 168 degrees. Sparged with 4 gallons 172 degree water. Add the 2 pounds dry ME and the 2 cups sugar. Bring to a boil. Add 1 1/2 ounces of hops. Boil 1 hour. Add 1/2 ounce of hops, turn off heat, and let stand for 15 minutes. Cool wort to 72 degrees, strain into fermenter, and pitch yeast.

Bottling: one to two days before bottling, sour two bottles of ale. To do this, pour two bottles of ale into a sterile glass container. Cover with a clean cloth secured with string or a rubber band. Put in the cupboard (or somewhere relatively dark and warm) and let stand one to two days. It should sour, but not mold. Add 2/3 cup corn sugar to the sour ale and boil for 10 minutes. Pour into bottling bucket. Add sour ale and bottle as usual.

Mackeson Triple Stout Clone

Category Stout
Recipe Type Extract

Fermentables
7 lbs Australian light syrup
1 lbs chocolate malt
1. 5 lbs, black patent malt
12 oz crystal malt

Hops
2 oz Kent Goldings leaf hops

Other
12 oz lactose
1 tsp salt
1 tsp citric acid

Yeast ale yeast

Procedure Bring extracts syrup and enough water to make 3 gallons to boil. Add crystal malt. Boil 10 minutes. Add hops. Boil 5 minutes. Turn off heat. Add chocolate and black patent malt in grain bag. Steep 10 minutes. Sparge grain bag with 2 gallons boiling water. Add lactose. Pitch yeast

and ferment. When bottling, prime with malt extract.
Submitted by: Doug Roberts

Mackeson's Stout

Category Stout
Recipe Type All Grain

Fermentables
5 lbs pale malt
. 5 lbs crystal malt
. 5 lbs roast black malt
1 lbs soft brown sugar

Hops
1.75 oz Fuggles hops

Yeast ale yeast

Procedure Treat the water with 1/4 ounce of magnesium sulfate and 1 ounce of common salt. Crush all grains and mash in 2 gallons of water at 165 degrees for 2 hours. Sparge with 2 gallons of 170 degree water. A few drops of caramel may be added at this stage if proper color has not been sufficiently achieved. Boil 1-1/2 hours with hops and sugar. Bring to 5 gallons, pitch yeast when at correct temperature. This recipe can be brewed at an O.G. of 1.045 by adding 1/4 pound of dark extract. May also add 1/4 pound of lactose in boil to provide a slightly higher gravity and a sweeter palate.

Mackeson's Stout

Category Stout
Recipe Type Extract

Fermentables
4 lbs dark malt extract
2 lbs soft brown sugar

Hops
1.75 oz Fuggles hops

Other
8 oz gravy browning (caramel)

Yeast ale yeast

Procedure Boil hops in 20 pints of water for 1 hour. Strain and dissolve extract, caramel and sugar. Boil for 15 minutes. Bring to 5 gallons, pitch yeast at correct temperature.
As in the previous recipe, this can be brought to a gravity of 1.045 by increasing the extract by 1/4 pound, and lactose may also be added. A few drops of caramel may be added at this stage if sufficient color has not been achieved. Saccharine can be added at bottling to increase apparent sweetness.

Maple Syrup Stout

Category Stout
Recipe Type Extract

Fermentables
6 lbs Australian dark extract syrup
12 oz maple syrup
. 75 cup corn sugar (priming)

Hops
1. 5 oz Bullion hops (boil)

Yeast ale yeast

Procedure Add six ounces of the maple syrup during the boil and the other 6 in the last couple minutes of the boil (much like a finishing hops). Total boil time was 1 hour.

Maple Syrup Stout

Category Stout
Recipe Type Extract

Fermentables
6 lb dark extract (syrup)
4 oz chocolate malt
8 oz crystal malt
. 75 cup, corn sugar (priming)

Hops
1. 5 oz Bullion boiling hops

12 oz MacDonald's Pure Maple Syrup

Yeast 1 pack Whitbread Ale Yeast

Procedure Place the grains in 150 waters, steep for 1/2 hour.
Remove grains.

Add extract syrup.

Bring to boil, and add hops.

I boiled for a full hour, adding the Maple syrup during the last five minutes of the boil, like a finishing hop. I didn't want to boil off the maple aroma.

Ferment took place at about 65 degrees. This stuff fermented fast! I racked to the secondary in 48 hours, and then bottled five days later.

Mega Stout

Category Stout
Recipe Type Extract

Fermentables
2 cans, Munton & Fison stout kit
3 lbs Munton & Fison extra dark, dry malt extract
2 cups chocolate malt
2 cups black patent malt
2 cups roasted barley

. 75 cup corn sugar (priming)

Hops

3 oz Fuggles hops (boil)

. 5 oz Cascade hops (finish)

Other

. 25 tsp Irish moss

Yeast ale yeast

Procedure Steep whole grains in 6 cups of water and bring to boil. Remove grains at boil. Add extract and boiling hops. Boil 1 hour. Add Irish moss in last 15 minutes. After boil, add Cascade hops and steep 15 minutes. Cool and pitch yeast.

Mocha Java Stout

Category Stout

Recipe Type Extract

Fermentables

7 lbs Glenbrew Irish Stout Kit

. 25 lbs Flaked Barley

1/8 lbs Black Patent Malt

. 75 cup Corn sugar (bottling)

Hops

. 5 oz Fuggles hop pellets (bittering - 60 min)

. 5 oz Fuggles hop pellets (flavoring - 10 min)

Other

4 oz Ghirardelli unsweetened chocolate
2 cups Brewed Coffee (Monte Sano blend)

Yeast 1 package WYeast #1084 Irish Stout Yeast

Procedure Brew coffee using 2 scoops coffee to 12 oz. cold water. Steep flaked barley and cracked black patent for 45 minutes. Bring 1. 5 gallons water to a boil in the brew pot, sparge in grains, and add extract and boiling hops. Boil for 50 minutes. Add chocolate and flavoring hops and boil for 10 more minutes. Remove from heat and carefully stir in coffee. Cool and pour into fermenter containing 3 gallons cold (pre-boiled) water. Pitch yeast. Rack to secondary when vigorous fermentation subsides. Bottle with 3/4 cup corn sugar.

Most Recent Oatmeal Stout

Category Stout
Recipe Type Extract

Fermentables

6.6 lbs Munton & Fison light unhopped extract
3.3 lbs Munton & Fison dark unhopped extract
. 5 lbs cara-pils malt
. 5 lbs black patent malt
. 5 lbs roasted barley
.75 lbs steel cut oats
. 5 lbs malt-dextrin

Hops
2 oz Sticklbrackt hops (boil)
1 oz Bullion hops (boil)
1 oz Cascade hops (finish)
1 oz Cascade hops (dry)

Other
. 25 tsp Irish Moss

Yeast 14 grams Whitbread ale yeast

Procedure Last in the series of experiments in brewing oatmeal stouts. It is an extract brew, with specialty grains being added in the standard stove- top method and removed at boil. Grains are cracked with a rolling pin and boiled for 30 minutes before straining. The Sticklbrackt are added in 1/2 ounce batches at 20 minute intervals, the Bullion 1/2 ounce at a time in between the Sticklbrackt. The finishing hops are added 5 minutes before the end of the boil. The dry hopping is done in the primary.

My Own Scotch

New Stout II
Category Stout
Recipe Type All Grain

Fermentables
9 lbs Munton & Fison English Pale malted barley

3 lb roasted barley (unmalted)
1/2 lb English Crystal malt (40L)
1/2 lb Black Patent malt

Hops
2 oz East Kent Goldings hops (60 minutes)

Other
2 tsp. Irish Moss (@30 minute mark)

Yeast Wyeast 1084 (Irish Ale)

Procedure Mash in a single infusion at 155F for 60 minutes. The hops were, and always are, whole flower. This batch did not use a starter for the yeast, although I highly recommend using a one-pint starter for ales. My system is somewhat inefficient, so your extraction may be higher than my reported gravities. As I generally realize 26 points/pound, you should adjust the grain bill accordingly.
Judges generally embraced this beer (although a couple was turned off by the large amount of roasted barley), but that has not prevented me from tweaking around the edges. While the above recipe served me throughout 1993, in 1994 I incorporated several suggestions from better judging sheets, resulting in New Stout III, which has remained unchanged since.

New Stout III

George Braun

Category Stout

Recipe Type All Grain

Fermentables

9 lb Hugh Baird English Pale malted barley
3 lb roasted barley (unmalted)
1/4 lb HB English Crystal malt (130L)
1/2 lb Black Patent malt
1/2 lb flaked barley

Hops

1. 5 oz Chinook hops (13.1 AA% for 60 minutes)
1. 5 oz EKG hops (15 minutes)
0. 5 oz EKG hops (1 minute)

Other

1 tsp. Irish Moss (@30 minute mark)

Yeast Wyeast #1084 Irish Ale

Procedure Mash in a single infusion at 151 or 152F for 60 minutes. Mash out between 168F and 176F. The hops are whole flower. My system is somewhat inefficient, so your extraction may be higher than my reported gravities. As I generally get 26 points/pound, you should adjust the grain bill accordingly.

No Decaff Here Stout

Category Stout
Recipe Type All Grain

Fermentables
4 lbs 2 row
1.25 lb chocolate malt
. 5 lb black patent
.75 lb roast barley
1 lb cara-pils (dextrine)
1. 5 lb dark crystal (about 120)
1 lb Munich malt
1 lb flaked barley

Hops
1.2 oz cascade (60 min)
1.2 oz cascade (30 min) 1.00
1 ox cascade (fresh, finishing)

Other
Irish Moss

Yeast English ale yeast

Procedure Protein rest at 125 {for 30 min.
Mash at 158 for 30 min
I'm slightly suspicious of the flaked barley; it seems to me that I balked at the $3/lb price at my local shop.

Not So Oatmeal

Category Stout

George Braun

Recipe Type Extract

Fermentables

3.3 lbs Munton & Fison plain light extract
4 lbs Alexanders pale unhopped extract
. 5 lbs, black patent malt
.25 lbs roasted barley
. 5 lbs crystal or cara-pils malt
. 5 lbs steel cut oats

Hops

1 oz Hallertauer hops (boil)
. 75 oz Fuggles hops (boil)
1 oz Cascade hops (finish)
. 5 oz Cascade hops (dry)

Other

. 5 tsp Irish Moss

Yeast 14 grams Muntona ale yeast

Procedure This is the third of a series of experiments in brewing oatmeal stouts. It is an extract brew, with specialty grains being added in the standard stovetop method and removed at boil. Grains are cracked with a rolling pin and boiled for 30 minutes before straining. The finishing hops are added 5 minutes before the end of the boil. The dry hopping is done after 4 days in the primary.

Oatmeal Cream Stout

Category Stout

Recipe Type All Grain

Fermentables

10 lbs pale ale malt

1 lbs roasted barley (500L)

. 5 lbs flaked barley (1. 5 L)

. 5 lbs crystal malt (60L)

. 5 lbs chocolate malt (400L)

1-1/3 lbs steel cut oats (from health food store)

2/3 stick brewers licorice (boil)

Hops

9 AAU Bullion pellets (9% alpha)

. 5 oz Fuggles pellets (3.4% alpha)

. 5 oz Fuggles pellets

Other

. 5 lbs lactose

Yeast Wyeast Irish ale #1084

Procedure Mash with 5 gallons 18 oz (48 oz/#) at 155-150F for 90 minutes. Sparge with 3 gallons water at 165F, collecting 6. 5 gallons for the boil. Boil 75 minutes, then force chill. Save 2 quarts boiled wort for priming, ferment the rest.

Oatmeal Stout 1

George Braun

Category Stout

Recipe Type All Grain

Fermentables

7 lbs pale malt

1 lbs roast barley

1 lbs rolled oats

. 5 lbs light caristan (15--20L)

Hops

1-1/4 oz Chinook pellets (13% alpha) (boil 60 minutes)

Yeast Whitbread ale yeast

Procedure Treat 7 gallons water with 5 grams gypsum and 1 gram chalk.
Mash in with 8 quarts 137 F. water, target temperature 123. After 30 minutes, step with 5 quarts boiling water, target temperature 154. Conversion is done in 20 minutes or so. Mash out at 168. Sparge with remaining water to collect 6 gallons. Boil 60 minutes with Chinook hops. Chill, pitch with dry Whitbread yeast.

Oatmeal Stout 2

Category Stout

Recipe Type Partial Mash

Fermentables

3 lbs English 2-row pale malt

3.3 lbs dark extract
3 lbs dark DME
1 lbs steel cuts oats

Hops
2 oz Centennial leaf hops (AU=11. 1, total=22. 2
1 oz Cascade leaf hops (AU=5)

Yeast Wyeast Irish Ale yeast starter (#1084?)

Procedure Mash pale malt and steel cut oats in 5 quarts of water. Sparge with 2 1/4 English 2-row pale malt, 1 lb. of steel cut oats, mashed in 5 qts. Added dark extract and dark DME to the wort and boiled with 2 oz. of Centennial leaf hops (AU=11. 1, total=22. 2 WHOOPS!) Good thing I like hops. Finished with 1 oz. of Cascade leaf hops. (AU=5) Pitched Wyeast Irish Ale yeast starter (#1084?), took 24 hrs. for active ferment.

Oatmeal Stout 3

Category Stout
Recipe Type Extract

Fermentables
8 lbs amber malt extract
. 5 lbs black patent malt
. 5 lbs roast barley
. 5 lbs chocolate malt
1 lbs steel cut oats

Hops
2 oz Eroica hops (boil)
1 oz Fuggles hops (finish)

Yeast Whitbread ale yeast

Procedure Crack all grains (except oats), add to 2 gallons cold water, add oats, and bring to boil. Remove grains with strainer when boil is reached. Add malt extract and boiling hops. Boil 60 minutes. Add finishing hops and boil another minute or so. Remove from heat, let steep 15 minutes. Put 4-6 inches of ice in bottom of plastic fermenter and strain wort into fermenter. Sparge. Bring volume to 5-1/4 gallons and mix. The temperature should now be below 80 degrees. Rack to 6 gallon glass carboy and pitch yeast. Bottle when fermentation is done (about 2-3 weeks).

Oatmeal Wheat Stout

Category Stout
Recipe Type Extract

Fermentables
3.3 lbs Edme Irish stout, extract
3.3 lbs Edme light beer extract
3 lbs pale
2 lbs crystal malt
1 lbs wheat malt
1 lbs old-fashion oatmeal

2. 5 cups roasted barley
4 cups black patent malt
1 stick brewers licorice

Hops
2 oz Hallertauer leaf hops
1 oz Tettnanger leaf hops

Other
. 5 tsp Irish moss
1 tsp diastatic enzyme powder

Yeast 1 pack Edme ale yeast

Procedure Crush pale and crystal malt. Loosely crush black patent malt. Place oatmeal in cheesecloth. Mash all except 2 cups of the black patent malt for 1-1/2 hours. Add diastatic enzyme. Sparge and begin boil. Add extracts and licorice. After 15 minutes of boil, add 1 ounce Tettnanger and continue boiling. After another 15 minutes, add 1/2 ounce Hallertauer. During last 15 minutes, add Irish moss and 2 cups black patent malt. During last 2 minutes of boil, add 1 ounce Hallertauer. Cool rapidly and pitch yeast. Ferment in 5-gallon carboy with blow tube attached. Proceed with normal single-stage fermentation.

Ohio Valley Mud Stout

Category Stout
Recipe Type Extract

Fermentables

6.6 lbs. Munton and Fison Old Ale Kit
3.3 lbs. Plain Light Malt Extract Syrup
. 5 lbs. Black Patent Malt
. 5 lbs. Roasted Barley
. 75 cup corn sugar

Hops

. 5 oz. Cascade Leaf Hops
. 5 oz. Cascade Leaf Hops

Other

3 tsp. Gypsum
4 oz. Ghirardelli Unsweetened Chocolate
2 cups brewed Mocha Java blend coffee

Yeast 2 packs Muntons yeast

Procedure Bring 1 1/2 gallons of water, crushed black patent malt and roasted barley to a boil. Remove grains when boiling begins. Remove from heat and add malt extract, bittering hops, and gypsum. Boil for 60 minutes. During the last 10 minutes, add chocolate by putting the chocolate in a strainer and holding over or just on the boil until melted. During the last 2-3 minutes, add the finishing hops. Remove from heat and stir in the coffee. Pour into 3 gallon of cold water and pitch yeast when cool.

Original Oatmeal Stout

Category Stout
Recipe Type Extract

Fermentables
6.6 lbs John Bull dark extract
1. 5 lbs plain dark extract
. 5 lbs steel cut oats

Hops
2 oz Bullion hops (boil)

Yeast 7 grams Muntona ale yeast

Procedure This is the first of a series of experiments in brewing oatmeal stouts. It is an extract brew, with some specialty grains (not in this particular recipe) being added in the standard stovetop method and removed at boil. When grains are used, they are cracked with a rolling pin and boiled for 30 minutes before straining.

Overly Acidic Stout

Category Stout
Recipe Type Extract

Fermentables
0. 5 kg dark DME
500 g flaked barley
500 g roasted barley
250 g crystal

Hops
1.8 kg Best Cellar Stout Kit (made in Ireland, I used the kit hoping to get
10 g Cascade (boiling)
40 g Goldings (boiling)
20 g Goldings (finish)

Yeast Wyeast 1084 Irish Ale

Perfect Guinness

Category Stout
Recipe Type All Grain

Fermentables
11 lb pale malt
1 lb British crystal (60L)
. 5 lb black patent malt
. 5 lb roast barley

Hops
1 Oz cluster hops (7.8%AA) (90 mins)
. 5 oz Willamette hops (4.8%AA) (30 mins)
. 5 oz EKG (5.2%AA) (30 mins)

Other
0-40 cc lactic acid (88% solution) to finished beer (to taste)

Yeast London, British ale yeast

Procedure Mash 90 mins; target 154F and pH=5. 2; soft water!

P-Guinness

Category Stout
Recipe Type All Grain

Fermentables
8 lbs PILSNER malt
1 lb roasted barley
1 lb barley flakes
4 oz. black patent

Hops
1.75 oz GOLDINGS ~5% AA hop plugs

Other
1-6 bottles of soured beer

Yeast Wyeast 1084 Irish ale yeast starter

Procedure The whole idea is to keep the protein in the beer, so you start with Pilsner malt & don't do a protein rest. Mash using your favorite technique, but keep it short - 1hr or so. Sparge w 170 F water (acidified). Do not recalculate excessively. The short mash and the pilsner malt will help avoid a stuck runoff. Bring the wort to a boil as quickly as possible. Normally I boil 30 min

to coagulate the protein before I add hops, but I in this case, add the hops right at the start of the boil, or even before. Use Goldings. Add the soured beer - preferably soured from a lactic infection. Boil 1 hour, or 45 min if you used hop pellets instead of plugs. Cool & pitch Wyeast 1084 Irish ale yeast starter. SG should be 1.045-1.050 or so, unless you get spectacular extraction rates (I don't). Ferment 60-65F.
Now if you bottle, use 3-4 oz corn sugar and let condition. If you keg, you've got an added element in how you imitate Guinness: Chill the beer to 50F, & turn the pressure up to 10-15 PSI & Serve. Do not agitate the keg. The beer will have a head, but very little carbonation in the beer itself, just like Guinness.

Right Thing Oatmeal Stout

Category Stout
Recipe Type All Grain

Fermentables
1. 5 lbs Briess Roasted Barley
8 oz Hugh Baird Black Malt
1 lbs Briess Cara-Pils
1 lbs Briess Wheat Malt
7 lbs Briess 2-Row
1 lbs Quaker Quick Oats, added to grist

Hops
2 oz Chinook, boiling (22 HBU's)

1 oz Willamette, finishing

Yeast WYeast London Ale (very dry finish)

RIS Marital Bliss

Category Stout
Recipe Type All Grain

Fermentables
20 lb 2-row births
2. 5 lb Belgian Carapils
2 lb Crystal (60L)
2 lb Munich 2-row
1 lb Belgian Special B
. 5 lb Chocolate Malt
1/4 lb black Patent
5 lb Amber Extract

Hops
6 oz Northern Brewer (60min)
3 oz Fuggles (5min)

Other
. 5 oz Irish moss at end of boil

Yeast, Yeast 1214 Belgian Liquid (And definitely make a starter!)

Simply Stout

Category Stout
Recipe Type All Grain

Fermentables
7 lbs. British 2 row pale malt
1 lbs. flaked barley
1 lbs. roasted barley

Hops
1 oz. Bullion whole hops (10.3% AA, 60 minutes)

Other
. 5 oz. gypsum (in mash water)

Yeast Wyeast 1084 Irish Ale Yeast

Procedure Mash schedule: Protein rest at 124 deg. F for 50 minutes. Saccharification at 150 deg. F for 3 hours. A sour mash was added to the main mash prior to the protein rest.

Stout 4

Category Stout
Recipe Type Extract

Fermentables
8.8 lbs unhopped dark malt extract
1 lbs roasted barley
1 lbs wheat malt
. 5 lbs, black patent malt
. 5 lbs chocolate malt

Hops

4 oz Bullion hops (boil)
1 oz Cascade hops (finish)

Yeast yeast

Procedure The bullion hops are added 30 minutes into the boil. I used pelletized hops and there was a huge amount of sediment when I racked it---not sediment in the normal sense---it was mostly beer with hops floating in it, but it was too thick to go through the siphon.

Stout 6

Category Stout
Recipe Type All Grain

Fermentables
9 lbs. Pale malt
. 75 lbs. Black patent malt
. 75 lbs. Crystal malt
10 oz. Roasted Barley

Hops
1 oz. Bullion hops-pelleted

Yeast Edme dry Ale yeast

Stout 5

Category Stout
Recipe Type Extract

George Braun

Fermentables

3.3 lbs amber NW extract
6.6 lb dark extract
1 lb crystal
1 lb roasted barley
0.4 lb chocolate malt
0. 5 lb black patent

Hops

2 oz brewers gold 15.2 (60 minute boil)
1 oz cluster 7.3 (60 minute boil)
0. 5 oz Willamette (10 minute boil)
1 oz cascades (10 minute boil)
0. 5 oz hersbrucker (5 minute boil)
1 oz cascade (5 minute boil)
0. 5 oz hersbrucker (5 minute boil)
0. 5 oz Willamette (5 minute boil)

Other

1 oz. roast aroma tea (10 minute boil)
1 oz. Roast aroma (after turning off heat)

Yeast, dry yeast and everything.

Stout ala Guinness

Category Stout
Recipe Type All Grain

Fermentables

8 lbs pale ale malt
. 75 lbs of crystal

1 lbs roasted barley
1 lbs flaked barley
. 25 lbs chocolate malt
.25 lbs wheat malt

Hops
12-12 HBU Hops

Yeast Wyeast Irish yeast

Procedure Standard mashing procedure used.

Stout Stout 7

Category Stout
Recipe Type All Grain

Fermentables
10 lbs pale malt (2-row)
1 lbs roasted barley
1 lbs flaked barley
. 5 lbs crystal malt

Hops
1+ oz Centennial whole hops (at 10.1 AAU) no finishing

Yeast Wyeast Chico ale slurry

Procedure Mash in 3 gallons of water at 170 degrees. Starch conversion at about 90 minutes. Mash out. Sparge with 170 degree water. Collect 5 gallons or so. Boil for 60 minutes with hops going it at beginning of boil.

Skwerl Stout

Category Stout
Recipe Type Extract

Fermentables
7.0 Lbs Light DME
1.0 Lbs Crystal 80L
1.0 Lbs Chocolate Malt
0.75 Lbs Roasted Barley
0.25 Lbs Black Patent Malt

Hops
2.0 Oz Yakima Kent Goldings

Yeast Wyeast 1098

Procedure Steep grains at 150F for 20min, and remove. Bring to boil, add hops, and boil for 50 min. Add DME 5min before end of boil. Add a BIG starter of 1098 or 1084. This recipe has gone over very well with all who have tried. A prominent yet mellow chocolate taste

Speedball Stout

Category Stout
Recipe Type Extract

Fermentables
6 lbs Dark Australian malt extract
. 5 lbs Dark Australian dry
4 oz black patent malt
4 oz Flaked Barley
4 oz Medium Crystal malt
4 oz molasses

Hops
2 oz cascade (bittering) at 4.7 AAU
2/3 oz northern brewer (aromatic)

Other
1/3 lbs Coffee

Yeast Sierra Nevada yeast culture

Procedure Steep flaked barley and crystal malt for 50 minutes at 153 degrees. Boil for 90 minutes. Add black patent malt and molasses at 45 minutes. Bittering hops in thirds each 30 min. Fill a hops bag with the coffee and aromatic hops and add to the hot wort just before chilling. If you don't have a wort chiller you'd better wait until pitching. Remove the bag after about 24 hours or when the fermentation is going strong, whichever is longer. Rack to secondary once initial fermentation has died down, about 5 to 6 days.

Summer Chocolate Stout

Category Stout
Recipe Type Extract

Fermentables
1 lbs chocolate malt
1 lbs crystal malt
4 lbs light malt extract syrup
2. 5 lbs dark malt extract powder
8 oz molasses

Hops
1. 5 oz Perle (boil) - 60 min.
1 oz Fuggle (flavor) - (1/2 ounce for 15 minutes
. 5 oz Willamette (leaf hops

Other
2 tbsp gypsum

Yeast Wyeast #1084 Irish Ale Yeast

Procedure Steep grains for 30 minutes at 180F in 3 gallons water. Sparge thoroughly with 2 gallons. Filter wort through leaf hops (this didn't work well, and I don't suggest it).

Swamp Dog Stout

Category Stout
Recipe Type Extract

Fermentables
7 lb dark plain extract
1. 5 lb plain dark dried extract
. 5 lb black patent malt
. 5 lb roasted barley
1 cup corn sugar for bottling

Hops
2 oz Nugget hops (14 AA) boil
1 oz Chinook hops (13.2 AA) finish
1 tsp Irish moss (w/finish hops)

Yeast Munson dry yeast

Procedure This was my first batch. I just last week made another batch `cause I was down to only a 6-pack of SDS. In the second, I also used 1# oatmeal and 1 cup of brown sugar. Left in the primary for 7-10 days. Secondary for at least 4 weeks. Try it, you won't be sorry!!!!

Sweet Tooth's Sheaf & Vine Stout

Category Stout
Recipe Type Extract

Fermentables
3.3 lbs John Bull Unhopped Dark Extract
3.0 lbs Laaglander Light DME

George Braun

0. 5 lbs Belgian Special-B
0. 5 lbs Belgian Cara-Munich
0. 5 lbs Belgian Roasted Barley
0. 5 lbs Belgian Roasted Malt
. 5 cup corn sugar for priming

Hops

2.25 oz Cascade 4.0% @ 60 minutes
1.15 oz BC Goldings 4.0% @ 15 minutes

Other

. 25 tsp Burton Water Salts
0. 5 lb lactose at bottling

Yeast Wyeast #1056 American Ale Yeast

Procedure Don't boil the grains, just crush them and steep them in 2 gallons of 170F water, then remove and add the rest of the 5. 5 gallon boil water. If you don't do a full wort boil, you will have to increase the hop rates (say, 25% more for a 2.75 gallon boil) to compensate for the lower efficiency. Better be very sure you keep good sanitation since lactobacillus can eat the lactose and will certainly make for gushers (or worse) if you get an infection.
Fermented at 68F.

Sweet Darkness

Category Stout
Recipe Type Extract

Fermentables
7 lbs Australian light syrup
1 lbs chocolate malt
1. 5 lbs, black patent
12 oz crystal malt

Hops
2 oz Kent Goldings hops (whole leaf)

Other
12 oz lactose
1 tsp salt
1 tsp citric acid

Yeast yeast

Procedure Bring the wort to boil (water and syrup to make 3 gallons), then add crystal. Boil 10 minutes, then add hops. Boil 5 minutes. Turn off heat and add chocolate and black patent malt in a grain bag. Steep about 10 minutes. Sparge grain bag with about 2 gallons of boiling water. Add lactose. Chill and pitch. When fermented, try priming with 3/4 cup of light dry malt extract.

Too Dry Stout

Category Stout
Recipe Type Extract

Fermentables
1 lb British Crystal
. 5 lb Black Barley
.25 lb Black Patent
7 lb Australian Dark

Other
2 oz. Perle (at beginning of boil)

Yeast ale yeast

Procedure Steep specialty grains. Remove grains, add extract and hops. Boil.

TBones Game Warden Stout

Category Stout
Recipe Type Partial Mash

Fermentables
5 lbs Briess 2 row
1 lb Flaked Barley
1. 5 lb Crystal 40L
3.3 lb John bull dark
3.0 lb dark M&F DME

Hops
2 oz Eroica pellets

Other

2 inches Brewers Licorice

Yeast Danstar Nottingham yeast

Procedure Crush Grains and mash at 150 for 60 minutes, really I got the Briess only to convert the flaked as an experiment in head and body. Sparge and get 3 gallons. Add to this (already surly looking' brew) the extract and hops. Boil 60-90 until 2.0 2. 5 gals remain in the pot. Pour into primary with 2. 5 cold water. Chill in ICE water for 76.
Pitched Danstar Nottingham... went off like a bomb... had to replace 1 1/4 inch blow off on day 2.. was spooged out... and it worried me... well.. not too worried... racked to secondary after one week in secondary for 2 weeks... primed with 1.25 cups Dark DME.

Terminator Stout

Category Stout
Recipe Type All Grain

Fermentables
12.0 Lbs Great Western 2-row
1.0 Lbs Briess 40L Crystal Malt
1.0 Lbs Black Barley
1.0 Lbs Briess Munich

Hops
30 IBUS Cascade Hops

Yeast Wyeast #1056

Procedure Single step, upward infusion mash with strike temp at 157.
Cascade Hops, additions at boil, and at 1 hour. Shoot for 30 ibus. The total boil time is 1. 5 hours.

Use liquid Wyeast #1056 and ferment around 69 degrees.

Terminator Stout (Scale to size)

Category Stout
Recipe Type All Grain

Fermentables
80.0 % Great Western 2-row
7.0 % Briess 40L Crystal Malt
7.0 % Black Barley
6.0 % Briess Munich

Hops
30.0 ibus Cascade Hops

Yeast liquid Wyeast #1056

Procedure Single step, upward infusion mash with strike temp at 157. Hops- Cascade additions at a boil, and at 1 hour. Shoot for 30 ibus. The total boil time is 1. 5 hours. Use liquid Wyeast #1056 and ferment around 69 degrees

Three Vice Stout

Category Stout
Recipe Type Extract

Fermentables
6.6 lbs Stout extract (2 cans if using canned)
. 25 lbs flaked barley
1/8 lbs black patent malt
. 75 cup brown sugar (priming)

Hops
. 5 oz Fuggles hops (bittering)
. 5 oz Fuggles hops (flavoring)

Other
4 oz unsweetened chocolate
5 cups brewed coffee

Yeast 1 package Wyeast #1084

Procedure Heat water to 160 degrees and steep barley and malt for 30 minutes. Remove grains and heat to boiling. Add extract and coffee and return to boil. Add bittering hops and boil 50 minutes. Add chocolate and flavoring hops and boil for 10 minutes. Cool and pitch yeast (I used a starter). Rack to secondary when active fermentation subsides. Leave in secondary 3-4 weeks. When ready to bottle boils brown sugar with a pint of water to prime.

CHAPTER 3- FRUIT BEERS

Apples in the Snow

Category Fruit Beers
Recipe Type Extract

Fermentables
6.6 lbs John Bull light malt extract (or other brand)
1 lbs corn sugar
. 75 cup corn sugar (priming)

Hops
2 oz Hallertauer hops (boil)
. 5 oz Hallertauer hops (finish)

Other
12 lbs apples (9 pounds Granny Smith

Yeast 2 packs Edme ale yeast

Procedure Cut apples into 8-10 slices. Put 1-1/2 gallons water into pot, add boiling hops and bring to boil. Add extract and corn sugar. Boil 40 minutes. Add finishing hops and apples. Steep 15 minutes. Pour wort into 3-1/2 gallons cold water. Push apples to one side and pitch yeast. Ferment 3 weeks.

Basic Fruit Beer

Category Fruit Beers
Recipe Type Extract

Fermentables
4-pound can Alexanders pale malt extract
. 5 lbs light, dry extract

Hops
10 HBU hops

Other
. 25 tsp Irish moss
2 gallons fruit juice (such as apple or raspberry)

Yeast yeast

Batch #14 Raspberry

Category Fruit Beers
Recipe Type Extract

Fermentables
5. 5 lbs dry, light malt extract

Hops
1 1/3 oz Willamette hop pellets 60 minutes
{alpha 4.3, beta 3.3}
1/3 oz Willamette hop pellets 10 minutes
1/3 oz Willamette hops 5 minutes

Other

1 can (96 oz) raspberry wine base
. 25 teaspoon Irish moss

Yeast 1 package wyeast Belgian ale yeast

Procedure Cultured the yeast in 1.020 starter 48 hours in advance. Bring water to a boil. Add extract. Add boiling hops after hot break. Flavor hops added as noted above. Add Irish moss for last 15 minutes. Remove from heat. Cool. Sparge into carboy. Boil more water. Cool. Fill carboy. Wine base added to secondary at time of racking.

Billy Bob's Blueberry Bitter

Category Fruit Beers
Recipe Type All Grain

Fermentables

9 lbs English Pale 2-row
10 lbs fresh blueberries

Hops

1. 5 oz Cascade hops for 60 minutes
0. 5 oz Cascade hops for 30 minutes
1.0 oz Kent Goldings hops for 1 minute

Other

1 tsp. gypsum added to mash

2 tsp. Irish Moss added 30 minutes prior to end of boil

Yeast Wyeast American Ale yeast -- no starter

Procedure Mashed in single infusion. Starch conversion around 156F for 60 minutes. Mash out at 168F for five. Sparge water @ 170F. The exact amount of sparge water unknown; I simply sparger until the desired yield was reached. The blueberries were crushed prior to adding to the wort. They were added to wort after the end of the boil, when temperature of wort was lower than 180F. The blueberries were allowed to sit in the hot wort for 15 minutes. The wort was then chilled with an immersion chiller. Then, the whole shebang (fruit, hops, and all) was poured into a plastic fermenter for primary fermentation. Primarily done for seven days, following which the beer was racked off of the gunk into glass. I think I left it in the glass for two days; fermentation was pretty much complete. Oh -- a tsp. of polyclar added 24 hours prior to bottling.

Blackberry Peach Lager

Category Fruit Beers
Recipe Type Extract

Fermentables
4 lbs. Laaglander extra light dried malt extract
2. 5 lbs. clover honey

George Braun

2 lbs. frozen blackberries (in retrospect, I would probably go w/ 2. 5 - 3 lbs.)

3 lbs. Fresh peaches (peeled, pitted & lightly mashed)

Hops

1. 5 oz. Cascade hops (boiling)

. 75 oz. Cascade hops (finishing -- final 4 minutes)

Yeast 1 pkg. Yeast Lab European Lager yeast

Procedure Extracts, honey, and boiling hops to 1. 5 gal boiling water; 1 hour boil. TURN OFF HEAT, allow wort to cool for a minute (ideally to temps between 160 &180F), and add fruit, juice and all. Allow to steep. Cover for about 15 minutes; add finishing hops for the final few minutes. Pour unsparged into 3 gal. cold water in primary fermenter. Pitch yeast when cool; O.G. 1.052 after 3-6 days fermentation, rack beer into secondary fermenter. (I had big problems w/ this step due to chunks of fruit clogging up my siphon, and ended up losing like 1/2 a gallon of beer. Renee suggested this solution: a nylon stocking as a filter -- leave it to a gal, huh?) Then you bottle the stuff. F.G. 1.018. Pretty good after 12 days, better after 3 weeks, delicious after a month.

Blackberry Stout

Category Fruit Beers

Recipe Type Extract

Fermentables
1 can Mount Mellick Famous Irish Stout extract
3 lbs M&F dark, dry malt extract
4 lbs frozen blackberries
1 lbs dark crystal malt
. 5 lbs, black patent malt
. 5 lbs roasted barley

Hops
1. 5 oz Hallertauer hops
. 5 oz Fuggles hops

Yeast ale yeast

Procedure Start grains in brew pot with cool water. Remove when boil commences. Add all malt and Hallertauer hops. Boil 1 hour. Add Fuggles and boil 5 more minutes. Remove from heat. Add thawed blackberries and steep 15 minutes. Cool. Dump the whole mess into primary. After a couple rack to secondary, straining out berries.

Blackberry Weizen

Category Fruit Beers
Recipe Type Extract.

Fermentables
1 cup crystal
1 cup cara-pils

George Braun
3 lbs blackberries (or raspberries)

Hops
1 oz Hallertauer or Saaz
. 5 oz Hallertauer or Saaz

Other
6.6 lbs Ireks wheat or two 3.3 pound cans of M & F wheat

Yeast Wyeast Bavarian Wheat.

Blackberry Stout

Category Fruit Beers
Recipe Type Extract

Fermentables
1 can Mount Mellick Famous Irish Stout extract
3 lbs M&F dark, dry malt extract
4 lbs frozen blackberries
1 lbs dark crystal malt
. 5 lbs, black patent malt
. 5 lbs roasted barley

Hops
1. 5 oz Hallertauer hops
. 5 oz Fuggles hops

Yeast ale yeast

Procedure Start grains in brew pot with cool water. Remove when boil commences. Add all malt and Hallertauer hops. Boil 1 hour. Add Fuggles and boil 5 more minutes. Remove from heat. Add thawed blackberries and steep 15 minutes. Cool. Dump the whole mess into primary. After a couple rack to secondary, straining out berries.

Blueberry Ale

Category Fruit Beers
Recipe Type Extract

Fermentables
7 lbs British amber extract
1. 5 lbs crystal malt
2 lbs fresh, frozen blueberries

Hops
2 oz Northern Brewer hops (boil)
1 oz Fuggles hops (finish)

Yeast Whitbread ale yeast

Procedure Steep crystal malt while bringing to boil. Remove grains and add extract and boiling hops. Boil 60 minutes. Add finish hops and let steep 15 minutes. Sparge into ice, mix. Rack for 7-gallon carboy. At peak of fermentation add blueberries. Ferment 1 week and rack to secondary. Prime with corn sugar.

Cherry Weiss et cetera

Category Fruit Beers
Recipe Type Extract

Fermentables
3.3 lbs wheat liquid extract (I used M & F)
3 lbs light dme (I used wheat)
3 cans good quality cherry juice concentrate

Hops
1 oz. 5% cascade hops

Yeast American ale yeast (didn't go with the Weiss yeast to reduce those

Procedure 3 gal. boil volume.
Very rapid fermentation for 4 days, slowed _finally_ and racked to secondary after 8 days, left it 6 more days in the carboy, great clarity! Once in secondary I added 2tbs. pure vanilla extract for flavor and mostly aroma, and I tbs. cherry essence for aroma (taste was great, didn't need any more flavor, wanted better aroma).

At bottling added 8oz malto-dextrin for better head and mouth feel - was of course very dry... and priming sugar.

Cherry-Honey-Weiss

Category Fruit Beers

Recipe Type All Grain

Fermentables
6 lbs 2 Row English Pale Malt
4 lbs Malted Wheat
10--1/2 lbs Cherries
1 lbs Honey

Hops
1 oz Saaz Hops - Boiling
. 25 oz Saaz Hops - Finishing

Other
Gypsum for adjusting PH
Irish moss (Clarity)

Yeast yeast

Procedure I mashed using 10 quarts at 140 F strike heat for a protein rest at 130 F. Then added an additional 5 quarts at 200 F to bring to a starch conversion at 150 F rose to 158 F, with a mash-out at 168 F. Sparged with 5 gallons of water at 168 F recovering over 7 gallons. Boil for two hours. Chill down to about 70 F, pitched yeast.

Christmas Cranberry Ale

Category Fruit Beers
Recipe Type Extract

Fermentables
1. 5 cups crystal malt
6.6 lbs Armstrong, Amber malt extract

Hops
2 oz. Hallertauer hops (pellets)

Other
3 cups fresh cranberries
. 75 cup corn sugar to prime

Yeast ale yeast

Procedure Brought 1 gal water to boil with crystal malt, removed crystal malt, Added amber malt, Boiled 45 min., added 1 oz. hops, boiled 15 min., added 1 oz. H-T hops, boiled 2 min. Cooked cranberries separately, added to primary with wort and filled with 5 gal (US).

Now, I know boiling fruit releases the pectin, but I couldn't figure a way around the need to both pasteurize the berries and to break the skin. However, I can't detect any negative influences in my beer. By using two stage fermentation, I was able to siphon off the beer and leave all the fruit pulp behind. The only thing really missing from the beer is a hop aroma - the H-T hops were just too mild for the cranberries...

Cranberry Beer

Category Fruit Beers
Recipe Type Extract

Fermentable
6 lbs extra light dry malt extract
1 lbs Munich malt
3 bags Cranberries

Hops
1 oz Juggles boiling
1 oz Juggles as finishing hops

Yeast

Procedure I thawed the berries and blended with enough water to make a little over 2 quarts of slush. Meanwhile, I did a normal extract brew using the Munich malt as a specialty grain (i.e., put in a double layered pair of clean pantyhose and stuck in the pot while I bring the cold water to a boil). At the end of the hour of boiling I put in the finishing hops and poured in the cranberry liquid for the final minute or two as I turned off the heat. I bottled after a week.

Cranberry Wheat

Category Fruit Beers
Recipe Type All Grain

Fermentable
9 lbs Schreyer 2-row malt
9 lbs DWC Wheat malt

Hops
20 IBU's kettles hop (I used 1.35 oz Perle @ 7. 5 % alpha)

Other
12 lbs cranberries

Yeast Edme ale yeast

Procedure *No* finishing hops (want to taste the cranberries) Mash at 124 F/30 min, 145-50 F/30 min, 158-60 F/30 min.
Added 12# of chopped cranberries after Krause fell. **note, a cheesecloth bag with some sort of weighting would be advisable to **keep the berry pieces from floating up & out of the liquid.

Fermented another 2 weeks, then seconded 'till clear & bottled.

Cranbeery Ale

Category Fruit Beers
Recipe Type Extract

Fermentables
5 lbs pale malt extract syrup
1 lbs corn sugar
6 lbs cranberries

Hops
2 oz Hallertauer hops (boil)
. 5 oz Hallertauer hops (finish)

Yeast ale yeast

Procedure Crush cranberries. Boil wort. Add cranberries to wort at time finishing hops are added. Turn off heat and steep at least 15 minutes. Pour wort into fermenter with enough water to make 5 gallons. Pitch yeast. After about 5 days, strain into secondary fermenter, avoiding sediment. Bottle after about 1 more week. Age bottles about 2 weeks.

Cranberry Ale

Category Fruit Beers
Recipe Type Extract

Fermentables
1 can Munton & Fison extra light unhopped extract
. 5 lbs 40 L crystal malt
. 5 lbs barley flakes
. 5 lbs corn sugar

George Braun

6 12-ounce bags of cranberries, juiced with pulp

Hops

1 oz Saaz (4.2% alpha) 1 hour boil
. 75 oz Willamette 1 minute boil

Yeast Wyeast 1056 (Chico)

Procedure Cranberry juice and pulp were steeped with boiled and slightly cooled water and a small amount of post-boil (and pre-chill) wort for about 10 minutes and then strained into carboy.
Escaped pulp required the use of a pantyhose (clean and sanitized) strainer over racking.

Dark as the Night Stout

Category Fruit Beers
Recipe Type Extract

Fermentables

8 cans blueberries (or 10 pints fresh
. 5 lbs roasted barley
1/3 lbs black patent malt
1 lbs crystal malt
6.6 lbs John Bull dark unhopped malt extract
. 5 cup corn sugar (priming)

Hops

1. 5 oz Fuggles hops (boil)

Yeast yeast

Procedure Crush and boil blueberries in 1-1/2 gallons of water for 10 minutes. Strain out berries. Add grains and steep. Add extract and hops and bring to boil. Strain into fermenter with enough cold water to make 5 gallons. Pitch yeast. Give these lots of time in the secondary fermenter or add champagne yeast after initial fermentation.

Extract Pumpkin Ale

Category Fruit Beers
Recipe Type Extract

Fermentables
6 lbs Northwestern Golden malt extract
1 lbs amber malt
10 oz pure maple syrup
3 lbs sliced up pumpkin (smaller "sweet" pumpkin, not bigger

Hops
1. 5 oz Fuggles hops for 60 minutes
. 5 oz Fuggles finishing hops

Other
1. 5 tsp Nutmeg
1. 5 tsp Allspice
2 tsp Cinnamon

George Braun

1. 5 oz fresh grated Ginger root

Yeast Wyeast #1056 (American Ale)

Procedures Cut the pumpkin into 1 inch cubes, but leave out the gooey inside and seeds. Add the pumpkin for the last 10 minutes of the boil along with all the spices.

Leave the pumpkin in the primary, then rack off the pumpkin after about 4 days. I'm going to leave mine in the secondary for two weeks, then bottle-age for another couple of weeks. I really can't wait to taste this one!

Feelix the Cat Dark Cherry Lager

Category Fruit Beers

Recipe Type Extract

Fermentables

3.3 lbs John Bull dark unhopped malt extract

2 lbs Munton & Fison light, dry extract

. 5 cup black patent malt

Hops

2 oz Cascades hops

3-5 lbs pitted, chopped cherries

. 5 oz Hallertauer hops

Other

2 tbsp gypsum

1 tsp salt

Yeast yeast

Procedure Steep black patent malt in 2 gallons of water, bringing to boil. Strain out grain. Add extract and boil with Cascade hops, gypsum, and salt. Boil 60 minutes. Remove from heat. Add finishing hops and cherries. Steep 30 minutes. Strain into fermenter with cold water to make 5 gallons. Pitch yeast.

Framboise

Category Fruit Beers
Recipe Type Extract

Fermentables
6-7 lbs light malt extract
. 25 lbs crystal malt
2. 5 cups raspberry puree
10 cups raspberry puree

Hops
1 oz boiling hops (Hallertauer)

Yeast yeast

Procedure Crack, steep, and strain crystal malt before boiling. Add extract and hops. Boil. Strain into primary. Add 2-1/2 cups raspberry puree. Add enough cold water to make 5 gallons. Pitch yeast. When racking to secondary, add another 10 cups raspberry puree.

Framboise

Category Fruit Beers
Recipe Type All Grain

Fermentables
7 lbs Lager Malt
7 lbs crushed raspberries
3 lbs Wheat Flakes

Hops
1 oz 2 year old Cluster hops that had been baked for 20

Yeast WYeast #1056 American Ale Yeast

Procedure We did a beta glucan rest at 120 degrees for 30 mins, a protein rest at 130 degrees for 30 mins, and a scarification rest at 155 for 1 hour. Be extra careful with the sparge because it has the potential to be very slow (although we managed to whip right through in 45 mins.). We boiled the wort for 2 hours, leaving the hops in for the entire boil. Cooled with an immersion chiller to 42 degrees and strained into a carboy. After 8 hours we racked the wort off of the trub and pitched the yeast. We left it in primary for 2 weeks and then racked it into a carboy and added the raspberries.

Free Time Raspberry Brew

Category Fruit Beers
Recipe Type Extract

Fermentables
. 53 kg Dried malt extract
1 kg Plain light malt extract

Hops
1. 5 oz Tettnanger Hops (boiling)
. 5 oz Tettnanger Hops (finishing, 1 min.)

Other
. 47 kg Dextrose
5 cans Welch's Frozen conc. raspberry cocktail (341 ml cans)

Yeast 1 pack Coopers Brewery Pure Brewer's Yeast

Procedure Boil wort for one hour. Sparge into a glass carboy, and then add raspberry canes. and water. Starting SG: 1.049. Wait. Bottle. Wait. Enjoy. The brew is named "FREE TIME" because it was brewed on Oct. 29, 1994, the end of daylight savings time

Fruit Galore

Category Fruit Beers
Recipe Type All Grain

Fermentables
10 lbs Klages pale malt
. 5 lbs amber crystal malt

Hops
2 oz Cascade (4.9%)

Other
3 lbs depitted & sliced fruit
7 ea oranges and peels diced (didn't remove pith)
2 ea lemon and peels diced (didn't remove pith)
1 tbsp ground nutmeg
3 tsp whole cloves 5 2" sticks cinnamon
. 5 cup fresh grated ginger root

Yeast William's English Brewery Ale yeast (from 12ounce starter)

Procedure Mash Klages and crystal malt at 158 degrees for 90 minutes. Sparge. Bring wort to a boil and add hops. Boil for 1 hour. Add fruit and spices during final 10 minutes of boil. Cooled to 80 degrees in a half-hour and pitched. Racked after 5 days, and noted rocky head from fruit pulp. Added 2 tablespoon dissolved gelatin after 12 days. Bottle after 15 days. NOTE: I forgot the Irish moss.

Great Pumpkin Bitter

Category Fruit Beers
Recipe Type Extract

Fermentables
1 can Cooper's bitter hopped malt syrup
1. 5 lbs M&F dry malt extract
. 25 lbs, black patent malt
1 cup Brer Rabbit molasses
10 lbs pumpkin mush

Hops
. 5 oz Tettnanger hop pellets (boil 30 minutes)
. 5 oz Tettnanger hops pellets (finish)
. 5 cup chopped cilantro

Other
2 sticks cinnamon
2-3 oz fresh grated ginger
. 5 oz fresh grated ginger

Yeast 2 packs Pasteur champagne yeast

Procedure Steep black patent malt. Remove grain and add extracts. Boil wort 60 minutes with 2-3 ounces ginger; add boiling hops at 30 minutes. At 10 minutes, add cinnamon. In the last couple minutes, add finishing hops. Prepare pumpkin while the wort is boiling: place pumpkin flesh in blender or food processor and mush. Mix chopped cilantro and 1-2 ounces fresh ginger in with mush. Place pumpkin mush, wort, and water to make 6-1/2 gallons in primary fermenter. Let primary fermentation proceed 1 week. Remove pumpkin mush and strain remaining liquid into 5 gallon carboy. Rack again after 3 weeks. Bottle after another 2 months.

Harvey's Blue Beer

Category Fruit Beers
Recipe Type All Grain

Fermentables
5. 5 lbs Hugh Baird Pale Malt
. 5 lb Crystal Malt
1 lb b Wheat Malt
. 5 lb Corn Sugar
4 Cups Blueberries

Hops
. 5 oz Willamette Hops (boil)
. 25 oz Saaz Hops (10 minutes)

Yeast Yeast of your choice Wyeast 1056 or Coopers Dry is preferred by us

Procedure Mash in 9 quarts 140 F. water, rise to 152 F and convert for 90 minutes. Mash out 5 minutes at 168 F. Sparge with 5 gal. of 168 F acidified sparge water. Boil 60 min to 90 min or until volume adequately reduced. Mash berries with potato masher in bowl with corn sugar until a pulpy mess. Add to hot wort when it has cooled to about 180 F and cover and let sit around 20 minutes, then chill as normal (we use an immersion chiller, berry bits could clog a counter flow) and ferment.

Jolly Rancher Beer

Category Fruit Beers
Recipe Type Extract

Fermentables
3.3 lbs Liquid Light Malt Extract
3.3 lbs Liquid Amber Malt Extract
. 75 cup priming sugar

Hops
1. 5 oz Hallertau hops

Other
4.0 oz L.D. Carlson Blueberry Extract

Yeast Ale yeast packet

Procedure Boil 1. 5 gal cold water, add all malts and.75oz hops, at last 10 min, add balance of hops, and at 5 min add blueberry extract.
I pitched the yeast at 70 deg. and racked into secondary after 3 - 4 days, and bottled after another 5 days. It is very smooth, and does taste like a grape jolly rancher

Michael's Raspberry Ale

Category Fruit Beers

George Braun
Recipe Type Extract

Fermentables
6.6 lb Light Malt Extract (John Bull unhopped)
. 5 lb British crystal Malt (cracked)
5 each 12oz boxes of frozen Raspberries

Hops
3 oz Hallertau hop pellets (3.1% Alpha)

Other
1 tsp Irish moss

Yeast Wyeast 1098 English Ale liquid yeast

Procedure Steep cracked crystal malt in your brew pot with 1-2 gal water coming to a boil. Remove crystal at 170 F. Bring to rolling boil and added malt extract. Boil for 15min and then add 2. 5 oz Hallertau hops in a hop bag. Boil for 45 more minutes and add Irish moss, 0. 5 oz Hallertau hops for aroma to hop bag and the frozen Raspberries (previously rinsed and drained). Leave on heat for 5 more minutes. Turn off heat, remove hop bag and let stand for 10 more minutes. Cool, top off to 5 gals and pitch yeast. Be sure to leave the raspberries in the wort during the primary ferment. Transfer to a secondary after 2-3 days and leave the raspberries behind.

My Framboise Recipe

Category Fruit Beers
Recipe Type Extract

Fermentables
6.6 lbs wheat malt extract
. 5 lbs crystal malt
5-6 bags frozen raspberries (12 ounce bags)

Hops
1 oz Hallertauer hops

Yeast 1 pack Wyeast #3056 Bavarian wheat

Procedure The wheat malt should ideally be a 60-40 mix of wheat and barley. The crystal malt is cracked and steeped in hot water for 20 minutes, then strained. The hops are then added and the mixture is boiled for 45 minutes. Chill and add yeast. Allow the beer to ferment for 7 days and then prepare raspberry mixture by defrosting berries and using blender to puree. Pitch in fermenter and after 48 hours, bottle. Next time I make this, I will modify the recipe to use 1 can (6.6#) of Ireks wheat malt, 3-4 pounds of light DME, 1 ounce of Hallertauer (35 minute boil), and again, Wyeast #3056. By using a 100% wheat extract, such as Ireks, I can control the amount of barley extract to assure 60% wheat to 40% barley.

Peach Wheat Ale

Category Fruit Beers

George Braun
Recipe Type Extract

Fermentables
6.6 lbs Northwestern wheat extract syrup
. 75 cup corn sugar (or malt extract) for carbonation
4 lbs fresh peaches (pitted and skinned)

Hops
5 AAU hops (maybe 1 ounce of Mt. Hood, Hallertau, etc.)

Yeast wheat yeast (Wyeast Bavarian wheat)

Procedure Boil malt and hops for 1 hour. Add cold water to fermenter to bring to 5 gallons. Add wort. Pitch ale yeast. On 2nd day of fermentation, skin, de-pit, and chop peaches. Add to fermenter. Three days later, rack to secondary. Bottle 10 days later.

Pick of the Season Cherry Ale

Category Fruit Beers
Recipe Type Extract

Fermentables
6 lbs Laaglander light, dry extract
. 25 lbs crystal malt

Hops
. 5 oz Chinook hops (boil)

. 5 oz Chinook hops (finish)
. 5 oz Hallertauer hops (dry)

Other
. 25 lbs lactose
7-8 lbs fresh sweet cherries
. 5 tsp Irish moss

Yeast Whitbread ale yeast

Procedure This recipe makes 5-1/2 gallons. Freeze cherries a couple days before brewing. Defrost in the fridge. While wort is boiling, remove stems and crush cherries. After boiling, pour wort over cherries in fermenter. Add cold water and pitch yeast. After a couple days, rack to secondary, straining out cherries.

Pumpkin Ale

Category Fruit Beers
Recipe Type Extract

Fermentables
6 lbs light Dried Malt Extract (or 2 cans light malt extract syrup)
6 lbs Pumpkin meat (2 small)
. 5 tsp Vanilla Extract

Hops
1. 5 oz Mt. Hood Hop Pellets
. 5 oz Tettnager Hop Pellets

Other

1 tsp Burton Water, Salt
1 tsp Irish moss
1 tsp cinnamon
. 5 tsp nutmeg
. 5 tsp allspice
. 5 tsp mace
.25 tsp cloves

Yeast Wyeast #1007 Liquid Yeast (or #1214)

Procedure Peel and remove seeds from pumpkin and cook until soft. In a large pot, heat 1--1/2 gallons of water - add your malt, Mt. Hood Hops and cooked pumpkin meat and boil for 30 minutes. Add Burton Water, Salt and 1 tsp. Irish moss and boil for 15 minutes more. Add finishing hops and boil for 5 minutes more. Remove from heat. Strain hops and pumpkin meat. Add boiled wort to prepared fermentor -make up to 5--1/2 gallons. Add prepared Liquid Yeast. Ferment to SG 1030, transfer to Secondary Fermenter, add the spices (BE SURE NOT to add the spices until the secondary fermentation or you will lose the intensity of the spices). Finish fermenting. Prime with 3/4 cup corn sugar, bottle and age for 3 to 4 weeks or more.

Category Fruit Beers
Recipe Type Extract

Fermentables
2 cans light malt extract (your choice)
6 lbs pumpkin meat (skin off)

Hops
1. 5 oz Mount Hood hops (boiling)
. 5 oz teenager hops (finishing)

Other
1 pack Burton salts
1 tsp Irish moss
. 5 tsp cinnamon
. 5 tsp allspice
. 5 tsp nutmeg
. 5 tsp mace
. 5 tsp clove
1 tsp vanilla extract

Yeast 1 package liquid yeast #1007

Procedure Bring to a boil 1 gallon and 1/2 water and pumpkin meat. Add 2 cans of malt, 1 and 1/2 oz. Mount Hood hops, and Burton Salts. Boil for 45 mins. Then add Irish moss, and finishing hops. Boil for another 15 min. Sparge into 3 and 1/2 gallons of water. Let cool and pitch yeast. Transfer to secondary fermenter at same time. Add all of your spices. When fermentation is complete shipon, carbonate, and bottle. (After you siphon give a gentle shake to mix spices around)

Purdue Red Hot Apple Ale

Category Fruit Beers
Recipe Type Extract

Fermentables
1 lbs Light DME
1 lbs Honey
. 5 lbs Crystal Malt
4 lbs Sliced Winesap Apples (from Purdue Hort. Farms--

Hops
4 lbs Mountmellick Brown Ale Kit (Hopped)

Other
2 tsp cinnamon
1 cup Cinnamon Imperials (Red hots)
10 grams Burton salts
1 tsp Irish moss

Yeast 1 package Brewer's Choice London Ale Yeast (#1028)

Procedure Bring 3 gallons water to boil and put in brew bucket to cool. Bring 1. 5 gallons water and crystal malt to boil. Remove grain. Add extract, honey, Burton salts, and Irish moss and boil for 15 minutes. Add red hot candies. Turn heat to low after candies melt. Add apples and cinnamon and steep 15 minutes. Dump into the brew bucket, and then transfer to primary. (I made malted applesauce out of the apples by the way!)

Pyramid Apricot Ale

Category Fruit Beers
Recipe Type Extract

Fermentables
4 lbs. Alexander wheat extract
1.4 lbs. Alexander wheat kicker
4 oz. Malto-dextrin
. 75 cup corn sugar

Hops
14 IBU domestic Hallertauer (60 minute boil)

Other
4 oz. apricot essence added to bottling bucket

Yeast Wyeast # 1056 liquid yeast

Raspberry Pilsner

Category Fruit Beers
Recipe Type Extract

Fermentables
2 cans Ironmaster European pilsner

George Braun
3-5 lbs raspberries (fresh or frozen, be sure to sterilize*)
2-4 lbs blackberries (")
DME to bring the OG to 1.048

Yeast 1 tsp yeast nutrient

Procedure That's the basic recipe... experiments with it a bit... I throw the berries on top of the wort in primary, and let the primary go until they have leeched all their colors out. At that point, I rack to secondary and let it all settle (use finings if you feel the need, I didn't). By the time it's done, you have a beautiful red brew that is then keg, conditioned, and aged for 3 months in the fridge. If you sterilized the berries right, there's not a trace of haze or cloudiness. It's almost like raspberry champagne, and a great dessert beer. The initial taste is beery, and then a lingering fruity aftertaste. I used the pilsner kit for its relatively low hop content, allowing the fruitiness to come out a little more.
(*) Sterilizing the berries because the berries are susceptible to wild yeast on the canes, it is advisable to sterilize the berries by heating them in water to a point a little below 85 degrees centigrade. (Adding some dextrose to the water will start leeching out the flavor and color). Any higher, and you will release some pectin into the solution, which will cloud the beer (not critical, it

just doesn't look as cool as it does when it's crystal clear and bubbling).

Raspberry Ale

Category Fruit Beers
Recipe Type Extract

Fermentables
5 lbs Munton & Fison light malt extract
. 5 lbs crystal malt
48 oz frozen raspberries

Hops
1. 5 oz Cascade hops (boiling)
. 5 oz Cascade (finish)

Yeast yeast

Procedure Added crystal to water, removed prior to boiling.
Boil wort. Added 24 ounces of raspberries, right after turning off the stove. Chilled, pitched. Primary fermented about 1 week. Rack to secondary and add another 24 ounces of raspberries. Let sit 2 weeks in secondary.

Raspberry Ale

Category Fruit Beers
Recipe Type Extract

Fermentables

George Braun

2 cans Alexanders pale malt extract
2 lbs rice-extract syrup
8 lbs frozen raspberries

Hops
1 oz Cascades hops

Yeast Edme ale yeast

Procedure I used about 8 lbs (11 12oz packages) and it turned out wonderfully, not at all overly raspberry-like. I blended them with just enough water to make it slurry and added it to the cooled wort (seeds, skins and all). I also added 2 campden tablets to ward off infection. It seems to have worked. No pectin haze at all. I racked into a secondary and left most of the raspberry sludge behind.

Raspberry Catastrophe

Category Fruit Beers
Recipe Type Extract

Fermentables
1. 5 kg Premier Reserve Gold Unhopped Ale Extract
1. 5 lbs Muntons Plain Light DME
(0. 5 lb Laaglander DME - see comments)
12 oz Frozen Raspberries
0.75 oz Fresh Raspberries
0. 5 cup Priming sugar

Hops
1.0 oz bittering Mt. Hood hop pellets (3.6% alpha acid)
1.0 oz flavoring Fuggle hop pellets (3.6% alpha acid)

Yeast Wyeast American Ale (No. 1056)

Procedure Boil 2. 5 gallons of water with Extract, DME, and bittering hops for 60 minutes. Add flavoring hops at 10 minutes before the end of the boil.
Cool to almost pitching temperature. Add wort and frozen raspberries to AT LEAST a six (6) gallon primary fermenter. Add another ~2. 5 gallon (to make five gallons total). Aerate (I put on the lid and shake) and pitch yeast. Fit primary with a blow off tube, NOT AN AIR-LOCK. Primary for two (2) weeks (some place where you don't care if it might erupt and check it daily), secondary for two (2) weeks, prime then bottle and drink in another two weeks.

Raspberry Imperial Stout

Category Fruit Beers
Recipe Type Extract

15-1/4 lbs bulk light extract
. 75 lbs roasted barley
.75 lbs black patent malt

George Braun

. 75 lbs chocolate malt
2 lbs English crystal malt
13 lbs fresh raspberries
1 cup corn sugar (priming)

Hops

3-3/4 oz Bullion pellets (9.6 alpha)
1-1/4 oz Northern Brewer pellets (6.7% alpha)
2 oz Kent Goldings pellets

Other

4 tsp gypsum

Yeast Sierra Nevada yeast

Procedure This makes 6-1/2 to 7 gallons. This is based on Papazian's recipe from the summer 1990 issue of Zymurgy, except that I use more raspberries than Charlie. Follow his directions, or E-mail me for directions. (The directions are pretty standard.)
The Bullion hops and Northern Brewer is used for bittering and are added to the boil. The Kent Goldings pellets are used for dry-hopping.

Slugbait Apricot Cobbler Ale

Category Fruit Beers
Recipe Type All Grain

Fermentables

5 lbs. British 2-row

3 lbs. German Wheat malt
4 oz. chocolate malt
4 oz. Munich malt
1 lbs. honey
1 gallon fresh apricot puree - ~ 7 lbs. (Previously frozen 'cots run through a juicer)

Hops
. 75 oz. Hallertau (5.3 alpha for ~17 IBU) @ 60 mins.

Other
1 ea 8" cinnamon stick

Yeast Wyeast 3068

Procedure Mashed all grains with a single infusion at 154F. Collect 6. 5 gal sweet wort, boiled down to 5 gals. Honey and cinnamon went into the pot @ 10 mins. Chill and pitch 1. 5 qt. Wyeast 3068 (Weihenstephan). Fermented in primary 24 hours and racked onto pasteurized 'cot puree in clean, sanitized carboy. Leave on the fruit for 5 days. Rack to secondary. Batch primed with corn sugar and bottled 10 days later.

Strawberry Beer 1

Category Fruit Beers
Recipe Type Extract

Fermentables

George Braun

1 lbs. Amber malt extract
1 lbs. light crystal malt
9 pints fresh strawberries

Hops

2 oz. hops

Other

6 lbs. pale male extract
a little Irish moss
About 3 tsp. pectin enzyme

Yeast 1 pkg. WYEAST Belgian Ale

Procedure I cleaned and pureed all the strawberries in a blender, added about half a gallon of water to them, and boiled them separately from my wort for about 15 mins. (My pot wasn't big enough to fit 'em). Cooled them and my wort and added the rest of the water. Pitch the yeast. The blow off was amazing! (I probably lost about 1 1/2 gallons of beer). Tons of it. I heated the pectin enzyme in a little water and added it to the secondary (to eliminate pectin haze). Let it sit in a secondary for three weeks. When I bottled it tasted tart as hell -- but a week later I started drinking it and it was great! It's a bit bitter, but the strawberry is very noticeable and everyone seems to enjoy it (especially me!).

Strawberry Beer 2

Category Fruit Beers
Recipe Type Extract

Fermentables
3--1/2 lbs dry, light malt
1 lb crushed crystal malt
8 pints fresh strawberries

Hops
3.3 lbs M&F amber hopped syrup
1 oz Northern Brewer leaf hops

Other
4 tbsp pectin enzyme

Yeast Ale yeast starter

Procedure Make a yeast starter by boiling 1 cup dry malt extract in a quart of water and cool to below 90 degrees F. Add four of Red Star Ale yeast and agitate. Let it set for two hours.
Steep crystal malt in 1 gallon of water for a while, then "rinse" in another 1--1/2 gallons. (I pre boil.) Add malt and boiling hops and boil liquid for 1 hour. Turn down heat to very low flame and add pureed strawberries, heat for 15-20 minutes. Remove hops, then cool wort. Dump in primary fermenter and add cold bottled water. The temp should be around 65-70. Dump in the yeast starter. The next day or sooner, add about 4 tablespoons of pectic enzyme, right into the beer.

George Braun
Rack after 3- 4 days. Bottle with 3/4 cup corn sugar.

Strawberry, Not Very Ale

Category Fruit Beers
Recipe Type Extract

Fermentables
7.2 lbs Alexander's pale malt extract syrup
. 5 lbs cracked crystal malt (10L)
6 pounds+ pureed previously-frozen strawberries

Hops
. 75 oz Saaz hops (5.9% alpha)
1 oz Fuggles (5.3% alpha)

Other
Pectin enzyme

Yeast Wyeast #1214 Belgian ale yeast

Procedure I used two 8 quart stockpots to cook this. I boiled one full pot of water, and set the sieve at the top with the crystal malt after I cut the heat. Waited 20 minutes, then took the sieve out and threw out the grains. I split the "tea" between the two pots, filled with water and started the boil. I added the extract and Saaz, boiled for 30 minutes, added the Fuggles, and boiled for 30 minutes or more. I cooled the 4 gallons to 75 degrees and pitched the yeast. Then I boiled (!) the strawberries with 1 gallon of water for 15 minutes, then cooled and racked the beer (lost some trub here) onto the strawberry mix. 4 hours later, I racked the mix again, losing all of the trub (so far). Primary fermentation was outrageous! With 5+ inches headroom in my primary, I blew the Saran Wrap up 3 inches then off 3 times! 3 days in the primary, then I racked to the secondary, and added the pectin enzyme. After 8 days in the secondary, I bottled with 1 1/2 cups of dried extract. I stored it for 3 weeks then tried it.

Washington Apple Ale

Category Fruit Beers
Recipe Type Extract

Fermentables
4 lbs Telford's Yorkshire nut brown ale hopped malt
1 lbs honey
. 5 lbs corn sugar
. 5 lbs dark crystal malt
4 lbs red apples

Other
2 tsp cinnamon

Yeast ale yeast

Procedure In cold water, place crushed dark crystal malt in a cheesecloth. Bring water to boil.

When boiling commences, remove grain and add Telford's. Boil 15-20 minutes. Add sugar and honey and boil another 10 minutes. Reduce heat so that boiling stops. Add cinnamon and sliced apples and steep 15 minutes. Remove apples with strainer and transfer wort to primary.

CHAPTER 4- PALE ALE

7--Mile Red Ale

Category Pale Ale
Recipe Type Extract

Fermentables
6.6 lbs of Northwestern amber malt extract
. 75 lbs 60 degree L Crystal Malt

Hops
2. 5 oz Fuggles hop plugs (4.6% alpha)
1 oz Cascades whole leaf hops. (5%-is alpha)

Yeast 1 package Glen-brew ale yeast

Procedure Steep crystal malt for 30 minutes in 150 degree water. Sparge into brew pot of hot water and add malt extract. Bring to boil and add 1 ounce Fuggles. 20 minutes later add another ounce. At the 40 minute mark, toss in the final half ounce of Fuggles. (Almost threw in a full ounce, but after tasting wort, decided against it---plenty bitter at this point.) Turn off heat and add Cascades. Stirred down the hops slowly and let sit for about 10 minutes. Strain all into fermenter containing ice water. Cooled. Pitched yeast. Single stage ferment. Keg and age a few days.
Submitted by: Karl Lutzen

Abbey Beer

Category Belgian Ale
Recipe Type All Grain

Fermentables

George Braun

9 lbs U.S. 2-row
1. 5 lbs Munich malt
0. 5 lbs 60L (or darker) crystal malt
. 5 oz of chocolate malt
1 lbs of honey or dark brown sugar

Hops

7 AAU bittering hops, a mix of Hallertauer and Kent Goldings (60 minute boil)

Yeast Chimay yeast of course

Procedure Add hops at 60 minutes before end of boil. You are not looking for high hop bitterness, nor should not there be noticeable hop aroma.
If you're not an all-grain brewer, then don't use the 2-row or Munich malt, but as, say, 7 pounds light, unhopped dry malt extract instead. Use crystal and chocolate malt for color. The honey or brown sugar will boost the starting gravity as well as contribute to the flavor and body of the finished beer. You might try doing the fermentation at a relatively "warm" temperature, say, and 70 to 75 degrees F. This should lead to more of that Chimay flavor in the finished beer. And, don't drink the beer all at once, as its flavor will evolve in the bottle over time.

Ale

Category Scottish Ale
Recipe Type All Grain

Fermentables

6 lbs Klages 2-row malt
1 lbs Munich malt (10L)
1 lbs Dextrin (Cara-pils) malt
. 5 lbs crystal malt (80L)
4 oz black patent malt

1 cup dark molasses
2/3 cup corn sugar (priming)

Hops
. 75 oz East Kent Goldings hops (6.2 alpha)

Yeast 1 pack Wyeast #1028 London Ale

Procedure Mash in 2 gallons water at 138 degrees, adjust pH to 5.2 using Calcium Carbonate. Protein rest 30 minutes at 158 degrees. Conversion rest 30 minutes at 158 degrees. Mash out 5 minutes at 168 degrees. Sparge with 5 gallons water at 165 degrees. Boil 90 minutes, adding hops in last 30 minutes. Chill wort, pitch yeast and ferment 1-2 days. Rack to secondary for 5 more days and bottle. Style.

American Pale Ale

Category Pale Ale
Recipe Type Extract

Fermentables
5 lbs unhopped light dry malt extract
. 5 lbs dark crystal malt

Hops
1 oz Cascade hops (60 minute boil)
. 5 oz Cascade (30 minute boil)
. 5 oz Cascade (10 minute boil)
1/2--1 oz Cascade (dry hop)

Yeast Wyeast American ale yeast

Procedure "Dry hopping" consists of adding hops not to the boil, but after boil and especially after fermentation. When your beer is done fermenting, you must rack it into a second sanitized vessel, preferably a glass carboy for which you have a fermentation lock. The beer and the hops are both added to that second vessel, and the beer is left from 1 to 3 weeks in the vessel. It isn't fermenting, but it's picking up flavors from the hops. If you don't want to do this, then instead of dry-hopping, add that last hop addition 2 minutes until end of boil. When you turn the flame off, let the beer sit with the lid on for 20 minutes before chilling it and racking it into the fermenter. But, I recommend that you try dry hopping sooner or later, as it adds flavor and aroma that is just right for this beer! English Pale Ale (previous recipe) also benefits from dry hopping.

Anchor Liberty Clone

Category India Pale Ale
Recipe Type Extract

Fermentables
6 lbs. Northwestern Pale liquid extract
. 5 lbs. Crystal 40L

Hops
3 oz. Cascade (whole leaf) 5. 5 %, 60min (Partial Boil)
1 oz. Cascade (whole leaf) dry hop, one week

Other
1 tsp. gypsum
1 tsp Irish moss

Yeast Wyeast London

Procedure If I were to use only 1/2 oz. dry hop I think they would be identical.
Primary ferment was one week at 68 degrees. Secondary ferment was one week.

For the dry hop I just threw them in the secondary. The hops float so you can siphon from underneath them. The longer you dry hop the more the hops get "water logged" and start to sink. You may want to try 5 days instead of 7. When I transferred it to the bottling bucket I did get some hops in there. Wracking to a second bottling bucket might help, but I was too lazy.
I did waste a little more beer than usual during bottling trying to avoid the hops. It is worth the extra effort to use whole hops. The hop nose is awesome.
If you do a full boil, you may want to cut back on the bittering

Arizona Pale Ale

Category Pale Ale
Recipe Type Extract
Hops were used for boiling (of course) and flavoring, not for aromatic qualities.

Fermentables
6-7 lbs pale malt extract
1 lbs Crystal malt, 1/2 pound toasted malted barley
2 cups steamed (sanitized) American Oak Chips (secondary)

Hops
2 oz Northern Brewer hops (boiling): 10HBU
1 oz Cascade hops (finishing)

Other
2 tsp. gypsum
1 tsp Irish moss
. 75 cups corn sugar (bottling)

George Braun
Yeast 1 package Wyeast American Ale Liquid yeast (#1059)

Procedure If using Victory malt, toasting is not necessary since it already is. If not, use standard procedures for toasting grains--spread the grains on a cookie sheet in a preheated oven, cook at 350 degrees for 10 minutes.
Combine all grains in a pot with 1 gallon water. Skipping a grain bag obtains a more intense color. Hold at 150 degrees for 30 minutes.
In another pot, heat water for sparging, 1 gallon should do.
Sparge grains into the brew pot.
Fetch water from a local Water Mart. This is Reverse Osmosis (RO) water, and could be too thin for a (India) Pale Ale. Thus, add gypsum. You can add Burton Water Salts at the expense of quaff ability.
Boil wort for 1 hour. Add the Cascade hops and Irish moss after the boil and for 5-10 minutes to sanitize, as well as obtain flavor instead of mealy imparting aroma.
Age four weeks in the bottle.

Alaskan Amber Ale

Category Amber Ale
Recipe Type All Grain

Fermentables
1. 5 Lbs Munich Malt
8.75 Lbs Pilsener Malt (2-Row)

Hops
0. 5 Oz Mt Hood Hops
0.75 Oz Spalter Spalt

Yeast Wyeast 1007

Procedure Single Step infusion mash at 152 degrees F. Used Mt Hood hops for bittering added 60 minutes before end of boil. Spalter Spalt hops added 15 minutes before end of boil.

Alex's Scottish Ale

Category Scottish Ale
Recipe Type Extract

Fermentables
8 lbs Munton's amber malt extracts syrup
2/3 lb crystal
1/3 lb roasted barley

Hops
2 oz. East Kent Goldings (10.6 hbu)
1 oz. Goldings ten minutes

Other
. 75 cup dextrose priming

Yeast Scottish Ale Yeast

Alki Point Sunset

Category German Ale
Recipe Type All Grain

Fermentables
5.0 lbs D-C Belgian Pilsener Malt
1.625 lbs D-C Belgian Wheat Malt
1.0 lbs Ireks German Light Crystal
1.25 lbs Clover honey (15 minute boil)

Hops
. 50 oz. Tettnang (4.3% AA) 60 min. 7. 5 IBU
. 50 oz. Liberty (4.3% AA) 60 min. 7. 5 IBU

George Braun
. 50 oz. Mt. Hood (4. 5 % AA) 60 min. 8.0IBU
. 50 oz. Tettnang (4.3% AA) 30 min. 2.0IBU
. 25 oz. Liberty (4. 5 % AA) 10 min.

Yeast Wyeast #2565 (Kolsch)

Procedure Mash In: 132F
Protein Rest: 30 min @ 124F
Saccharification: 90 min @ 150F
Mash Off: 10 min @ 168F

Sparge to collect 5.75 gallons of sweet wort (until SG of runoff is 1.010-1.012).
Boil for 90 minutes. Add 1.125# clover honey for the last 15 minutes of the boil.
Force cool to 62F and pitch slurry from 1.25L starter of Wyeast #2565 Kolsch.

All Grain American Brown

Category Brown Ale
Recipe Type All Grain

Fermentables
9 lbs 2-Row (Old)
. 75 lbs Crystal Malt (40L)
.6 lbs Belgian Choc Malt

Hops
1 oz Northern Brewer (Alpha=10. 0) 60 min boil
. 5 oz Cascade 15 min boiling
.25 oz Cascade Dry hop (upon transfer to secondary)

Other
. 5 tsp Gypsum (Adjusting mash pH)

Yeast Wyeast 1028

Procedure Mash: Protein Rest: 123F for 30 min Bump to 154 for 90 min (or what suits you.)
Ferment at 60F and condition at 13psi of CO2 for carbonation.

ALT 2

Category German Ale
Recipe Type All Grain

German ales include: Alt (Dusseldorf), Kolsch (Koln) and Weizens (Bavaria). Alt is made from the German Ale yeast and then cold conditioned for up to four weeks. These ales are usually fermented at colder temps than British ones (55 Fahrenheit) the longer cold maturation yields a smoother, cleaner ale than the British ones.

Hops
2 oz Perle hops (boil 60 minutes)
1 oz Perle (boil 30 minutes)

Other
Pale malt 90% of the mash
Crystal malt 7% of the mash
Wheat malt 3--10% of the mash (vary percents accordingly)

Yeast 1 liter cultured German ale yeast

Procedure Mash grains, sparge. Add hops according to schedule above. Chill and pitch yeast. Ferment at 55 degrees for 1--2 weeks. Rack and cool to 40 degrees for 4 weeks. Dry hop lightly, if desired.

Alt 1

Category German Ale

George Braun
Recipe Type All Grain
Grains and hops used should be German.

Fermentables
8 lbs pilsner malt (or 6 pounds lighter
4 oz 10L crystal malt
4 oz 60L crystal malt
4 oz 120L crystal malt (assumes 75% extraction

Hops
6 oz German hops (Hallertauer

Yeast Wyeast #1338 or #1007

Procedure Cold condition in secondary.

Alt 3

Category German Ale
Recipe Type All Grain

Fermentables
4 lbs U.S. 2--row malt (Klages/Harrington)
3--1/4 lbs Munich malt (10 L.)
. 25 lbs crystal malt (80 L.)
. 5 lbs wheat malt
. 5 oz black patent malt
2/3 cup corn sugar (priming)

Hops
. 5 oz Willamette hops (5. 5 % alpha) (boil)
. 5 oz Kent Goldings (6.1% alpha) (boil)
1 oz Hallertauer (2.9% alpha) (finish)

Yeast Wyeast #1056 American ale yeast

Procedure Mash in 11 quarts water at 137 F. and pH 5.2. Protein rest 30 minutes at 131. Conversion rest 60 minutes at 155. Mash out 5 minutes at 168. Sparge with 5 gallons of water at 170. Boil 90 minutes. Add hops at 45 minutes and 10 minutes before end of boil.

America Discovers Columbus

Category Pale Ale
Recipe Type All Grain

Fermentables
11 lb Schreier 2-row pale malt
1 lb DWC Munich
0.6 lb DWC CaraVienne
0. 5 lb DWC Biscuit
0. 5 lb Gambrinus Honey Malt
0.25 lb DWC carapils

Hops
1. 5 oz Columbus hop pellets (12. 5 % alpha, 60 minute boil)
. 5 oz Columbus hops (15 minute boil)
. 25 oz Cascade hops (4.1% alpha, 15 minute boil)
. 5 oz Columbus (dry hop one week in primary)

Other
. 5 oz Columbus (finish)

Yeast ale yeast (Wyeast 1272 or 1056---see notes)

Procedure Mashed at 157-155F for 65 min. Water - essentially deionized with = tsp gypsum
I split a 5 gallon batch into two glass fermenters. Wyeast 1272 was pitched into the first 2 gallons siphoned out of the kettle and Wyeast 1056 got the last 2. 5 gallons with a

little more trub. Both yeasts were pitched from 3 cup starter.

American Brown Ale

Category Brown Ale
Recipe Type All Grain

Fermentables
5.33 lbs. Klages
2 lbs. D-C Pilsen
2 lbs. Vienna (American 6-row)
0. 5 lbs. German wheat
0. 5 lbs. Caravienne
0. 5 lbs. Caramunich
0. 5 lbs. chocolate malt
0.125 lbs. black malt

Hops
1. 5 oz. Cascade (5.8%) 60 min.
0. 5 oz. Tettnang (3.4%) 10 min.
0. 5 oz. Cascade (5.8%) finish

Other
0. 5 lbs. D-C Aromatic

Yeast

Procedure Single-step infusion 155F, ~1 hr.

American I.P.A.

Category Pale Ale
Recipe Type All Grain

Fermentables
90-92%, 2 row pale malt
8-10%, Crystal 40L

Hops
1-1. 5 oz Whole Cascade 60 minute boil
1 oz Cascade 30 minutes
2 oz Cascade added a handful at a time the last 15
Yeast

Procedure Mash in at 123 degrees for 30 minutes. Rise to 153 degrees for 60 minutes. Mash off at 172 for 10 minutes. Ferment at 60-68 degrees. Dry hop with 1 ounce whole Cascades, preferably in secondary but primary will work.

Amber Ale

Category Amber Ale
Recipe Type All Grain

Fermentables
10 lbs American 2-row pale malt
1 lb Vienna Malt
. 5 lb Cara-pills malt
1 lb light Crystal malt
. 5 lb crystal malt (60L)
. 5 cup chocolate malt

Hops
1 oz Cascade hops (boil)
. 5 oz Fuggles hops (flavor)
. 5 oz Cascade hops (finishing)

Yeast 1000 ml Yeast starter- Wyeast Chico Ale

Procedure Mash grains in 4.3 gallons of water at 75 deg C, to bring temp to 67 deg C. Hols at 64-67degC for 1 hour and 20 minutes. Sparge with 4 gallons of 77 deg C water. (Mash pH was between 5.0 and 5. 5). Collect wort, boil for one hour etc etc. Chill with wort chiller. Pour into fermenter, allowing pelletized hops and cold break to settle for a few hours. Rack wort to another clean fermenter. Aerate, pitch yeast.

American Pale Ale

Category Pale Ale
Recipe Type All Grain

Fermentables
9.0 lbs US 2-row pale malt (Briess)
1.0 lbs crystal malt (combo of British 50L, US 40L, Special B)
0. 5 lbs US dextrin malt

Hops
27-32 IBU from Goldings (bitterness)
0. 5 oz Cascade or Goldings (flavor)
0. 5 -1.0 oz Cascade or Goldings (aroma)
0. 5 -1.0 oz Cascade or Goldings (dry-hop)

Other
1 tsp rehydrated Irish moss

Yeast Wyeast Irish 1084 repitched

Procedure Mash: 1. 5 quarts per pound total water 90 min @ 152 F. Boil 90 minutes. 1 week primary, 2-week secondary, one of which is for dry-hopping. Add gelatin finings 2 days before kegging.

Angie's Ale

Category Brown Ale
Recipe Type Extract

Fermentables

6 lb Light Liquid Malt Extract
1 lb Crystal Malt 60L
. 75 cup Corn Sugar (priming)

Hops
2 oz Fuggles Hops (3.6% AA 30 min)
1 oz Willamette Hops (4.3% AA 10 min)

Other
5 gals Bottled Drinking Water
. 5 tsp Non-Iodized Salt

Yeast 1 pkt - Nottingham Dry Ale Yeast

Procedure Place Crystal Malt in a grain bag and heat with 2 gallons water in a pasta pot. Remove grain at 160 F. Mix green tea and Malt Extract in a cool brew pot, and add another gallon or two of hot water. Bring to a boil, add hops and salt. Cool wort. Rehydrate yeast, and pitch at 80 F. Ferment in primary for 4 days at room temp. Rack to Secondary. Ferment for additional 10 days at room temp.

Bah Humbug Brew

Category Brown Ale
Recipe Type Extract

Using an orange peel will give good results. Add a small quantity of orange peel at the beginning. Rapid start with the fermentation. This is a great winter brew and has some residual sweetness. The flavor is very complex.

Fermentables
8 lbs Light LME
. 25 lbs Black Patent
1 can Welch's Cranberry juice concentrate

George Braun

Hops

1 oz Willamette Hops
. 5 oz Kent Goldings (last 10 min of the boil)

Other

2 Tbsp pumpkin pie spice
peels from 4 oranges (without the white gunk)
6. 5 gallons water

Yeast 1 pkg. EDME ale yeast

Procedure Peel oranges with a Potato peeler, and set aside
Add grain (in grain bag) to water and heat to 152F, steep for 15 min.
Continue to heat to 170F and pull out the grains.
Heat to boiling, remove from heat, and add honey, LME, and Willamette hops
Boil for 30 min.
Add spice and orange peel
At 45 min add Kent Goldings hops
Turn off heat at 50 min and add cranberry juice cans.
Steep above 170F for 10 min
Cool asap
Ferment

Barrel Bottom Black Bitter

Category Brown Ale
Recipe Type Extract

Fermentables

6 lbs Australian dark malt extract syrup
2/3 lbs chocolate malt
1/3 lbs crystal malt

Hops

2 oz Perle hops
1. 5 oz Cascade hops

Yeast Burton liquid ale yeast

Procedure Soak malt in a pot of hot water for 1 hour. While soaking, begin boiling Australian dark malt with the Perle hops. After 1 hour, add Cascade hops and turn off heat. Steep about 30 minutes. Strain everything into primary and add cold water to bring volume to 5 gallons. Pitch yeast when cool.

Bass Ale

Category Pale Ale
Recipe Type Extract

Fermentables
7 lbs Steinbart's American Light Extract
1 lbs Crystal malt 40L
1 lbs Dark brown sugar; be damned German purity law!

Hops
1 oz Northern Brewer (60 minute boil)
1 oz Fuggle (30 minute boil)
. 5 oz Fuggle (10 minute boil)
. 5 oz Fuggle (15 minute seep)

Yeast yeast

Procedure Steep crystal malt and remove grains before boil begins. Add malt extract and brown sugar. Bring to a boil and boil for 60 minutes. Add 1 ounce Northern Brewer at beginning of boil, 1 ounce of Fuggle at 30 minutes and 1/2 ounce of Fuggle for the last 10 minutes. Turn off heat and add final 1/2 ounce Fuggle. Let steep for 15 minutes. Cool. Pitch yeast.

Bass Ale

Category Pale Ale
Recipe Type All Grain

Fermentables
6-7 lbs pale malt (2-row)
1 lbs crystal malt
1 lbs demarara or dark brown sugar

Hops
1 oz Northern Brewer hops (boil)
1 oz Fuggles hops (boil 30 min.)
. 5 oz Fuggles hops (finish)

Yeast ale yeast

Procedure This is an all-grain recipe---follow the instructions for an infusion mash in Papazian, or another text. The Northern Brewer hops are boiled for a full hour, the Fuggles for 1/2 hour, and the Fuggles finishing hops after the wort is removed from the heat, and it is then steeped 15 minutes.

Bass-Alike

Category Pale Ale
Recipe Type Extract

Fermentables
2 lbs light DME
3 lbs plain light malt extract
2 oz roast barley
8 oz crushed crystal malt

Hops
2 oz Fuggles (pellets)
1 oz Goldings (pellets)
. 25 oz Goldings (pellets)
. 5 oz Goldings (pellets)

Other
gypsum and if necessary

Yeast Ale yeast (I used Edme but wanted to try Wyeast)

Procedure This is a 5 gallon batch. Boil up a couple of gallons of water; add DME and LME, Fuggles, and 1 ounce of Goldings. Make tea out of roast barley, and strain into main boiler. Make tea out of crystal malt and strain into main boiler (half way through boil, add local water ingredients and Irish moss if required). After boil, add 1/2 ounce of Goldings, cover and let stand for 15 minutes. Pour into primary, make up to 5 gallons and pitch yeast. Rack and add 1/4 ounce Goldings and complete fermentation.

Bass Ale Clone

Category Pale Ale
Recipe Type Extract

Fermentables
3 lbs Munton & Fison Light DME
. 5 lbs Medium crystal (50L)
1/2 lb Dark brown sugar

Hops
1 oz Fuggles @ 60 min
. 5 oz Kent Goldings @ 30 min
. 5 oz Kent Goldings @ 2 min

Yeast Wyeast 1098

Procedure This was a three gallon batch. I steeped the crystal in 170F water for about 20 min or so, and then added it to the pot. I pitched from a 1 pint starter at 75F, and fermented (primary only) at about 62F for ten days. I didn't get an OG (forgot), but the FG was down to 1.004, so I bottled it last weekend

Batard de Belgique

Category Belgian Ale
Recipe Type All Grain

Fermentables
6 lbs U.S. 2--row malt
3--1/4 lbs dextrin malt
2 lbs unmalted wheat
1 lbs light brown sugar
1 cup blackstrap molasses
2/3 cup corn sugar (priming)

Hops
1. 5 oz East Kent Goldings hops (6.1% alpha)

Yeast Chimay yeast

Procedure Cook 1/2 pound 2--row malt and 2 pounds of unmalted wheat in 4--5 quarts of water until gelatinized (about 45 minutes). Mix cooked wheat in main mash water and stir until well mixed. Mash in: 12 quarts at 138F. Protein rest: 30 minutes at 126--131F. Mash: 2 hours at 148--152. Mash out: 5 minutes at 170. Sparge: 6--1/2 gallons at 170. Boil 2--1/2 hours, adding hops 60 minutes from the end of the boil.

Batch #28

Category Belgian Ale

Recipe Type Extract

Fermentables
10 lbs Northwest Gold liquid malt extract
1. 5 lbs. corn sugar

Hops
1.3 oz Hallertauer hops (4%) 60 min.
. 3 oz Saaz hops (3%) 60 min.
.3 oz Saaz hops (3%) 2 min.

Yeast Wyeast 1214 Belgian ale yeast

Procedure Boil extract, sugar, 1st hop addition 58 minutes. Add 2nd hop addition and boil 2 minutes. Cool and pitch yeast (I used a 1. 5 liter starter). Ferment cool (about 60 F.). Bottle when fermentation completes.

Batch #62 Brain Wipe

Category Belgian Ale
Recipe Type All Grain

Fermentables
10 lbs Dewolf and Cosyn pilsner malt
1 lbs. Briess 2-row malt
1. 5 lbs. Corn sugar
2 lbs Laglaander Extra pale dry malt extract

Other
1. 5 oz. Tettenager (4.4%) 60 min.
0. 5 oz. Tettenager (4.4%) 5 min.

Yeast Wyeast White beer yeast

George Braun

Procedure Mashed malts with step infusion mash, 30 min. 122 F., 75 min. 150 F., 10 min. 168 F. Boil thirty minutes. Add corn sugar, malt extract, 1st hop addition. Boil 55 minutes. Add 2nd hop addition. Cool and pitch yeast (2 liter starter). Ferment 65-70 until completion.

BB IPA

Category India Pale Ale
Recipe Type Extract

Fermentables
3.7 kg Cooper Real Ale Extract
450.0 Grams Crystal malt
500.0 Grams dextrose

Hops
52.0 Grams Hallertauer Hops

Other
1.0 Tsp Irish Moss

Yeast Gervin ale

Procedure Steep grains at 65 degrees C for 30 mins and remove. Add extract and dextrose and bring to the boil. Add 20g of the hops and boil for 30 mins. Add 20g of the hops and boil for another 25 mins. Add the Irish Moss and 12g of hops and boil for 5 mins. Pitch the yeast when less than 25 degrees C. Leave in the fermenter for 12 - 14 days and bottle. Ready to drink after 10 days in the bottle

Beekeeper's Brown

Category Brown Ale
Recipe Type Extract

Fermentables

1 Each Ironmaster Brown Ale beer kit
5. 5 cups corn sugar
2 lbs honey (*NOT* boiled)
. 5 cup corn sugar for priming

Yeast

Procedure Started Sun 30 April, O.G.: 1.045
Bottled Sun 14 May, F.G.: 1.000 (*)
Sampled today, 21 May, and it's already *VERY* nice! (*) It needed that full two weeks---as usual with honey, the fermenting started very early, went full steam for a long, long time, and went very much to completion.

Belgian Strong Ale

Category Belgian Ale
Recipe Type Extract

Fermentables
. 75 cup Belgian special roast malt
. 75 cup English crystal malt (80L)
10 lbs Northwestern gold extract
. 25 lbs light brown sugar

Hops
1 oz Fuggles pellets (boil)
. 75 oz Cascade pellets (boil)
.75 oz Saaz whole hops (1/2 hour)
. 75 oz Styrian Golding pellets (1/2 hour)
2 oz fresh Cascade (aroma
. 25 oz Saaz (finish)
. 5 oz Olympic pellets (finish)
. 5 oz Cascade pellets (finish)

Other
. 25 tsp cinnamon

George Braun
1 tsp Irish moss

Yeast Wyeast #1214 Belgian

Procedure Brought to boil the Belgian and English crystal. Remove grains. Boiled 1 hour to extract, Fuggles and Cascade, brown sugar, cinnamon and Irish moss.

Belgian Trappiste / Abbey Ale

Category Belgian Ale
Recipe Type Extract

Fermentables
3.3 Lbs M&F Plain Dark Extract
3.3 Lbs M&F Hopped Amber Extract
3.3 Lbs M&F Hopped Light Extract
1.0 Lbs Clover Honey

Hops
1.0 Oz Hallertauer Pellets

Other
5.0 Tbsp Freshly Grated Orange Peel

Yeast White Labs Abbey Ale (WLP530)

Procedure Bring extract and honey and 2 gallons water to 155 - 160 degree Fahrenheit for 15 mins. Bring wort to a rolling boil for 1 hour. Add the hops for the last two minutes of boil. Add the fresh orange peels after removing the wort from the burner. Sparge in primary fermenter with 3 gallons water. Primary ferment was one week and secondary ferment was two weeks at approx. 73 degrees Fahrenheit. Notes: Because of the large amounts of liquid extract used, the batch exceeds 5 gallons. Primary fermentation was done in a 6-gallon glass carboy. Krausen was quite excessive and made a mess. Next batch might be best used with 4. 5 gallons of water. Alcohol % in the area of 12%.

Belgian Wheat Ale

Category Belgian Ale
Recipe Type All Grain

Fermentables
6 lbs pale malt
3 lbs wheat malt
. 25 lbs crystal malt (light)

Hops
2/3 oz Bramling Hops (boil 50 min.)
1/3 oz Bramling Hops (boil 10 min.)
. 25 oz Centennial Hops (boil 1 min., and then steep for 15 min.)

Other
1 tsp gypsum in mash water

Yeast Wyeast Belgian Ale yeast

Procedure Two-stage mash: 50 deg C. for 30 min., then 66 deg C. for 45 min. The two-stage mash is because of the wheat malt component. Ferment at cool room temperature (around 16 deg C.). That's it. The light hopping is to let the wheat and yeast flavors shine through, and they do, very nicely. Although the ale, I found it tasted best well-chilled. It also needed a little while (about a month) in the bottle for the yeast and hop flavors to reach an optimum balance.

Best Pale Ale

George Braun
Category Pale Ale
Recipe Type All Grain

Fermentables
9 lbs pale two row malt
. 5 lbs pils 2-row
. 5 lbs crystal 55L

Hops
1 oz Perle at 45 min remaining
. 5 oz Cascade at 15 min remaining
1 oz Hallertauer (10 min. Steep)

Yeast Wyeast American pale ale

Procedure I used a three step mash with a mash in of 132 f., conversion at 152 f., and mash out of 168. Sparged with 168.
Surprisingly the beer was not exceptionally hoppy with full body resembling full Sail ale.

I used wyest American pale and my original gravity was 1.053. I do not know the final as I have broken my hydrometer. Mash efficiency was 75%. IBU's were 35.7 without the Hallertau steep and 41.7 with.

Bierre de Garde

Category Belgian Ale
Recipe Type All Grain

Fermentables
9 lbs Vienna
. 25 lbs Crystal 80
. 5 lbs wheat

Hops

. 5 oz Northern Brewer (8.8%) 60 minutes
. 5 oz Northern Brewer 20 minutes
. 5 oz Hallertau (5.25%) 2 minutes

Other
1/3 lbs aromatic

Yeast, Yeast Labs' Munich Lager

Procedure Infusion mash (RIMS) per Dr. Fix (40-60-70C). Boil 120 minutes.

Big Bang Pilsner Ale

Category Lager
Recipe Type Extract

Fermentables
2 lbs Liquid extract
3 lbs DME
1 lbs Rice extract

Hops
1. 5 oz Willamette for bittering
. 5 oz Willamette for dry hopping aroma

Yeast American liquid Wyeast yeast

Procedure Boiled 1 hour OG 1.042 at 72 degrees Added dry hops 3 days later when I moved the beer to a secondary fermenter. The dry hopping gives a unique taste and the beer is already at 3-4% alcohol to protect itself from hop contamination.

Black Bear Ale

Category Porter
Recipe Type Extract

George Braun

Fermentables
6.0 Lbs Briess Amber Malt Extract
1.0 Lbs Munton & Fison dark DME
0. 5 Lbs Crystal Malt - 80 Lov
0.25 Lbs Chocolate Malt
0.25 Lbs Black patent Malt

Hops
2.0 Oz Fuggles Hops (boiling)
1.0 Oz Fuggles hops (aroma)

Yeast Wyeast European Ale (pitchable tube)

Procedure Pour 1 1/2 gallons of water into the brew pot and turn the heat to high. Pour the cracked grains into the pot. When the temperature reaches 180F, remove the grains with a strainer. Add the malt extract... wait until boiling commences and then add the boiling hops. Boil for 45 minutes and add the aroma hops for another 2 minutes. Remove the pot from the heat and sparge into the fermenter.

Blackout Brown Ale

Category Brown Ale
Recipe Type All Grain

Fermentables
7 lbs Klages malt
. 25 lbs chocolate malt
.25 lbs black patent malt
. 5 lbs 80 L. crystal malt
. 75 cup corn sugar (priming)

Hops
1 oz Willamette hops (3.8% alpha) (boil 60 minutes)

4/5 oz Perle hops (8. 5 % alpha) (boil 30 minutes)
. 5 oz Willamette hops (3.8% alpha) (dry hop)

Other
. 5 tsp Irish moss (boil 15 minutes)

Yeast Wyeast English ale yeast

Procedure I use Papazian's temperature-controlled mash (30 minutes at 122, 90 minutes at 155-145, sparge at 170). Total boil time was 1 hour. Cool and pitch yeast. After 6 days, rack to secondary and dry hop. One week later, prime and bottle

Brew Free or Die IPA

Category Pale Ale
Recipe Type Extract

Fermentables
4 lbs Munton and Fison light DME
4 lbs Geordie amber DME
1 lbs crushed Crystal Malt

Hops
1. 5 oz Cascade leaf hops (boil 60 minutes)
1. 5 oz Cascade leaf hops (finishing)

Other
1 tsp Irish Moss

Yeast Wyeast #1056 Chico Ale Yeast (1 quart starter made 2 days

Procedure Add the crystal malt to cold water and apply heat. Simmer for 15 minutes or so, then sparge into boiling kettle. Add DME, top up kettle and bring to boil. When boil starts, add boiling hops and boil for 60 minutes. 10 minutes before end of boil add 1 teaspoon of Irish moss. When boil is complete, remove heat, add finishing hops and immediately begin chilling wort. Strain wort into fermenter and pitch yeast starter. Primary fermentation took about 4 days. Let the beer settle for another 2 days and then rack to a sanitized, primed (1/3 cup boiled corn sugar solution) and oxygen purged keg and apply some CO2 blanket pressure.

British Bitter

Category Pale Ale
Recipe Type Extract

Fermentables
5 to Alexander's pale malt extract
. 5 lbs crystal malt

Hops
1-1/4 oz Cascade hops (boil)
. 25 oz Cascade hops (finish)

Other
10 oz dextrose (optional)

Yeast Munton & Fison ale yeast

Procedure Steep crystal malt and sparge twice. Add extract and dextrose and bring to boil. Add Cascade hops and boil 60 minutes. In the last few minutes add remaining 1/4 ounce of Cascade (or dry hop, if desired). Chill and pitch yeast.

Brown Ale

Category Brown Ale
Recipe Type Extract

When I'm looking for a batch with a quick turnaround, it's time to whip up this Brown Ale recipe. It's ready to drink within 3 weeks and excellent within the month.

Fermentables
1 Lb. Special 'B' malt (VERY dark Crystal)
6 Lbs. Amber malt syrup
. 75 cup corn sugar boiled in 2 cups water for priming

Hops
1 oz. Fuggles hop pellets - 45 minutes
. 5 oz. Fuggles hop pellets - 5 minutes

Yeast Wyeast 1084 - Irish Ale yeast

Procedure Add the grains to the cold water in the pot, heat nearly to boiling (180-190 degrees), remove and sparge with more hot water (I use the tea kettle and a SS colander). Bring to a boil, turn off heat and add malt syrup and dissolve (this is to avoid burning it to the bottom of the pot). Bring back to a boil, add the boiling hops, and after 40-45 minutes add the finishing hops. Remove from heat, cool (I put the whole pot in an ice water bath), transfer to carboy and top up to 5 gallons if needed. Pitch yeast, mix and aerate thoroughly.
Fermentation should be done in a week, but I leave it sit for another just to be sure. After bottling it should be carbonated and tasty in another week.

My water is fairly hard so a dose of brewing salts might also be in order.

Brown Ale

Category Brown Ale

George Braun
Recipe Type Extract
This beer tastes fine. It is brown, malty, and slightly bitter. I don't get much nutty flavor, so I would increase the chocolate malt.

Fermentables
6 lbs English Amber malt syrup
. 5 lbs Light English dried malt extract
. 5 lbs crystal malt (40L)
. 5 lbs chocolate malt
1 lbs light brown sugar

Hops
10 HBU Cascade
1 oz Cascade (finishing; 5.8% alpha)

Yeast Wyeast English Ale yeast

Brown Ale

Category Brown Ale
Recipe Type Extract

Fermentables
. 25 lbs chuck. malt
. 5 lbs. De Wolf-Cosyns special B malt
6 lbs. amber syrup (I used Briess)
2 lbs. dark syrup

Hops
1 oz. Northern Brewer hops (boiling)
. 5 oz. fuggle hops (finishing)

Other
. 5 lbs. Briess special roast
. 75 cup corn sugar to prime

Yeast European Ale yeast

Procedure In case your homebrew store doesn't have the specific brands of grains I listed here--the "special roast" is toasted barley, about 50 Lovibond, and the "special B" is very dark crystal malt--221 Lovibond. If it's not available, substitute in the dark crystal malt you can find.
You asked for specific directions, so here goes:
1) Heat about 2 gals of water in your brew pot. Steep the choc malt, special B, and special roast while the water heats up. Putting the grains in a muslin steeping bag helps make removing the grains a lot easier.
2) When the water begins boiling, remove the grains, and add the amber syrup, dark syrup, and Northern Brewer hop.
3) After 50 min, throw in the fuggle hops, and boil for 10 more minutes.
4) Cool down your wort, and add to your carboy with 3 gal water. When it's all reached 78F, pitch your yeast.

Brown Ale

Category Brown Ale
Recipe Type Extract

Fermentables
1 can Munton's Plain Amber Malt Extract 3.3 lbs
2 lbs. Munton's Plain Light Dry Malt Extract
1 lbs. Crushed Grain Mix (1/2 50 L Crystal & 1/2 Chocolate)
3/4 cup 3/4 cup Corn Sugar (priming)

Hops
2 oz. Willamette Whole Flower Hops 4.9%

Other
1 teaspoon Irish moss 1/2 way through boil

Yeast WYeast #1028 London Ale or RTP English Ale Yeast

Procedure Steep grain until boiling, remove - add extracts - bring to boil, drop in hopes for the entire 45 min. boil (Irish moss 25 min. into boil) 2 weeks fermentation. 2 weeks bottled. All at room temp.

Brown Ale #3

Category Brown Ale
Recipe Type Extract

Fermentables
. 5 lbs. #60 Crystal malt grains
. 25 lbs. Chocolate malt grains
. 25 lbs. Black patent malt grains

Hops
2 oz. Fuggles (4. 5 %) boiling
. 5 oz. Willamette (5.3%) finishing

Other
7 lbs. Alexander's Dark LME
2 tsp. Gypsum
2 tsp. Ground cinnamon

Yeast 1 pkg. Brewer's choice (Wyeast) #1095 British ale yeast

Procedure Cinnamon and finishing hops went in during last 10 minutes of boil.
Sorry, didn't do SG or FG. But, experience tells me it is about 4. 5 %. Another pound or two of the LME would probably raise the alcohol level to about 5. 5 % or so.

Brown and Blue Ale

Category Fruit Beers
Recipe Type All Grain

Fermentables
6--1/2 lbs pale malt
. 5 lbs wheat malt
.75 lbs crystal malt (80L)
4 oz black patent malt (uncracked)
2 oz roasted barley (uncracked)
5 lbs fresh blueberries

Hops
1 oz Goldings (4.9% alpha)
. 5 oz Fuggles (4. 5 % alpha)

Yeast Wyeast #1084 (Irish ale)

Procedure Mash in 2 gallons at 130F, protein rest 30 minutes at 125F, add 1.25 gallons, mash 30 min at 150F, raise temp to 158F until converted (15 minutes), mash out 10 minutes at 170F. Sparge with 4 gallons to yield 5- -1/2 gallons at 1.046. Add Fuggles and 3/4 ounce of Goldings after 20 minutes of boil, boil 60 minutes, add last 1/4 ounce of Goldings and boil 15 minutes more. Rinse blueberries in a dilute sulfite solution (after weeding out the fuzzy ones), puree, and add to primary along with yeast.

Brown Rye Ale

Category Brown Ale
Recipe Type All Grain

Fermentables

George Braun

5 lbs Mild Ale Malt (Munton and Fison)
1. 5 lbs Rye Flakes (in the bulk section of your health food store)
8 oz Cara-Munich (DeWolf-Cosyns)
3 oz Roasted Barley (DeWolf-Cosyns)
1 lbs of Sucanat (evaporated cane juice, IE. Natural brown sugar)

Hops

2.0 oz 8.0 AAU Fuggles (60 min)
1. 5 oz 5.2 AAU Spalt (10 min)

Yeast ale yeast

Procedure Mash at about 142 F for 90 minutes. Sparge as usual. Boil wort 60 minutes with sucanat, hop as indicated above. Chill as usual. The original gravity comes to 1.048 (for 5 gallons). Pitch any of the plethora of British and German ale yeasts marketed by Wyeast. (I generally use London Ale.)

Brown Rye Ale

Category Brown Ale
Recipe Type All Grain

Fermentables

5 lbs Mild Ale Malt (Munton & Fison)
1. 5 lbs Rye Flakes (in the bulk section of your health food store)
8 oz Cara-Munich (DeWolf-Cosyns)
3 oz Roasted Barley (DeWolf-Cosyns)
1 lbs of Sucanat (evaporated cane juice, ie. natural brown sugar)

Hops

2.0 oz = 8.0 AAU Fuggles (60 min)

1. 5 oz = 5.2 AAU Spalt (10 min)

Yeast London Ale or German Ale Wyeast

Procedure Mash malt and rye at 142 for 90 minutes. The three times I've made this, the mash temperature has always been on the low side. The beer came out great every time, so I'm not worried.
Sparge as usual. Add sucanat and boil 60 minutes.

Chill as usual. The original gravity comes to 1.048 (for 5 gallons).

Pitch London Ale or German Ale Wyeast. Actually, I'm going to try the California Steam/Lager yeast next time. It sounds like the steamy esters would complement the rye flavor quite nicely.

Buzzy Beer

Category Strong Ale
Recipe Type All Grain

Fermentables
11 lbs DWC Pilsen malt
8 oz Ireks Wheat malt
1. 5 oz Black Patent

Hops
1 oz Northern Brewer
. 25 oz Hallertauer (last 15 minutes)

Other
. 25 tsp Irish Moss

Yeast American ale Wyeast 1056

Procedure Mash in and hold at 122-125 deg far for 1/2 hour, rose to 145 deg far for 1 hour. I use 11 1/2 quarts water in mash. Sparge to 7-7. 5 gal, boil 1 hour. You should have an OG of around 1.058 to 1.060 Use a very attenuating yeast, I use American ale, Wyeast 1056 Primary ferment for 7 days, rack to secondary and let it sit another three to four days. Mine normally finishes at around 1.006.

Carp Ale

Category Pale Ale
Recipe Type Extract

Fermentables
3 lbs Munton & Fison light DME
3 lbs M&F amber DME
1 lbs crystal malt

Hops
2.6 oz Fuggles hops (4.7% alpha= 12.22 AAU)
1 oz Kent Goldings hops (5.9% alpha = 5.9 AAU)

Other
1/4 tsp Irish moss

Yeast 1 pack Brewer's Choice #1098 (British ale yeast)

Procedure Break seal of yeast ahead of time and prepare a starter solution about 10 hours before brewing.
Bring 2 gallons water to boil with crushed crystal malt. Remove crystal when boil starts. Fill to 6 gallons and add DME. After boiling 10 minutes, add Fuggles. At 55 minutes, add a pinch of Irish moss. At 58 minutes, add Kent Goldings. Cool (I used an immersion chiller) to about 80

degrees. Pitch yeast and ferment for about a week. Rack to secondary for 5 days. Keg.

Cat's Claw Blackberry Ale

Category Fruit Beers
Recipe Type Extract

Fermentables
6 lbs Alexander's Pale extract syrup
1 lbs Orange Blossom Honey
1 lbs (4 cups) Crystal Malt, 10L
. 25 lbs (1 cup) Victory Malt
8 lbs Blackberries
2/3 cup Orange Blossom Honey (for priming)

Hops
1 oz Cascade Pellets (bittering - 60 mins)
. 5 oz Cascade Pellets (finishing)

Yeast 1 pint WYeast #1084 Irish Ale Yeast (recultured)

Procedure Place crushed grains in cold water and steep for 45 minutes at 155 degrees. Sparge into brew pot and bring to a boil. Add extract and bittering hops and boil for 50 minutes. During the boil, mash berries through a strainer to extract the juice. Add honey and boil for 10 more minutes, skimming off any scum that forms. Remove from heat and pour blackberry juice into the hot wort. Stir well and allow to steep for 15 minutes. Cool and pour into primary containing 3 gallons cold (previously boiled) water. Pitch yeast and aerate well. Rack to secondary when vigorous fermentation subsides. When fermentation completes, make a "hop tea" with the finishing hops. Cool, add to bottling bucket along with a honey priming solution, and bottle.

Cat's Paw Brown Ale

Category Brown Ale
Recipe Type All Grain

Fermentables
7 lbs Klages malt
. 25 lbs chocolate malt
.25 lbs black patent malt
. 5 lbs crystal malt (90L)

Hops
1 oz Willamette hops (boil)
4/5 oz Perle hops (boil)
. 5 oz Willamette hops (finish)

Other
1 tsp gypsum
. 5 tsp Irish moss

Yeast Whitbread ale yeast

Procedure The mash was done using Papazian's temperature-controlled mash. The boiling hops (Willamette and Perle) equal 9.84 AAUs. The finishing hops are added after the boil (while chilling with an immersion chiller). The ale yeast is rehydrated in 1/2 cup of 100 degree water.

Celis Clone

Category Belgian Ale
Recipe Type All Grain

Fermentables
0.4 lbs rolled oats
3 lbs. 10 oz. flaked wheat

4 lbs. DWC pilsner malt

Hops
1.3 oz Tetnang. pellet AA 4.3 for 70 min boil
0. 5 oz of Saaz pellets last 5 min. of boil

Other
. 5 oz bitter orange peel last 20
1.25 oz of coriander seed (crushed) (last 5 minutes
120 grams of dextrose
5 ml of 88% lactic acid

Yeast Wyeast 394

Procedure Step infusion mash with 1 hour at 124 F; 1 hr 10 min at 145 to 150 F; mash out at 160 and sparge at 160 with 1. 5 h sparge to get 6.75 gallons. Use 1.3 oz of Tetnang. pellet AA 4.3 for 70 min boil, 1/2 oz bitter orange peel last 20 min of boil; last 5 min added 1.25 oz of coriander seed (crushed); and about 0. 5 oz of Saaz pellets. Chilled and pitched with Wyeast 3944. (5 gallons with o.g. 1.040). Ferment between 70 to 74 F. Racked 8 days later with gravity at 1.011. Bottled with 120 grams of dextrose at f.g. of 1.011. Added 5 ml of 88% lactic acid to last 2.25 gallons bottled.

Notes: Sparge went beautifully with no problems. Hard time grinding coriander seeds with mortar and pestle.

Charlie Brown Pumpkin Ale

Category Fruit Beers
Recipe Type Extract

Fermentables
7 lbs light dried malt extract
1 lbs 40 L Crystal malt

George Braun
2 lbs pale ale malt
1 whole pumpkin (10 - 15 lbs)
1 tsp pumpkin pie spice
. 5 cup brown sugar mixed with 1 teaspoon cinnamon and 1 teaspoon pumpkin pie spice (for priming)

Hops
2 oz Fuggles (90 min)
1 oz hallertauer (90 min)
. 5 oz Fuggles (5 min)

Other
1 tsp ground cinnamon

Yeast Wyeast liquid ale yeast in starter

Procedure Clean and quarter the pumpkin, bake for 30 minutes at 350 F. Puree the pulp in food processor or blender. The grains and pumpkin were mashed for 90 minutes at 154 F. This thick mess was then strained into the brew pot (a long process!), and then a standard 90 minute boil took place. When done, cool with a chiller, and WYEAST starter was pitched. Sorry about the WYEAST number, I forgot to record it. I know it was an ale yeast and most probably a German ale yeast to be specific, but I am not certain. Standard fermentation and bottling except the spices were added at priming time with the priming sugar.

Chronos' Kin Kolsch

Category German Ale
Recipe Type Extract

Fermentables
5.0 Lbs Light DME
8.0 Oz CaraMunich Malt
1.0 Lbs Acacia Honey

Hops
0.5 Oz Zeus (13.3% AA 60 min)
0.5 Oz Zeus (13.3% AA 30 min)
1.0 Oz Zeus (13.3% AA 2 min)

Other
1.0 Tsp Gypsum
1.0 Tsp Irish Moss

Yeast WLP011 European Yeast

Procedure Steep Cracked Caramunich Malt in 150 F water for 30 minutes. Discard Malt and bring water to boil. Dissolve DME and Honey in boiling water, add 60 minute hops. After 30 minutes of boiling, add flavor hops. After 45 minutes of boiling, add Irish moss. Steep aroma hops either two minutes from the end of the boil or after turning off the brew pot.

Clara Bell

Category Pale Ale
Recipe Type Extract

Fermentables
7 lbs lighter
1 lbs Cara-pils malt

Hops
1.5 oz Hallertauer hops pellets

Other
1 tsp salt
1 tsp citric acid
2 tbsp Irish moss

George Braun
Yeast 2 packs Munton & Fison yeast

Procedure Put cara-pils and crystal malt in 2 gallon pot with 170-180 degree water for one hour, stir occasionally. Sparge into boiling pot with enough water to bring volume to 3-1/2 gallons. Add syrup and 1 ounce of hops. Boil one hour, adding Irish moss in last 1/2 hour and 1/2 ounce hops in last 10 minutes. Add salt, citric acid, and nutrient. Put in primary with enough water to bring volume to 5 gallons. Pitch yeast at about 75 degrees

Cranberry Ale

Category Fruit Beers
Recipe Type Extract

Fermentables
5 lbs light malt extract
1 lbs sugar
3 lbs pureed frozen Cranberries

Hops
1--1/4 oz Fuggles (Boiling 30 minutes)
. 75 oz Fuggles (Finishing 10 minutes)

Other
. 75 cup brown sugar for priming

Yeast Munton & Fison Dry Ale yeast

Procedure I used a little under 3 pounds of frozen cranberries and pureed them right before adding to the wort right after turning off the heat. Their semi-frozen state brought the boil straight down. I had a strainer over the funnel hole and would let the wort drip through it. Then I would press it a bit with the ladling spoon and scoop it out into a bowl. This took a little while, and some of the wort was left behind in the saturated cranberries (I used hop bags and grain sacks so that there wasn't a lot of other stuff). But I topped it off with some tap water (gasp!) and got a nice two cases out of it.

Cranberry Ale

Category Fruit Beers
Recipe Type Extract

Fermentables
3 kg liquid pale malt extract
1 kg honey
1.2 kg crushed frozen cranberries (steeped 10 min)

Hops
1. 5 oz Hallertauer (~4% AAU) boiling hops (60 min)
0. 5 oz Hallertauer flavoring hops (5 min)

Yeast Wyeast German Ale #1007

Procedure Standard 1hr boil with 3 gal wort, cool in ice water, pour into 2. 5 gal boiled, cooled water. Add yeast starter, rack after 7 days, and bottle after 14 days with 3/4 cup corn sugar.

Cranberry Beer

Category Fruit Beers
Recipe Type Extract

Fermentables
6 lbs extra light dry malt extract
1 lbs Munich malt
3 bags Cranberries

Hops

George Braun
1 oz Fuggles boiling
1 oz Fuggles as finishing hops

Yeast yeast

Procedure I thawed the berries and blended with enough water to make a little over 2 quarts of slush. Meanwhile, I did a normal extract brew using the Munich malt as a specialty grain (i.e., put in a double layered pair of clean pantyhose and stuck in the pot while I bring the cold water to a boil). At the end of the hour of boiling I put in the finishing hops and poured in the cranberry liquid for the final minute or two as I turned off the heat. I bottled after a week.

Delightful IPA

Category Pale Ale
Recipe Type Extract

Fermentables
0. 5 lbs amber crystal, steep until boil
6 lbs. English light malt extract: boil 60 min.

Hops
1 oz. Galena (11% a. a.): boil 60 min
1 oz. Willamette whole leaf hops (4% a. a.): boil 10 min.
1 oz. Willamette:

Yeast English brewer's yeast

Procedure You can carry the hop bag over into the secondary if you rack. This English brewer is so fast it really finishes before you need a secondary. If you do rack, or when you bottle, the hop nose will hit you like a baseball bat. Oh, it's good.

Diaper Pail Ale

Category Pale Ale
Recipe Type Extract

Fermentables
7. 5 lbs Coopers Light Malt Extract Syrup
0.75 lbs. Crystal 40 L

Hops
2 oz. Nugget hops (11% AA)
1 oz Cascade hops (6.1% AA)

Other
1 tsp gypsum

Yeast Wyeast 1056 American Ale

Procedure Steep Crystal malt at 155 degrees F for 45 min.
Add gypsum, extract, and bring to boil for 60 min.
1. 5 oz Nugget @ 15 min
0. 5 oz Nugget @ 30 min
0. 5 oz Nugget, 0. 5 oz Cascade @ 45 min
Dry hop for 2 weeks with 0. 5 oz Cascades.

Don's Most Wickid Ale

Category Porter
Recipe Type All Grain

Fermentables
6 lbs pale ale malt
. 75 lbs crystal malt
.25 lbs black patent malt
1 lbs corn sugar
1 cup blackstrap molasses

Hops

George Braun
10 AAU Northern Brewer
6 AAU Cascade

Other
. 5 cup corn sugar to prime

Yeast Wyeast 1028 London Ale yeast

Procedure Mash grains in 10 quarts water at 150 degrees for 90 min. Mash pH 5. 5 . Mash-out 5 min. @ 168 degrees. Sparge with 5 gallons water @ 168 degrees. Dissolve sugar and molasses into running. Boil 90 minutes. Add Northern Brewer hops 30 minutes into boil. Turn off heat and add Cascades. Cool. Let it sit over night. Rack off trub and pitch yeast. Temp at pitching: 62 degrees. After five days in primary, rack to secondary. Let sit for ten days, then rack into bottling bucket with dissolved priming sugar and bottled.

Double Diamond

Category Pale Ale
Recipe Type All Grain

Fermentables
9 lbs Pale ale malt
1 lbs crystal malt
. 75 lbs, Brown sugar
. 5 lbs malto-dextrins (or 3/4# cara pils)

Other
2 oz Williamette (60m)

Yeast 1/2 ounce Williamette Whitbred dry yeast

Procedure This is an infusion mash at 156 degrees. Sparge, and add brown sugar, and malto-dextrins. Bring to boil and add 2 ounces Williamette hops. After 60 minutes, turn off heat and steep 1/2 ounce Williamette hops for 10-15 minutes.

Dr. Bruce's Skull and Crossbones Old Ale

Category Pale Ale
Recipe Type All Grain

Fermentables
9 lbs light malt (6-row)
1 lb Cara-pils
1 lb Crystal malt (medium or dark)

Hops
4 oz Fuggles hops

Yeast ale yeast

Procedure Using light malt only, proceed with protein rest @ 122 degrees f for 30 minutes. Raise temp to 158 f, and add toasted, cara-pils and crystal malts. Mash until conversion is complete, raise temp to 180 and hold for 20 minutes. Sparge until 5-5. 5 gallons are obtained. Use 2 oz. hops for boiling, 1 oz for flavoring 10 minutes before end of boil and another oz 2 minutes before for aroma. Primary fermentation is one week, secondary ferm for another week. Bottle you have to leave this stuff for a while to mellow it out a bit. Yield will be less than 5 gallons, don't worry as long as your OG is about 1.050 (of course a little higher is fine

Dry Ale

Category Pale Ale
Recipe Type Extract

Fermentables
3 lbs light Scottish malt extract

3 lbs 2-row pale malt
1 cup corn sugar (priming)

Hops
9 AAU Kent Goldings hops

Other
1 tsp gelatin
1 oz PolyClar-AT

Yeast Edme ale yeast

Procedure This beer was made using the small-scale mash procedure described by Miller in The Complete Handbook of Home Brewing

English Special Bitter

Category Pale Ale
Recipe Type All Grain

Fermentables
6. 5 lbs English 2-row
8 oz. Belgian CaraMunich
4 oz. Flaked Wheat
1. 5 oz Chocolate

Hops
35 IBU's East Kent Goldings + 1 oz Goldings dry-hopped in the keg

Yeast Wyeast #1968

Procedure No process problems other than a difficult sparge (culprit: the flaked wheat?)
Primary fermentation 7 days @ 68F

English Strong Spice Ale

Category Strong Ale
Recipe Type All Grain

Fermentables
12 lbs 2-row pale (Gambrinus)
1/8 lb roasted barley
1. 5 lb Munich (gambrinus)
. 5 lb victory
. 5 lb malted wheat
. 5 lb carapils

Hops
1. 5 oz Chinook 60 min
. 5 oz Hallertauer 10 min
. 5 oz Hallertauer 1 min

Other
1/8 lb chocolate
1 tsp Irish moss for 15 min
. 5 oz. Ginger
9 inches of cinnamon stick
1 oz sweet orange peel
. 25 tsp Nutmeg
.25 tsp Cloves

Yeast Wyeast London ESB #1968

Procedure Mash is using single-step infusion mash at 153 degrees F. Sparge as usual. Hop according to times listed. Ferment at 65-70, rousing after for 3 days to extend fermentation. Rack to secondary at 50-55 for two weeks. Add spice tea to secondary. To do this, combine spices with boiling water and steep for 3 minutes. Add tea with spices to fermenter.

George Braun

Et Tu Brute?

Category Pale Ale
Recipe Type Extract

Fermentables
2 lbs. (Guesstimate) Munton & Fison light DME
3.3 lbs. Munton & Fison amber DME
1 lb crystal malt

Hops
2. 5 oz Cascade hops (boiling)
1 oz Fuggles hops (flavor)
. 5 oz Fuggles (aroma)

Yeast Edme dry ale yeast (forgot to start the Wyeast English Ale)

A procedure I did the usual

Procedure of bringing 2-gal of water to a high-but-not-boiling temperature (I have no thermometer), and steeped the crushed crystal malt for 30 min, then strained out. I then upped the heat to a boil, added the DME and stirred to dissolve. Then, I added the boiling hops. Boiled 1 hour uncovered. I added the flavor hops, boiled 10 min, covered, then added aroma hops, boiled 2 min, removed from heat. I skimmed out the hops, ran the hot wort through my chiller into my primary, and diluted to 5 gal. Then, I pitched the hydrated Edme yeast.
I racked to a secondary after seven days, and gave it a 2-week secondary fermentation. I primed with 3/4 cup of M&F light DME and bottled.

First All-Grain

Category Pale Ale
Recipe Type All Grain

Fermentables
9 lbs. Munton & Fison Lager (purchased precrushed, don't have a mill)
. 5 lbs. same grain toasted for 10 min at 350 in oven
. 5 lbs. Munton & Fison Crystal Malt (No idea about L. rating)

Hops
1 oz. Kent Goldings 60 min boil
. 5 oz. Hersbrucker Hallertau 30 min boil
. 5 oz. Hersh. Hall. 10 min boil

Other
1/4 tsp Irish Moss 10 min boil

Yeast 1 pack Edme dry yeast

Procedure I used a step mash ala THCOHB. Lauter-tun got filled up to the top with grain so there was no way to keep the sparge water above the grain bed, still seemed to go smooth. I only have small pots so I had to use 4 of them to hold and boil all of the wort. I also split up the hops between the pots so they all got some. I chilled with my new immersion chiller thanks to a non brewer friend that found a copper coil in his travels and gave it to me. Boy it sure beats the cold bath tub bit. It is now fermenting as we speak.

George Braun

First Ames Brew American Pale Ale

Category Pale Ale
Recipe Type All Grain

Fermentables
7 lbs pale malt
1 lb Munich malt
1 lb special roast malt (45L)
. 25 lb crystal malt (40L)
. 5 lb wheat malt
. 25 lb dextrine malt
1/8 lb black patent
. 5 cup corn sugar priming

Hops
1 oz cascade hops 5. 5 % AA (1 hour)
1 oz Tettnang hops 3.8% AA (1 hour)
. 75 oz hallertauer 2.6% AA (1/2 hour)
.75 oz hallertauer 2.6% AA (10 minutes)

Yeast Wyeast American Ale #1056

Procedure This was the first beer I brewed when I moved back to Ames, IA hence its name. Crush all grains and add to hot tap water (approximately 2. 5 gallons). Let mash set for 15 minutes. Raise temperature to 122 F for protein rest and hold for 35 minutes. Add 3/4 gallon of boiling water to bring mash to 140 F, hold for 30 minutes. Add additional 3/4 gallon of boiling water to bring temperature up to 155 F. Hold at this temperature for 1 hour. Sparge till your heart's content and begin boil. Boil hops for indicating times (I put the hops in boiling bags). After 1 hour, stop boil and chill wort and siphon into primary fermenter. Pitch yeast from starter.

Frane's House Ale

Category Pale Ale
Recipe Type All Grain

Fermentables
9 lbs British ale malt
. 5 lbs British crystal
2 oz Flaked barley

Hops
. 75 oz Eroica hops
1 oz Mt. Hood hops

Yeast WYeast American Ale yeast

Procedure Mash with 3-1/2 gallons of water at 155 degrees (our water is very soft; I add 4 grams gypsum and 1/4 gram epsom salts in mash; double that in the sparge water) for 90 minutes or until conversion is complete. Sparge with 6 gallons, boil 90 minutes. After 15 minutes, add 3/4 ounce Eroica hops. At end of boil, add 1 ounce Mt. Hood hops. Ferment at 65 degrees with WYeast American Ale yeast (in starter). Bottle two weeks later, drink one week later

Frosty Toad British Ale

Category Pale Ale
Recipe Type Extract

Fermentables
1 CAN Edme DMS malt syrup (3.3 LB.)
3 LB. Amber Dry Malt Extract
1 LB. English Crystal Malt 50/60 L

George Braun
. 75 Cup Dextrose for priming or 1 1/4 cup Dry Malt Extract

Hops
2. 5 oz Cascade hop pellets (11 HBU) - (Boil) 60 min.
. 5 OZ. Fuggles hop pellets - (Finish) when heat is removed

Other
2 Tbsp. Gypsum
1 tsp. Irish Moss (add 15 min. before end of boil)

Yeast Liquid British Ale Yeast (Yeastlab A04 or Wyeast 1098)

Procedure Add the gypsum to cold water and heat to 170 degrees. Steep the crushed crystal malt in a straining bag for 15 minutes at 170 degrees. Remove the straining bag, add malt extracts, the cascade hops and bring to a boil. Boil for 60 minutes. Add Irish Moss 15 minutes before the end of the boil. Add the Fuggles when the heat is turned off.

Full Moon Ale

Category Scottish Ale
Recipe Type Extract

Fermentables
6 lbs dark Australian DME
1 lbs caramel crystal malt
. 75 cup corn sugar (priming)

Hops
1. 5 oz Willamette hops
1. 5 oz Fuggles hops

Yeast 1 pack Wyeast #1098: British Ale

Procedure Boil 2 gallons of water and turn off heat. Add crystal malt and steep about 15 minutes. Strain through muslin into kettle. Heat another gallon of water to 170 degrees. Pour through grain into pot. Heat to boiling and add DME and 1/3 of hops. After 45 minutes, add another 1/3 of hops. Turn off heat after 15 minutes and add last 1/3 of hops. Steep. Cool wort and add 2 gallons of cold water. Pour in wort and pitch yeast. Rack to secondary after 4 days top off with enough water to make 5 gallons. After 4 weeks, prime and bottle.

Full Sail Ale

Category Pale Ale
Recipe Type Extract

Fermentables
7 lbs Australian Light Malt Syrup
. 75 lbs Light Crystal Malt
1 oz Dextrin Malt
. 75 cup Corn Sugar (priming)

Hops
2--1/4 oz Nugget Hops (1--3/4 ounce for boiling

Other
2 tsp Gypsum

Yeast Wyeast London Ale Yeast

Procedure Crack and steep crystal malt at 155 - 170 F for about 45 minutes in 1/2 gallon of water. Add extract, gypsum, dextrin and 2 gallons of water. Bring to boil, then add 1 3/4 oz. hops. Boil for 45 minutes, then add 1/2 oz. hops at the end of the boil for 15 minutes.

Full Sail Amber

George Braun
Category Amber Ale
Recipe Type All Grain

Fermentables
10. 5 lbs Klages malt
8 oz 90 L crystal malt
2 oz chocolate malt

Hops
. 75 oz Chinook (11.3 %), 90 minutes
1 oz cascade plugs (5.7 %) 15 minutes
. 5 oz cascade plugs (finish)
. 5 oz cascade plugs (dry hop)

Yeast culture of Brewers Resource's English Draft Ale yeast

Procedure Mash at 152 F, 90 minutes.
I used a culture of Brewers Resource's English Draft Ale, which has worked well for me in a couple of batches that I've made with it.

Generic Ale

Category Pale Ale
Recipe Type All Grain

Fermentables
9 lbs 2--row Harrington malt

Hops
1 oz Chinook hops

Yeast Edme ale yeast

Procedure Use standard mashing

Procedure I always add 1/4 of the hops after the boil so a nominal attempt at aroma is SOP.

Geordie Brown Ale

Category Brown Ale
Recipe Type Extract

Fermentables
2 cans Geordie Extra Strong ale, extract
1 cup dark brown sugar
2 cups corn sugar
. 5 lbs crystal malt
. 5 cup malt dextrin

Hops
1 oz Willamette leaf hops

Other
. 5 tsp Irish moss

Yeast

Procedure Bring grain to boil in 1 gallon water; remove grain when water starts to boil. Add another 1/2 gallon of water and bring to boil again. Add extract and sugars, boil for 15 minutes. Add Irish moss and hops for last 5 minutes of boil. Put it in fermenter with enough water to make 5 gallons. Add ale yeast and wait.

Golden flower Ale

Category Pale Ale
Recipe Type Extract

Fermentables

George Braun
3--1/2 lbs Laaglander dry extra light malt
1 lbs fragrant clover honey

Hops
8 grams Galena hops (8% alpha) (boil)
. 5 oz Fuggles hops (dry hop)

Yeast Wyeast American ale yeast

Procedure Boil water, malt, honey, and galena hop. Cool, transfer to fermenter (preferably with blow-off tube) and add started yeast. After krausen subsides, rack to carboy with Fuggles in it, ferment until hydrometer readings stabilize, about 5 days, probably. Bottle Drink young. Primary fermentation should be around 68-71 degrees Fahrenheit. Secondary should be closer to 61-63.

Granolabrau

Category Pale Ale
Recipe Type All Grain

Fermentables
6 lbs 6-row cracked pale malt
1 lbs white or brown rice
1 lbs yellow corn grits or flaked maize
6 oz flaked barley
4 oz oatmeal
1. 5 lbs clover or orange blossom honey

Other
4 oz millet

Yeast Wyeast German ale yeast (#1007)

Procedure Cook rice, grits, oatmeal and millet together in plenty of water for 3 hours to gelatinize. The result should be a mushy, gummy mess.

Mash malt, barley and gelatinized grains in moderately hard water at 150F for 1-1/2 hours. Raise to 168F to deactivate enzymes. Sparge with hot water (168F) to collect 250+ degrees of extract (e.g., 6 gallons at S.G. 1.042).

Boil 1-1/2 hours, adding all but 1/2 ounce of hops after 1 hour, honey towards the end of boil. Chill wort and add cold water to bring S.G. to 1.050. Pitch with working starter. Dry-hop with reserved hops in hopping bag. Primary fermentation takes 5-7 days. Wyeast 1007 will require 3-4 weeks in secondary fermenter to settle out. Bottle, then age 2 months. Drink and enjoy!

Grizzly Peak Pale Ale

Category Pale Ale
Recipe Type All Grain

Fermentables
8 lbs Klages malt
1 lbs Munich malt (20 L.)
1 cup Cara-Pils malt
. 75 cup corn sugar (priming)

Hops
3. 5 oz Kent Golding hops

Other
1. 5 Tbsp gypsum
. 5 tsp Irish moss

Yeast Wyeast Chico ale yeast

George Braun

Procedure User Papazian's temperature controlled mash (30 minutes at 130--120 F., 120 minutes at 155--145 F., sparge at 170). Add 1 ounce Kent Goldings at beginning of boil. Add another ounce 30 minutes later. In last 15 minutes, add another ounce of Kent Goldings and Irish moss. Chill, strain, pitch yeast.

Honey Bitter

Category Bitter Ale
Recipe Type Extract

Fermentables
4 lb Brew maker Victorian Bitter kit (1.8 kg)
2.2 lbs clover honey (1.0 kg)

Yeast yeast as supplied in kit

Procedure Half of supply yeast nutrient in primary, other half goes into secondary. 15 min. boil. I have only used this particular bitter kit, but if it isn't available to you then just try another brand and let me know what you think.

Hot Summer Nights

Category Pale Ale
Recipe Type Extract
This beer is light and crisp with a great Hallertau aroma.

Fermentables
6 lbs extra light liquid malt extract (30% corn in mash)
. 5 lbs light crystal malt (Lov 10) steeped before boil.

Hops
1 oz Hallertau 5 minutes into boil (1 hour boil)
. 5 oz Hallertau in muslin bag @ 55 min to boil, and left in primary

Yeast Wyeast German Alt liquid yeast

Hot Weather Ale

Category Pale Ale
Recipe Type Partial Mash

Fermentables
3 lbs pale malted barley
3 lbs Blue Ribbon malt extract
1 cup corn sugar (priming)

Hops
2 oz Willamette hops
. 5 oz Kent Goldings hops

Yeast 1 pack Red Star ale yeast

Procedure Mash the 3 pounds of plain malted barley using the temperature-step process for partial grain recipes described in Papazian's book. Boil 30 minutes, then add the Blue Ribbon extract (the cheap stuff you get at the grocery store) Add Willamette hops and boil another 30 minutes. Add Kent Goldings in last 5 minutes. When at room temperature, pitch yeast. Ferment at about 68 degrees using a 2-stage process.

Ides of March Ale

Category Pale Ale
Recipe Type Extract

Fermentables
1 can Coopers Ale Kit
1. 5 lbs light dry malt extract
1 lbs rice syrup
. 25 lbs Black Patent malt
.25 lbs chocolate malt

George Braun
. 25 lbs 40 deg crystal malt
. 5 cup corn sugar - bottling

Hops
1. 5 oz Willamette whole hops

Other
1 cup brewed Kenya AA coffee

Yeast

Procedure In three gallons of brewing water, put Black Patent and Chocolate malt. Bring to a boil. After boil just starts, strain out grains. Add coffee, crystal malt, rice syrup, dry ME and 1. 5 ounces Willamette hops. Boil 45 min. Add Cooper Ale Kit, and continue to boil 3 to 5 min. (Much longer and the finishing hops in the Coopers kit make the brew bitter). Cool and pitch with Ale yeast from the Cooper Kit. Ferment 7 days. Rack and add finings (or polychlar). When settled, bottle with corn sugar.

India Pale Ale

Category Pale Ale
Recipe Type All Grain

Fermentables
9 lbs Pale Malt
. 75 lbs Crystal Malt
. 5 lbs Carapils Malt

Hops
1. 5 oz (4.9%) Kent Goldings (60 Minutes)
1. 5 oz (4.9%) Kent Goldings (15 Minutes)
. 25 oz Kent Goldings (dry)

Other

1 tsp Irish moss (15 Minutes)
2 tsp Gypsum
2 oz Oak Chips

Yeast Wyeast 1059 American Ale

Procedure Mash Pale malt at 153 F for 30-60 minutes. Test after 30 minutes. Add Crystal and Carapils and mash-out at 168 F for 10 minutes. Sparge. Bring to boil. In a saucepan, boil the oak for no more than 10 minutes, then strain the liquid into your boiling kettle. Boil the wort, adding boiling hops after 30 minutes and the flavor hops and Irish moss after 75 minutes. Chill and pitch a quart of 1059 starter. Dry hops in a secondary fermenter. The beer will clear in the bottle.

India Pale Ale (2gal)

Category India Pale Ale
Recipe Type All Grain

Fermentables
2. 5 lb pale malt
5 oz crystal malt (80L)

Hops
1 oz Willamette hops 5%
. 5 oz Willamette hops (finish)

Yeast Wyeast #1028 London ale

Procedure This is a 2-gallon batch. Mash in 5 quarts 132 degrees (140 degree strike heat). Adjust mash pH to 5.3. Boost temperature to 150 degrees. Mash 2 hours, maintaining temperature at 146-152 degrees. Mash out 5 minutes at 168 degrees. Sparge with 2 gallons of 165 degree water. Boil 90 minutes, adding hops in last hour.

George Braun
Add finishing hops 5 minutes before end of boil. Ferment at 70 degrees, 6 days in primary, 4 days in secondary.

IPA 1

Category India Pale Ale
Recipe Type Extract

Fermentables
1 lb Crystal Malt
5 lb Pale Malt Extract Syrup
4 lbs Amber Malt Extract Syrup
1/2 lb Toasted Malted Barley

Hops
. 75 oz Cascade hops (finishing)
2 oz. Northern Brewers Hops (boil)

Other
2 Tsp Gypsum

Yeast Wyeast Britsh Ale (w/starter)

Procedure Hold grains at 150 for 30 mins. Remove, add extracts and proceed as normal within one hour boil. This time I plan to toast my own barley, add Irish moss and use dry yeast because I don't have time to wait for the starter (and I'm getting cheap :). Sorry, don't have the O.G. and F.G. only the ingredient list with me.

IPA 2

Category Pale Ale
Recipe Type Extract

Fermentables
8 lbs. Alexander's Sun Country Pale (Klages) Extract

1 lbs. 64l Crystal malt

Hops
. 75 oz. Northern Brewer Hops (about 9.8 alpha)
1 oz. Cascade hops (4.6 alpha)
1. 5 oz. Cascade hops (4.6 alpha) (dry hopping)

Other
2 tsp. gypsum

Yeast Wyeast American Ale Yeast

Procedure Crack grains and steep in two quarts 150-155 degree water for 45 minutes. Collect runoff and sparge with additional 1. 5 gallons water at 170 degrees. Add malt extract & gypsum and bring to boil. Add Northern Brew hops. After 30 minutes, add Cascades. After another 15 minutes, turn off the heat, let cool and then strain into enough cold water to make 5 gallons. Pitch yeast once the wort's at 75 degrees. Ferment for one week. Rack to secondary, adding 1. 5 oz. Cascade at this time. Bottle after another week. Serve very cold.

IRS IPA `92

Category Pale Ale
Recipe Type Extract

This one works for me, but is a bit under hopped, I think.
Fermentables
6.6 lbs Northwestern Gold Extract
1 lb Laaglander Light Dried Malt Extract
1.1 lb Roger's (Canadian) Demerara-Style Brown Sugar
. 5 lbs 6 row Crystal Malt (40L)

Hops
2 oz Bullion Pellets (%AA unknown) -- (90 min boil)

George Braun
. 5 oz East Kent Goldings Whole (4%AA) (15 min boil)
1 oz East Kent Goldings Whole (4%AA) (dry hop - last 7 days before bottling)

Other
1/3 oz Wines Inc. Burton Water Salts
5 gallons distilled water
1 gallon Chicago (soft) tap water

Yeast yeast recultured from 3 bottles of Sierra Nevada Pale Ale

Procedure Nothing special -- crush the crystal (actually, I used a rolling pin and a zip lock bag) and put the crystal into a mesh grain bag. Suspend the bag in the pot from the spoon as the water and Burton Water Salts go from cool to 165F. Remove and let drain. Bring to boil, add malt extracts and hops in hop bags at the proper times. Chill as quickly as possible. Aerate and pitch. Use a blow off method.

KGB Bitters

Category Pale Ale
Recipe Type Extract

Fermentables
1 can Alexanders Sun Country pale malt extract
3.3 lbs Northwestern Amber malt extract
. 5 lbs dark crystal malt

Hops
3 oz CFJ-90 Fresh hops

Other
. 25 tsp Irish moss

Yeast ale yeast

Procedure Start grains in brew pot with cool water. Remove when boil commences. Add malt extract and 1-1/2 ounce of hops. Boil 1 hour. Strain out boiling hops and add 1/2 ounce more hops and Irish moss. Boil 5 minutes. Remove from heat and add another 1/2 ounce of hops. Steep 10 minutes and cool. Strain wort into primary fermenter with cold water to make 5 gallons. Add final 1/2 ounce of hops.

Killer Party Ale

Category Pale Ale
Recipe Type Extract

Fermentables
2 cans Pilsner/Lager or American light malt
15 cups corn sugar
2 jar Lyle's golden syrup (22 oz.)
2 lbs flake maize

Hops
2. 5 oz Hallertauer hops

Yeast 1 pack Brew Magic yeast

Procedure In 1 gallon water, boil malt, golden syrup, sugar and 1-1/2 ounce hops for 8 minutes. Add remaining hops and boil another 2 minutes. Pour into primary fermenter with 2 gallons water. Bring another gallon of water to a boil and add flaked maize. Turn off heat and 1/3 pack of Brew Magic. Let sit 10 minutes. Add another 1/3 pack of Brew Magic. Let sit 10 more minutes. Strain maize into primary fermenter, and rinse with cold water. Discard maize. Fill primary to 5 gallon mark.

KiWheat Ale

Category Wheat Beer
Recipe Type Extract

Fermentables
6 lbs William's Weizenmalt Extract (60% wheat, 40% barley)

Hops
1. 5 oz Hallertauer hops (2.9% alpha acid) - 60 min
1 oz Hallertauer hops - 5 min

Other
0. 5 tsp Irish moss

Yeast Wyeast Belgian Ale yeast

Procedure Fermented at ~70^F.
After 5 days, I peeled and diced about 7# of kiwi fruit, added 2 campden tablets, and put them in the freezer overnight to help break down the cell walls.

The next day, racked to secondary and added the kiwifruit (brought up to room temperature.

After 1 week, when the secondary fermentation was complete, I bottled.

Koelsch 1

Category German Ale
Recipe Type All Grain

Fermentables

7 lb British pale malt or German pilsner malt (or 3. 5 lbs of each)
1 lb Vienna malt
. 5 lbs wheat malt

Hops
12 AAU Tettnanger 60, 30, 10

Yeast West German ale (1007) Wyeast Kolsch

Procedure Step mash according to Miller's recipe.

Koelsch 2

Category German Ale
Recipe Type Partial Mash

Fermentables
3 lbs Brit. pale malt
1. 5 lbs wheat malt
3.3 lbs Munton & Fison light malt extract
1.0 lb laaglander light, dry extract (for a little body)

Yeast Wyeast Kolsch (Cologne) yeast

Procedure Hop 7 IBU at beginning of boil, 3 at 30minutes and the rest 10 minutes before the end of boil. The key to this style beer is the use of WYEAST KOLSCHE or COLOGNE yeast and the use of wheat to give it the kolsche snap.

Koelsch 3

Category German Ale
Recipe Type All Grain
Fermentables
7. 5 lb Belgian Pils Malt
1 lb Wheat Malt

George Braun
. 25 lb 40L Crystal

Hops
1. 5 oz Tettnanger (aa = 5. 5 %) 60 min
. 25 oz Tettnanger 20 min
.25 oz Saaz (aa = 2.8%) 20 min
. 25 oz Tettnanger 5 min
.25 oz Saaz 5 min

Other
1 tsp p Irish moss

Yeast 1. 5 qt Wyeast Kolsch yeast starter

Procedure Rest 25 min @ 135F, 25 min @ 145F, 60 min @ 155F.

Lageresque Ale

Category Pale Ale
Recipe Type Extract

Fermentables
4 lbs Alexanders light unhopped malt extract
1-1/2 lbs Light dried malt extract (DME)

Hops
5 AAU's of your favorite bittering hops (e.g., 1/2 ounce. Of 10% alpha chinook)
1-1/2 oz Hallertauer or Tetnanger hops for finishing

Yeast Ale yeast (Wyeast American Ale #1056 aka Sierra Nevada

Procedure Dissolve the extracts in 5 gallons of brewing water. Bring to boil. After 15 minutes, add bittering hops. Boil 60 minutes total. Turn off heat and add finishing hops.

Cool as rapidly as possible to 60-70F. Rack to fermenter, fill to 5 gallons, pitch yeast, relax, etc.

Lambic

Category Belgian Ale
Recipe Type All Grain

Fermentables
7 lbs 2-row Pale Malted Barley
. 5 lbs crystal malt

Hops
1 oz Chinook hops
1 oz Willamette hops
1 oz Northern Brewer leaf hops

Other
3 1/2 brewers' flaked wheat
. 75 cup dextrose (priming)

Yeast 1 teaspoon yeast nutrient

Procedure Baked all hops for 1 hour at 300 degrees and left 3 days in the open air. Mash grains and flaked wheat in 14 quarts of 130 degree water with 1 tsp gypsum added, for 5 minutes. Let the protein rest for 20 minutes at 140 degrees. Start conversion for 60 minutes at 158-155 degrees. Mash out 10 minutes at 170 degrees. Sparge with 170 degree water. Boil 2 hours with hops added near the beginning. Cool. Pitch yeast. After 12 days I pitched the Pediococcus. I have to admit, I didn't much care for the taste of either the beer or the starter solution. It only took about 10 days (and some premature hot weather) to produce decided ropiness, so I pitched the Brettanomyces.

Light Ale

George Braun
Category Pale Ale
Recipe Type Extract

Fermentables
4 lbs light malt extract (Northwestern)
2 lb rice extract (from a Chinese grocery)
1/2 lb crystal malt

Hops
2 oz low alpha hops

Yeast Wyeast Chico ale yeast

Light Lager

Category Lager
Recipe Type Extract

Fermentables
1 Ea Coopers Lager kit (3.75lbs) or any lager or pilsner kit
2 lbs light dry malt

Other
1 packet of pilsner enzyme (amylase enzyme)

Yeast 2 Fresh packets of ale yeast

Procedure Wort boiled for 15 minutes. This preserves the light color of the wort.
Fermentation will also take longer, about 3 to 4 weeks at 68F, because the enzymes will take a while to convert and unfermentable sugar (body) to sugars the yeast can convert to alcohol.

Light Pale Ale

Category Pale Ale

Recipe Type Extract

Fermentables
6 lbs Alexanders Pale malt extract
. 75 cup corn sugar (for bottling)

Hops
1. 5 oz cascade hops pellets

Other
1 packet Knox unflavored gelatin

Yeast 1 packet dry ale yeast

Procedure Add malt extract and 1 ounce hops pellets to 1. 5 gallons boiling water. Boil for 30 minutes and add remainder of hops (0. 5 ounce). Boil for 10 more minutes. Place wort in primary fermenter and add water to make 5 gallons. Wait for temperature to reach 70 degrees F and pitch yeast.

After most fermentation activity stops (3 to 4 days), rack to secondary fermenter. Dissolve gelatin in one cup boiling water and add to wort. Keep in secondary fermenter one week.

Dissolve 3/4 cup corn sugar in 2 cups boiling water, add to wort and bottle. This beer clears nicely after one week.

Limey Bastart Pale Ale

Category Pale Ale
Recipe Type Extract

Fermentables
7.0 Lbs Light LME

George Braun
0. 5 Lbs Crystal Malt 60L
1.0 Oz Chocolate malt

Hops
1.0 Oz East Kent Golding (5 AAU)
0. 5 Oz Fuggles (5 AAU)

Other
1.0 Pinch Irish moss

Yeast White Lab Burton Ale Yeast

Procedure Bring 5 Gal water to 150-160 degrees. Steep grains in grain soak for 20 min. Bring water to boil Add LME Add 1 oz EKG's (60 min) Add. 5 oz Fuggles (last 20 min of boil) Add Irish Moss (last 2 min)

Long Island Winter Warmer

Category Strong Ale
Recipe Type All Grain

Fermentables
7 lbs mild ale malt
3 lbs US 6-row malt

Hops
2 oz Cascade (leaf) - boil 75 min.
1 oz Cascade (leaf) - boil 30 min.
. 5 oz Cascade (leaf) - boil 15 min.
. 5 oz Cascade (leaf) - steep for 15 min. after the boil
. 5 oz Cascade (leaf) - dry hop in the secondary

Yeast ale yeast

Procedure The Cascade hops were fresh and very aromatic, from the fall '91 harvest. Alpha acid was about

5%; alas, I didn't write it down. I used Edme yeast, although I doubt if I would ever again use dried yeast on a beer like this (or any beer?). Fortunately, I got no infections.

Lord Stanley Dark Ale

Category Porter
Recipe Type Extract

Fermentables
6 lbs light malt extract syrup
1+ lb NW Gold dry malt extract
8 oz crystal (60 l.)
8 oz carapils
4 oz chocolate malt
2 oz roasted malt

Hops
1 oz perle pellets (boil)
. 5 oz cascade pellets (boil)
. 5 oz cascade (flavor)
1 oz Williamette (Aroma)

Other
2 tsp gypsum

Yeast Wyeast American Ale II

Marginally Pale Ale

Category Pale Ale
Recipe Type All Grain

Fermentables
7 lbs Pale Ale (Hugh Baird)
8 oz EPC (CaraStan or 40 degrees)
7 oz D/C Aromatic Malt

George Braun
3 oz Biscuit Malt
2 oz Toasted Barley (such as Briess Special Roast)
4 oz CaraPils
8 oz Flake Barley
. 5 cup raw clover honey
. 5 cup dark brown sugar

Hops
4 oz E. Kent Goldings

Yeast Wyeast London ESB yeast (starter)

Procedure I used a standard step-infusion mash schedule Sparge with 15 quarts water at 165 degrees. Prime with honey/brown sugar (1 cup nut).

Midwest Mild Ale

Category Brown Ale
Recipe Type All Grain

Fermentables
6 lbs mild ale malt
4 oz chocolate malt

Hops
1. 5 oz Fuggles (pellets) - boil
. 5 oz Fuggles (pellets) - finish

Yeast yeast

Procedure Bottled on day 13. At its best fresh; weeks 3-6. I believe the original gravity figure (which suggests more than 80% efficiency) was in error. Around 1037 seems more likely.

Mild Ale

Category Brown Ale
Recipe Type All Grain

Fermentables
5 lbs Klages 2-row malt
4 lbs mild malt
2 lbs crystal malt (80L)
. 5 lbs English pale malt
. 5 lbs flaked barley
1/5 lbs chocolate malt

Hops
1 oz Willamette leaf hops (5.9% alpha)
1/8 oz Cascade leaf hops (6.7% alpha)
1/8 oz Eroica leaf hops (13.4% alpha)
. 5 oz Willamette leaf hops (finish)

Yeast yeast

Procedure Water was treated with 2 gm each MgSO4, CaSO4, KCl, and CaCO3. Mash grains in 3 gallons of water at 134 degrees. Hold 120-125 degrees for 55 minutes, rise to 157 degrees for 55 minutes. Rise to 172 degrees for 15 minutes. Sparge with 5-3/4 gallons water. Boil 15 minutes. Add bittering hops. Boil 55 minutes. Add finishing hops and boil 5 more minutes. Chill and pitch with Sierra Nevada or Wyeast Northern Whiteshield yeast. Ferment and bottle or keg.

Millennium Amber Ale

Category Amber Ale
Recipe Type All Grain
American Amber Ale

Fermentables
0.25 Lbs Crystal 40L

George Braun
0.67000002 Lbs Biscuit Malt
0.67000002 Lbs Wheat Malt (American)
0.33000001 Lbs Caramel Pils Malt
8.25 Lbs Pale Malt (2 Row)
2.0 Lbs CaraMunich 60

Hops
0. 5 Oz Cascade Hops 60min
0. 5 Oz Cascade Hops 30min
0. 5 Oz Cascade Hops 10min

Other
1. 5 Tsp Irish moss

Yeast Wyeast 1272 American Ale II

Procedure It pretty much fits the profile of the "American Amber Ale", but is a few SRM points darker -- not to worry. We can't taste, color :-) However, if it's a real concern, you can use slightly less than 1/4 lb Roast Barley to get it back within profile range (needs to go down about 4 or 5 points).

Mittelfrueh Brew

Category Pale Ale
Recipe Type Extract

Fermentables
0.25 lb roasted barley
0.75 cup corn sugar - priming
6.6 lb Amber LME (I used Northwestern)
1.0 lb Amber DME
0.75 lb med crystal malt
0.25 lb chocolate malt

Hops

1. 5 oz Cluster hops - bittering - 60+ min
1.0 oz Mittelfrueh hops - 15 min
0. 5 oz Mittelfrueh hops - end of boil
1.0 oz Mittelfrueh hops - dry hop

Other
1.0 tsp gypsum
1.0 tsp Irish moss

Yeast Liquid ale yeast (I used William's California Ale aka Wyeast

Procedure Steep grains with gypsum @ 150 deg F for 30 minutes. Add Irish moss whenever you think it should be added. Ferment in primary for about 1 week, transfer to secondary and add dry hops. Bottle after a few more weeks (I waited 3).

Mirror Pond Pale Ale (Clone)

Category Pale Ale
Recipe Type All Grain

Fermentables
6. 5 Lbs Pale Malt
1.0 Lbs Crystal Malt 20L

Hops
12.0 AAU Cascade Hops (Boil)
10.0 AAU Cascade Hops (Finish)

Yeast Wyeast 1056 or equiv

Procedure Mash grains in 2. 5 gallons of water at 152 degrees. Sparge with 3 gallons.
Boil, add the 6 AAUs of hops. After 45 minutes, add 6AAUs of hops. Boil for 15 more minutes.

Ferment at 68 degrees for 2 weeks. Then transfer to secondary fermenter and add 10AAUs of cascade hops. Keep cool for 3 to 4 weeks and bottle.

Mo' Better Bitter

Category Pale Ale
Recipe Type Extract

Fermentables
3 lbs M&F dry, light malt extract
3 lbs M&F dry amber extract
1. 5 lbs Laaglander dry, light extract
. 5 lbs cracked toasted 2--row malt
Small handful roasted barley
Hops
1 oz Galena hops 8% alpha (boil)
1 oz Fuggles hops 4% alpha (boil)
. 5 oz Fuggles (finish)

Yeast Wyeast Irish ale yeast

Procedure Substitute boiling hops at will, as long as you end up with 12 HBU. The roasted barley is to add a hint of red color and just a touch of flavor; if you despise the taste of roasted barley use chocolate malt instead. The toasted barley is essential. I used Wyeast Irish, but London ale would probably be even better. I wish I had dry hopped this batch with an extra 1/2 ounce of Fuggles.

Motor City Madhouse Ale

Category Brown Ale
Recipe Type All Grain

Fermentables
8 lbs English 2-row

1 lbs wheat
2. 5 lbs clover honey

Hops
1 oz Willamette
1 oz Hallertau

Yeast WYeast 1007

Procedure The mash schedule was:
95 degrees for 15 minutes (Acid Rest)
122 degrees for 30 minutes (Protein Rest)
152 degrees for 45-60 minutes (until passed iodine test)

Northern Lights

Category Pale Ale
Recipe Type All Grain

Fermentables
13 lbs 2--row pale malted barley
2 lbs 20L crystal malt
1 lbs wheat malt

Hops
2 oz Cascade leaf hops (boil)
. 5 oz Perle leaf hops (boil)
. 5 oz Fuggles leaf hops (boil)
1 oz Chinook leaf hops (boil)
. 5 oz Chinook leaf hops (finish)
. 5 oz Fuggles leaf hops (finish)
1 oz Northern Brewer hops pellets (dry hop in

Other
1 lbs corn flakes, optional

Yeast Wyeast German ale yeast #1007

Procedure I did a step mash, following normal procedure.

Nebraska Red

Category Pale Ale
Recipe Type Extract

Fermentables
6.6 Lbs Munton & Fison Amber Malt Extract (Unhopped)
1.0 Lbs Crystal Malt (Steeped 45 minutes at 150-170 F)
2.0 Oz Roasted Barley (Same as above)

Hops
1.0 Oz Cascade Hops (for bittering, First wort Hopped, added with specialty
0. 5 Oz Cascade Hops (For flavor, Boiled 15 minutes)
0. 5 Oz Cascade hops (for aroma, Boiled 2 minutes)

Other
1.0 Tsp Irish moss, (Rehydrated and added for fining added for last 15

Yeast 2 - 6 gram packets of Muntons Dry yeast.
(Rehydrated and started in a

Procedure Wort cooled to 85 F, aerated by stirring, and pitched the yeast starter at 85F.

Net Brown Ale

Category Brown Ale
Recipe Type Extract

Fermentables
. 75 lb Cara-Munich, Crystal
. 25 lb Special B
1/8 lb Chocolate Malt
6. 5 lbs Amber Malt Extract Syrup

Hops
1 oz Brewers Gold - 60 min
1 oz Fuggle - 5 min

Yeast ale yeast

Procedure Single stage fermentation between 65 and 72 Deg F (ie room temp) for 1 to 2 weeks. The original recipe (from Austin Homebrew Supply) called for Whitbread dry yeast, but I've also used Windsor & Nottingham dry and Wyeast 1098 & 1968 all with good results. I've used tap water, bottled water, and softened water w/ water crystals. Occasionally I've used Irish moss, but I don't think it does anything.

Net Brown Ale

Category Brown Ale
Recipe Type Extract

George Braun

Fermentables

. 75 lb Cara-Munich, Crystal
. 25 lb Special B
1/8 lb Chocolate Malt
6. 5 lbs Amber Malt Extract Syrup

Hops

1 oz Brewers Gold - 60 min
1 oz Fuggle - 5 min

Yeast ale yeast

Procedure Single stage fermentation between 65 and 72 Deg F (ie room temp) for 1 to 2 weeks. The original recipe (from Austin Homebrew Supply) called for Whitbread dry yeast, but I've also used Windsor & Nottingham dry and Wyeast 1098 & 1968 all with good results. I've used tap water, bottled water, and softened water w/ water crystals. Occasionally I've used Irish moss, but I don't think it does anything.

New Peculier

Category Strong Ale
Recipe Type Extract

Fermentables

6.6 lbs dark extract
. 5 lbs crystal malt
. 25 lbs, black patent malt
2 tsp water crystals

Hops

1. 5 oz Fuggles (45 minute boil)
. 5 oz Fuggles (10 minute boil)

Other

1 tsp Irish moss
. 5 cups black treacle

Yeast Whitbread ale yeast

Procedure Put malts into a boiling bag and place into 2--1/2 gallons of cold water. Bring to boil and remove, sloshing about and draining well (as one would with a [giant] tea bag). Add extract, 1. 5 oz Fuggles and boil 45 minutes. During the last 10 minutes, add the remaining hops. Cool (I take my pot outside and put it in a baby bathtub full of circulating cold water from the garden hose). Rack into a carboy and add yeast (I started the yeast with cooled-boiled water, but recently I have taken to putting the yeast directly into the warm wort). I let it go for 4 days, then racked into a second carboy where it sat for another week before bottling. Bottle as usual.

Newcastle Brown

Category Brown Ale
Recipe Type Extract

Fermentables
3.3 lbs. British pale malt extract
3.3 lbs. British amber malt extract (or less)
1 lbs. turbinado sugar (from health food shop)
8 oz. British dark crystal
4 oz chocolate malt
. 5 C. priming sugar

Hops
2 Oz Fuggles at 45 minutes (Williamette or strain Goldings good as)
. 5 oz Fuggles at 10 minutes (optional)

Other

George Braun
4 oz. wheat

Yeast Wyeast 1028 London ale yeast

Procedure Steep grains in a bag 30 minutes in 1 Gal. of 150 degree water. Rinse a bit with 170 degree water. Add extracts. 60 minute boil, chill to 75 degrees, rack to leave behind cold break, pitch with 1. 5 quarts of yeast and starter. Aerate 12 hours by air and a.22 u air filter. Rack at end after 3-4 days. Rack at 2 weeks and bottle. Style has low hops and low carbonation. Nut flavor I think is from the barely refined sugar. The English have a dark brown sugar (raw sugar) that we in the states do not, British recipes call for it.

Norman Conquest Strong Ale

Category Strong Ale
Recipe Type Extract

Fermentables
3.3 lbs American light Malt Extract Syrup
3.3 lbs Coopers bitter ale kit
3.3 lbs Coopers Draught ale kit
1 lbs amber malt extract
. 75 lbs crystal malt

Hops
2 oz Northern Brewer hops (boil)
2 oz Willamette hops (finish)

Other
2 tsp gypsum

Yeast 1 pack MEV 031 high-temp ale yeast

Procedure Start yeast 2 days ahead and add to a quart of sterile wort 3 hours before brewing. Add gypsum to 2 gallons water, add crystal malt. Bring to boil. Strain out grain. After 10 minutes, add Northern Brewer hops. 30 minutes into boil add Willamette hops. Boil a few more minutes. Remove from heat. Strain into fermenter with cold water to make 5 gallons. Pitch yeast.

Not So Pale Ale

Category Pale Ale
Recipe Type All Grain

Fermentables
8 lbs Munton & Fison 2-row pale malt
2 oz U. S. Chocolate malt

Hops
1 oz Northern Brewer pellets (60 min. boil)
. 5 oz Willamette flowers (30 min. boil)
. 5 oz Herrsbrucker plug (15 min. boil)
. 5 oz Herrsbrucker plug (add at end of the boil; steep 15 min.)
. 5 oz Herrsbrucker plug (dry hops, last 5 days in secondary)

Other
. 5 tsp Irish moss

Yeast WYeast 1098 (white-bread)

Procedure Infusion mash for 75 minutes at 150-155 F. 3 days in primary. 11 days in secondary. Finings and dry hops added after day 6.

Nuggets Pale Ale

Category Pale Ale

George Braun
Recipe Type Extract

Fermentables
1.6 Lbs Light DME
0.40000001 Oz 237 Lovibond Crystal DME

Hops
0.1 Oz Perle hops, 6.6% a/a
0.15000001 Oz Nugget hops, 11.7% a/a
0.1 Oz Cascade hops, 6.0% a/a

Yeast Winsor Ale

Procedure Note that crystal dme was in color and is optional. Boil: 60 minutes @ 0 mins: add malts + nugget hops @ 30 mins: add perle hops @ 55 mins: add cascade

Number 23

Category Pale Ale
Recipe Type Extract

Fermentables
4 lbs plain light malt extract syrup
1.1 lbs (750 grams) Maltose

Hops
2/3 oz Chinook Hops
1/3 oz Cascade Hops
. 5 oz Cascade Hops

Yeast Ale Yeast cultured from Sierra Nevada Pale Ale

Procedure About a week before, make a starter from 2 bottles of Sierra Nevada Pale Ale. Use about 4 tablespoons of plain light malt extract syrup and a couple of hop pellets. Boil major ingredients, ala Complete Joy of Home Brewing, in 2 gallons of water. (60 minute boil). Add 1/3 ounce Chinook hops at start of boil, 1/3 ounce Chinook at 30 minutes and 1/3 ounce of Cascade hops in the last two minutes of the boil. Then combine with 3 gallons of ice cold tap water (which was boiled the previous night, and cooled in the freezer) in a 7 gallon carboy. Ferment in primary for a week. Put 1/2 ounce of Cascade pellets in bottom of secondary and rack beer into secondary. Bottle three weeks later.

Oktoberfest Ale

Category Pale Ale
Recipe Type All Grain

Fermentables
6 lbs Light DME
0. 5 lbs CaraMunich crystal (or 60L crystal if you can't find CaraMunich)
0. 5 lbs CaraVienne crystal (or 20L crystal if you can't find CaraVienne)
2 oz Roasted barley (optional)

Hops
4 HBUs Noble hops (Hallertau, Tettnang) for 60 min.
4 HBUs Noble hops for 30 min.
4 HBUs Noble hops for 15 min.

Yeast Wyeast 1056

Procedure Steep crushed crystal malt in 1 gallon of hot (160F) water for at least 30 minutes, and strain into boiling kettle.
For a full-volume boil, use the hopping schedule shown.
For a 1/2-volume boil, double the first two hop additions.

George Braun

Use natural ale yeast (e.g. Wyeast 1056), make a starter and ferment cool (65-68F) to minimize esters.

After bottling and conditioning, keep it in the fridge near 32F for as long as you can before drinking.

Old Man Pyle

Category Strong Ale
Recipe Type All Grain

Fermentables
7.0 lbs British pale 2-row malt
1.0 lbs Vienna malt
1.0 lbs Munich malt
0. 5 lbs 80L Crystal malt
1.0 lbs 120L Crystal malt
0.25 lbs Chocolate malt
0. 5 lbs Dark brown cane sugar
0. 5 cup Corn sugar for bottling

Hops
0. 5 oz Northern Brewer pellets (AA=7. 1) at 60 min. (IBU=15)
0. 5 oz Northern Brewer pellets (AA=7. 1) at 30 min. (IBU=8)
1.0 oz Fuggles plugs (AA=4. 2) at 30 min. (IBU=10)
0. 5 oz Fuggles plugs (AA=4. 2) at 5 min. (IBU=2)
0. 5 oz Fuggles plugs (AA=4. 2) dry hopped (IBU=0)

Yeast Wyeast 1338 European Ale yeast (1-2 pint starter)

Procedure Mash pale, Vienna, and Munich malts at 154F for 1. 5 hours. Add crystal and chocolate malts at mash-out. Add sugar to the boil; adjust amount to hit OG (not more than 1# though). Hop as listed above; dry hops added after primary fermentation slows.

Old Peculier

Category Strong Ale
Recipe Type Extract

Fermentables
4 lbs dark malt extract
. 5 lbs roast barley
. 5 lbs crystal malt
2 lbs dark brown sugar

Hops
2 oz Fuggles hops

Other
5 saccharin

Yeast yeast

Procedure This recipe uses saccharin, but I will not use this in my beer; instead I may add brewer's licorice or lactose for sweetness. The amount of fermentables also seems low; I would add a pound or two of light extract to increase the gravity to the mid-fifties. The recipe also calls for priming with 3 ounces of black treacle, which is molasses. This seems low, and it also seems that different brands would contain different amounts of fermentable sugar.

Orange Blossom Amber

Category Amber Ale
Recipe Type Extract

Fermentables

George Braun
6.6 lbs Northwestern Amber Extract
2 cups Orange Blossom Honey (boil)
0. 5 lbs crystal malt

Hops
1. 5 oz Hallertauer hops (boil)
0. 5 oz Hallertauer hops (finish)

Other
1 tsp. Irish Moss
5/8 cup Orange Blossom Honey (priming)

Yeast M&F ale yeast

Procedure Steep crystal malt while bringing water to a boil. Remove crystal malt and add extract, honey and boiling hops. Boil for 15 min., add Irish moss, boil for another 30 min. Add finishing hops for 1-2 min. boil. After fermentation is complete, bottle using 5/8 cup of honey with one pint water for priming.

Ordinary Bitter

Category Pale Ale
Recipe Type All Grain

Fermentables
5. 5 lb pale malt
0. 5 lbs Maris otter crystal malt 60L
0. 5 lbs corn sugar

Hops
1 oz Northern Brewer hops (7% alpha acid) - 60 min
0. 5 oz East Kent Goldings hops (5.2% alpha acid) - 15min
OPTIONAL: dry hop with 0. 5 to 1.0 oz of Kent Goldings or Styrian Goldings

Yeast, Yeast lab YLA01 liquid Australian ale

Procedure Single infusion mash 90 minutes at 150 to 151 degrees F. Raise to 168 degrees F for mash out. Sparge with 170 to 175 degree F water. Boil 90 minutes. Burtonize your water. Ferment at 65 to 68 degrees F at least seven days. Rack with priming sugar.

Pale After Math Ale

Category Pale Ale
Recipe Type Extract

Fermentables
6.6 lbs American classic light extract
1 lbs crystal malt
2 lbs British pale malt

Hops
3 oz Fuggles leaf hops
1 oz Cascade leaf hops

Other
2 tsp gypsum
. 5 tsp Irish moss

Yeast 1 pack MEV high-temperature British ale yeast

Procedure Mash grains at 155 degrees. Sparge with 170 degrees water. Boil, adding extract and boiling hops; the hops were added in stages, 1 ounce at 50 minutes, 1 ounce at 30 minutes, and 1 ounce at 20 minutes. The Cascade hops were sprinkled in over the last 10minutes of the boil.

Pale Ale

Category Pale Ale

George Braun
Recipe Type All Grain

Fermentables
7-8 lbs English 2-row malt
1/2-1 lbs crystal malt

Hops
3 oz Fuggles hops (boil)
. 75 oz Hallertauer hops (finish)

Yeast ale yeast

Procedure You'll get good yield and lots of flavor from English malt and a 1-stage 150 degree mash. In the boil, I added the finishing hops in increments: 1/4 ounce in last 30 minutes, 1/4 ounce in last 15 minutes, and 1/4 ounce at the end (steep 15 minutes) don't have to be Fuggles; almost any boiling hops will do, I usually mix Northern Brewer with Fuggles or Goldings (just make sure you get.12-. 15 alpha) Conversion will probably only take 60 minutes rather than 90. Depending on when you stop the mash your gravity may vary as high as 1.050. That's a lot of body!

Pale Ale

Category Pale Ale
Recipe Type All Grain

Fermentables
5 lbs pale malt
1 lbs crystal malt
3. 5 lbs pale dry extract
1-1/3 lbs light brown sugar

Hops
1 oz Willamette hops (boil)

1. 5 oz Hallertauer hops
1 oz Clusters hops pellets

Other
1 tsp gypsum
1 tsp Irish moss

Yeast Red Star ale yeast

Procedure Mash pale malt, crystal malt, and gypsum in 2-3/4 gallons of 170 degree water; this should give initial heat of 155 degrees (pH 5.0). Maintain temperature at 140-155 degrees for 2 hours. Sparge. To wort, add extract and brown sugar. Boil with Willamette hops. After 15 minutes, add Hallertauer and Irish moss. Dry hop with clusters and steep. When cool, add wort to carboy and pitch yeast.

The posted recipe called for 4 pounds of dry extract with 2 cups reserved for priming. This seemed excessive and a good way to get exploding bottles, so we reduced the amount of extract to 3-1/2 pounds and assumed that standard priming techniques would be used, maybe replacing corn sugar with 3/4 to 1 cup of malt extract.

Pale Ale

Category Pale Ale
Recipe Type All Grain

Fermentables
9. 5 lbs. Klages 2-row
1. 5 lbs. Crystal 40L
1 lbs. Cara-Pils
1 lbs. Red wheat malt
2 TBS Dextrin powder in bowl

George Braun

Hops

1. 5 oz. Northern Brewers - 60 min.
. 5 oz. Cascade - 60 min.
. 5 oz. Northern Brewers - 30 min.
. 25 oz. Cascade - 15 min.
. 75 oz. Cascade - dry hop in primary

Other

2 tsp gypsum in mash water
1 Tsp. Irish moss and boil
. 5 oz. Crushed coriander and boil (yeah, yeah)

Yeast Wyeast 1056 Chico Ale yeast

Procedure 1.4 qts. /lib. mash water
Protein rest @ 125 deg. - 30 min.
Conversion @ 155 deg. - 60 min.
Mash-out 170 deg.
5. 5 gals. sparge water, pH 5. 5 w/citric acid
Ferment w/Wyeast 1056 Chico Ale yeast - 68 - 70 deg.
5 days primary, 12 days secondary, 10 days bottle before drinking.

Pale Rye Ale

Category Pale Ale
Recipe Type All Grain

Fermentables

8 lbs pale malt
4 lbs rye malt

Hops

. 75 oz Northern Brewer, finish

Other

. 5 oz Centennial 6.6% bittering

. 5 oz Centennial finish

Yeast Sierra Nevada yeast or Wyeast 1056

Procedure Single-step infusion mash or step mash. 90 minute boil.

Perle Pale

Category Pale Ale
Recipe Type All Grain

Fermentables
8 lbs Klages malt
1 lbs flake barley
. 5 lbs toasted Klages malt
. 5 lbs Cara-pils malt

Hops
1. 5 oz Perle hops (boil)
. 5 oz Willamette hops (finish)

Other
1 tsp gypsum
. 5 tsp Irish moss

Yeast 14 grams Muntona ale yeast

Procedure The 1/2 pound of Klages malt was toasted in a 350 degree oven for 10 minutes. The mash was done using Papazian's temperature-controlled method. The Willamette hops are added after the boil, while chilling with an immersion chiller. The yeast is rehydrated in 1/2 cup of 100 degree water.

Pete's Wicked Ale

Category Pale Ale
Recipe Type Extract

George Braun

Fermentables
2 cans Unhopped light Extract
1 lb Crystal Malt

Hops
1 oz. Bullion hops
1 oz. Cascade hops
1 oz. Fuggles

Yeast Ale Yeast

Procedure Put the 1 lb crystal malt in hop bag and put in a gallon of cold water. Bring water up to a boil, then remove bag of crystal with strainer and throw away (you made a tea with the crystal). Remove from heat and add 2 cans of Unhopped light extract. Bring back to a boil and add 1 oz bullion simmer for 30 minutes. Then add 1 oz. cascade hop and simmer for another 15 minutes. Then add 1/2 oz Fuggles simmer for 15 minutes. At last minute add another 1/2 oz. of fuggles.

Pete's Wicked Clone 1

Category Pale Ale
Recipe Type All Grain

Fermentables
8-9 lbs pale malt
1 lbs crystal malt
.25 lbs chocolate malt mash at 155F

Hops
. 5 oz Cascade (60 min boil)
. 25 oz Chinook (60 min boil)
. 5 oz Cascade (10 min finish)

Yeast Wyeast #1056

Procedure Mash malts at 155 F. Add 1/2 ounce Cascade and 1/4 ounce of Chinook for boil. Use 1/2 ounce Cascade to finish.

Pete's Wicked Clone 2

Category Pale Ale
Recipe Type All Grain

Fermentables
8 lbs domestic 2-row
1 lbs Dark German
8 oz CaraPils
6 oz chocolate

Hops
4.4 aau Fuggles for 60 minutes
4.4 aau Fuggles for 30 minutes
5.2 aau Kent Goldings for 2 minutes

Yeast Wyeast 1098

Procedure Mash-in 4 gallons at 57 C (135F) strike heat.
Falls to 52C (126F). Protein rest 30 minutes.
Raise to 68C (154F),
Scarification 2 hours.
No mash out due to brain-cloud. (You should mash out).
Sparge with 6 gallons at 75C (167F)
Got 7-1/2 ~ 7-3/4 gallons. Gravity is 1046.
Extraction = 29.7 points/#/gallon.

Boil 90 minutes.

Chill to 25C (75F). Pitch yeast.

George Braun

If your extraction rates are routinely below mine, add grain accordingly in your recipe. Just add to the two-row, don't bother to adjust the specialty malts, it's just not necessary. My water is fairly soft, and slightly alkaline. I use two tsp gypsum in my mash water. Your mileage, of course, may vary. If you want a 1055 beer, lose 1# of two-row. But I like mine at 1060. FG was 1018. I had to add 1/2 gallon water at bottling to bring volume up to 5 gallons.

Pete's Wicked Red Clone

Category Pale Ale
Recipe Type Extract

Fermentables

. 5 lb Roasted Barley
. 5 lb Munich
. 5 lb Caramel
1 can of John Bull amber
1 can of M&F amber

Hops

1 oz EKG fresh hops.. bittering.. @ 60 min to go
1 oz Tettnanger hops. aroma @ 10 Min to go

Yeast ale yeast

Procedure I steeped the grains till the boil and then removed. I added the cans of malt extract and boiled for about 60 min... add the hops as shown above. I forget the OG and FG (I know the people on here love those figures) but it came out a little over 5% alcohol. After it was done fermenting I put it in the beer ball and primed with a little over a half a cup of corn sugar. I threw out the first cup full of yeasty beer, but the rest was awesome

Pirate Ale

Category Pale Ale
Recipe Type All Grain

Fermentables
8 lb British 2-row
. 5 lb crystal malt
. 5 lb Wheat Malt
. 5 lb Golden Brown sugar

Hops
. 75 oz Willamette (60 mins)
. 5 0 oz East Kent Goldings (EKG) (60)
1 oz EKG leaf hops (60)
1 oz EKG leaf hops (30)
1 oz EKG leaf hops (5)

Pugsley's Pseudo Celis White #5

Category Belgian Ale
Recipe Type All Grain

Fermentables
4. 5 lbs. 6 rows (or 2 rows)
4.0 lbs. Unmalted Wheat (Bulgar from Health Food Store)

Hops
1 tsp. Alpha-Amalase enzyme
1 oz. Hallertauer

Other
4 grams dried orange peel
4 grams crushed coriander seeds
1 tsp gypsum

Yeast 1 pack Wyeast #3056 Bavarian Wheat

George Braun

Procedure Bring 2 gallons water to boil. Add unmalted wheat and hold at 185-195 degrees for 20 minutes. Add cold water and 6 row malt to bring down to 130 degrees. Add 1 tsp. amylase and gypsum (pH 5.3). Allow protein rest for 25 minutes. Raise temperature to 150 degrees and hold 20 minutes. Complete conversion by raising temperature to 158 degrees and holding for 20 minutes. Mash out at 168 degrees for 5 minutes. Acidify sparge water to pH 5.7 with lactic acid. Sparge with 4-5 gallons of 170-180 degree water. Boil wort for 90 minutes. Add hops and crushed spices 15 minutes before end of boil. Cool wort and pitch yeast.

Raspberry Brown Ale

Category Brown Ale
Recipe Type Extract

Fermentables
3.3 lbs hopped dark liquid malt extract
3 lbs light dry malt extract
5 lbs fresh raspberries

Hops
1 oz. cascade hops (1/2 brewing 1/2 finishing)

Yeast Wyeast liquid English Ale yeast

Procedure I mixed the wort and cooked it for 30 minutes, then lowered the temp to 170 and kept it there for about ten minutes. After one week I transferred the brew from primary to secondary fermenter. I kept it in the secondary fermenter for 3 1/2 weeks then bottled.

Rocky Raccoon Ale

Category Pale Ale
Recipe Type Extract

Fermentables
1 can M&F light malt extract (unhopped)
3 lbs clover honey
1/3 cup clover honey (priming)

Hops
2 oz Williamette hops (5.0 AAU's)

Yeast Wyeast London liquid ale yeast

Procedure The malt extract, honey, and 1 oz. of the hops were boiled in 3 gallons of water for 1 hour; the remainder of the hops were then added and steeped for 15 minutes. The wort was passed through a strainer into a plastic primary and diluted to 5 gallons. After reaching room temperature, the yeast was added. The initial SG was equal to 1.040. After 6 days in the primary (60-65 F) and 10 days in a glass secondary fermentor (60-65 F) the final SG was equal to 1.000 (Ed:, 1.010). The beer was then primed with honey and bottled.

Red Ale

Category Pale Ale
Recipe Type Extract

Fermentables
6 lb amber syrup (I use Stoma Brewery)
1 lb crystal malt
2 oz roasted barley

Hops
1. 5 oz Cascade hops for bittering (depending on taste)
.25 oz Cascade hops for flavor
.25 oz Cascade hops for aroma

George Braun
Yeast 115 g dry ale yeast

Procedure Steep the specialty malts in 1 1/2 gal water, remove grains, add syrup to liquor, and boil 60 minutes with the bittering hops Add flavor hops 10 min before end of boil, add aroma hops end of boil and steep for 5 min Add 3 1/2 gal cold water and pitch at a suitable temperature

Richard's Red

Category Pale Ale
Recipe Type All Grain

Fermentables
5 lbs 2 row
1 lb Munich
1 lb dark crystal
1 lb cara-pils
1 lb toasted 2 rows

Hops
1.33 oz Olympic hops at boil
2/3 oz cascade as power cut

Yeast ale yeast

Procedure Toast the 2-row grain for 10 minutes in an oven preheated at 350 before crushing.
Cover crushed grains with 130 degree water hitch will stabilize at 123. Add boiling water to bring to 158 for another half-hour or until conversion is complete.

Toss the hops in the fermenter along with the wort & add the oak as well (I suggest leaving them all in cheesecloth bags). Transfer the oak chips to your secondary as well. If you use a keg, toss them in.

Rusty Cream Ale

Category Pale Ale
Recipe Type Extract

Fermentables
2 lbs pale malt
1 lbs flaked corn
1 lbs crystal malt (about 50 l)
4 lbs Alexanders Pale Malt

Hops
1 oz Tettanger Hops (3.8%) (boil @ 45 min)
1 oz Liberty Hops (3.2%) (half and half boil/finish)

Yeast Whitbread ale yeast

Procedure It appears that the Whitbread yeast that I used was really attentive. The % alcohol/Vol is around 6. 5 . The preliminary tastes puts it nice, smooth, a bit thin (its' been aged about 2 weeks). It should have some character in about 1-2 months.

George Braun

Scotch Ale

Category Scottish Ale
Recipe Type Extract

Fermentables
3.1 lbs Superbrau Light Malt Extract
3.0 lbs Laanglander DME
3.0 lbs bulk Malt Extract (Laanglander)
1 lb Crushed Crystal

Hops
2 oz Northern Brewers (boiling)
5 oz Cascade (FInishing)

Yeast 1 pkg Red Star or Nottingham yeast

Procedure - Put gain in muslin bag into 1. 5 gals of cold water; bring to boil
- Remove grain; add malt extracts, DME, and Northern hops; boil for ~35min
- Last 10min add Cascade hops and Irish Moss (1 tb)

Second Try

Category Stout
Recipe Type Extract

Fermentables
6.6 lbs John Bull plain light extract
1. 5 lbs plain dark, dry extract
. 75 lbs, black patent malt
.25 lbs roasted barley
. 5 lbs chocolate malt
. 5 lbs steel cut oats

Hops
. 5 oz Fuggles hops (boil)

1 oz Hallertauer hops (boil)
1. 5 oz Cascade hops (finish)

Other
1/2 tsp Irish Moss

Yeast 7 grams Muntona ale yeast

Procedure This is the second of a series of experiments in brewing oatmeal stouts. It is an extract brew, with specialty grains being added using the standard stovetop method and removed at boil. When grains are used, they are cracked with a rolling pin and boiled for 30 minutes before straining. The finishing hops are added in the last 5 minutes of the boil

Sierra Nevada Clone

Category Pale Ale
Recipe Type Extract

Fermentables
6.6 lbs light unhopped malt extract

Hops
1 oz. Perles (boil) 8. 5 alpha
. 5 oz. Cascade 4.6(?) alpha (15 min. remaining)
. 5 oz. Cascade 4.6 (?) alpha (5 min.)

Yeast Wyeast 1056

Procedure Specialties steeped 1 hour at 155-160 deg. F (68-71 deg. C). 1 hour boil. The %AA of the Perles is higher than Tony's recipe. His calls for 6. 5 % The %AA of the Cascades were lower (his, 6.3%).

George Braun

Sierra Nevada Pale Ale

Category Pale Ale
Recipe Type All Grain

Fermentables
9 lbs U.S. 2--row pale malt
. 5 lbs crystal malt (60L)
. 25 to cara-pils malt

Hops
1 oz Perle (alpha 6. 5)
. 5 oz Cascade (alpha 6.3) (15 minute boil)
. 5 oz Cascade (steep at end of boil)

Yeast Wyeast "American Ale" yeast

Procedure Mash at starch conversion temperature of 153/5 degrees F. Hop according to schedule above. This recipe assumes 75% extract efficiency. Chill and pitch.

Sierra Pale Ale

Category Pale Ale
Recipe Type All Grain

Fermentables
8 lbs. Great Western domestic 2-row malt
. 75 lbs. 50L crystal malt
. 5 lbs. CaraPils malt

Hops
1 oz. 8.3 AAU whole Perle hops (75 min. boil)
. 5 oz. 6.0 AAU whole Cascade hops (15 min. boil) (Total IBU is about 33)
1 oz. whole Cascade hops (steep while cooling)

Yeast 1 pint starter Wyeast #1056 (Chico)

Procedure 1 1/2 tsp gypsum (my water is rather soft) in mash. Lactic acid added to sparge water for pH 5.7.
122 degree protein rest for 30 min (I know I could have skipped this, but I have never used this malt before), 155 degree saccharification rest for 60 min., mash out at 168 degrees for 10 min. Sparge, boil, pitch, etc.etc. My pre-boil yield is about.033 pts/gal/lb, but since I whirlpool and settle the wort after chilling, then rack off from the trub, my yield drops to about.027 due to the amount of wort left behind in the kettle.

Simple Pale Ale Recipe

Category Pale Ale
Recipe Type Extract

Fermentables
4 kg white sugar, (corn if preferred)
2 cans (1.13kg) Brewmix malt
1 can Doric malt

Hops
various types of hop pellets to taste.

Yeast

Procedure I start with half a preserving kettle of water and when that is boiling I dissolve the sugar therein. If I don't forget, I usually add the hops first. Next I pour in the three cans of malt stirring as I do so. When this mix is about to return to a boil I shut off the heat. I then put the mix in a clean hard finish, plastic garbage pail (I thought that might get to some of you.), and add sufficient water to make the 14 doz. bottles.
The whole thing is then set on a wooden case about a foot high with a light bulb under it. (40watts) I then cover the

George Braun

lot with a heavy quilt and leave it alone for 7 or 8 days. After that, I check with the Hydrometer to see if the SP is up to about 1.0. If it is I bottle it using a plastic syphon.

I prefer not to drink any of this for at least a month, preferably longer, but then I have about 45 doz. bottles at my disposal. There is a certain amount of sediment in the bottles but if you pour carefully it comes out crystal clear. There is no taste to the sediment anyway and I drank it straight out of the bottle on occasion. Cheers.

Singularity Stout

Category Stout
Recipe Type All Grain

Fermentables
8 lbs Pale English 2-Row
1 lbs American 6-Row Crystal
1. 5 lbs Oatmeal
0. 5 lbs American 6-Row Chocolate
0. 5 lbs American 6-Row Black
0.25 lbs American 6-Row roasted barley

Hops
2 oz fresh Northern Brewer's hops
0. 5 oz Clusters hop pellets

Other
1 lbs Dextrin

Yeast Wyeast 1098 British yeast

Procedure 1-step infusion mash at 156 deg for 60 minutes. 60 minute boil: at 30 minutes, add N. Brewer's, at 55 minutes, add clusters.

Six Cooks Ale

Category Pale Ale
Recipe Type Extract

Fermentables
10 lbs English pale malt (DME) extract
1. 5 cups corn sugar (priming)

Hops
4 oz Cascade hops pellets (boil)
2 oz Hallertauer hops pellets (finish)

Other
4 tsp gypsum

Yeast 2 packs Edme ale yeast

Procedure This recipe makes 10 gallons. Bring 3 gallons of water to a boil. Add 4 teaspoons of gypsum, four ounces of hops, and 10 pounds of the DME extract. Bring to boil. Boil 45 minutes. Add 2 ounces of Hallertauer hops in last 1 minute of boil. Strain wort into a large vessel containing additional 7 gallons of water (we used a 55 gallon trash can). Allow wort to cool and siphon into 5-gallon carboys. Add yeast. Caveat Brewer: Trash cans are generally not food-grade plastic, digest wisdom calls for avoiding non-food-grade plastic. Brewer discretion is advised.

Stacie's Wicked Ale

Category Brown Ale
Recipe Type Extract

Fermentables
6.6 lbs Northwestern Malt Extract - Gold
4 oz Chocolate malt

George Braun
8 oz Klages Malt
8 oz 60 Lovibond Crystal Malt
8 oz Black Barley

Hops
1. 5 oz Northern Brew Hops at 60 min
1.0 oz Hallertau Mittelfreu at 10 min
0. 5 oz Hallertau Mittlefreu dry (in secondary)

Yeast Bell's amber ale yeast (or Wyeast 1056)

Procedure Steep grains in 150 to 160 degree F water for 60 minutes. Remove grains and bring to boil.
Primary for 3 weeks
Secondary for 3 weeks
Bottled for 2 weeks.
(I should racked earlier. But I got busy... didn't even read the HBD! Can you believe it?)

Stacie's Wicked Ale

Category Brown Ale
Recipe Type Extract

Fermentables
6.6 lbs Northwestern Malt Extract - Gold
4 oz Chocolate malt
8 oz Klages Malt
8 oz 60 Lovibond Crystal Malt
8 oz Black Barley

Hops
1. 5 oz Northern Brew Hops at 60 min
1.0 oz Hallertau Mittelfreu at 10 min
0. 5 oz Hallertau Mittlefreu dry (in secondary)

Yeast Bell's amber ale yeast (or Wyeast 1056)

Procedure Steep grains in 150 to 160 degree F water for 60 minutes. Remove grains and bring to boil.
Primary for 3 weeks
Secondary for 3 weeks
Bottled for 2 weeks.

Striped Cat I.P.A.

Category Pale Ale
Recipe Type Extract

Fermentables
6 lbs pale dry extract
1 lbs amber dry extract
1 lbs crystal malt
. 75 lbs toasted pale malt
.25 lbs pale malt
. 5 cup corn sugar for priming

Hops
1 oz Bullion hops (8.2 alpha)
. 5 oz Brewers Gold hops (7. 5 alpha)
1 oz Cascade hops (4.2 alpha)

Other
2 tsp. gypsum
. 25 tsp. Irish moss

Yeast 1 pack Wyeast #1098

Procedure

Procedure is that described by Papazian...steep grains, boil 1 hour (boil Brewers Gold and Bullion). Remove from heat and add the cascades. Cool wort. Pitch yeast.

Summer Pale Ale

Category Pale Ale
Recipe Type All Grain

Fermentables
8 lbs 2-row pale malt
1 lbs Munich malt
. 5 cup dextrin malt

Hops
20 grams Nugget leaf hops (14 alpha)
15 grams Brambling leaf hop

Other
1 tsp gypsum
1/4 tsp Irish moss

Yeast 1 pack Edme ale yeast

Procedure Use the standard temperature-controlled mash

Procedure described in Papazian. Use a 30 minute protein rest at 122 degrees, 20 minutes at 152 degrees, and 20 minutes at 158 degrees. Sparge with 4 gallons of 180 degree water. Boil 1 hour with Nugget hops. Add Irish moss in last 10 minutes. Remove from heat and steep Brambling hops for 15 minutes. Cool wort and pitch.

Taking Liberty Ale

Category Pale Ale
Recipe Type All Grain

Fermentables

14 lbs Klages
4 oz 40L Crystal Malt
4 oz 90L Crystal Malt

Hops
. 5 oz Chinook (12%)
1 oz Cascade (5. 5 %)
2 oz Cascade (5. 5 %)

Other
1 tsp Irish moss
. 75 cup corn sugar to prime

Yeast Wyeast 1056 American ale

Procedure Mash all grains for 90 minutes at 150F, adjust PH as needed. Mash off at 170F, sparged with 170F water. This has a total BU of 43.7. If you don't reach around 1.060, adjust the dry hopping accordingly.

TGIF Pale Ale

Category Pale Ale
Recipe Type Extract

Fermentables
6 lbs Light Dry Malt Extract
1 lb Crystal Malt 40L

Hops
. 5 oz Northern Brewer Hops 60 min. (pellets)
. 5 oz Northern Brewer Hops 30 min. (pellets)
. 5 oz Cascade Hops 10 min. (plug or whole)
. 5 oz Cascade Hops dry (plug or whole)

Other
1 tsp Irish moss 30 min.

Yeast 1 package Whitbread dry yeast

The Claude Bonaire Belgian Strong Ale

Category Belgian Ale
Recipe Type Extract

Fermentables
6. 5 999999 Lbs Light DME
2.25 Lbs Amber DME
1.0 Lbs Dark Belgian Candy Sugar
1.0 Lbs Brown Sugar
8.0 Oz Belgian Special B
4.0 Oz Belgian Aromatic
2.0 Oz Malted Barley

Hops
1.0 Oz UK Kent Goldings (60)
0.75 Oz Hallertauer (45)
0. 5 Oz Saaz (2min)

Other
2.0 Tbsp Coriander Seed (crushed)
5.0 Tbsp Sweet Orange Peel (last 15min w/ coriander)
1.0 Tbsp Cinnamon (boiled and added to secondary w/ the pound of Brown Sugar)

Yeast WLY500

Procedure all grains were in a grain bag. Brought to 150 and held for 10min. Raised to 175 for 20min. Finally, raise water to boiling and removed grain at 208, approximately 40min totally time actual boiling time: 75 min. So I initially had no intention of putting the brown sugar in or the cinnamon, but when I racked to the secondary they yeast had attenuated so well in 7days, I figured I'd give them something else to do, as they were almost done, and surely getting bored. Early on, it had a very phenolic nose. Granted, it was flat and 70. After that, the Special B really shined through with good plum and a little banana. Nothing too special... yet, but it's only been 18days. We'll see what comes. The orange and Coriander are there, but just barely, I didn't use a lot considering the "size" of the beer.

The Drive Pale Ale

Category Pale Ale
Recipe Type Extract

Fermentables
6.6 lbs light, unhopped malt extract
5 lbs light dry malt extract
2 cup corn sugar
. 75 cup medium crystal malt
1/4 cup black patent malt

Hops
3.75 oz Cascade hops pellets (4.4 alpha)
1. 5 oz Willamette hops pellets (4.0 alpha)

Yeast Whitbread ale yeast

Procedure This is a 10-gallon recipe; cut ingredients in half for 5 gallons. Steep grains in a mesh bag until water reaches boiling. Remove grains. Follow standard extract brewing process, adding extract and Cascade hops. I boiled the wort in an 8-gallon pot and added 4 gallons of cold water. Pitch yeast at about 80 degrees. I fermented this in a 20-gallon open container for 4 days, then racked to glass carboys for 24 days.

George Braun

This Pete's Wicked Red Ale

Category Pale Ale
Recipe Type Extract

Fermentables
2. 5 oz roast barley
8.0 oz crystal malt (20 L)
5 lb Canadian light malt extract
1 lb Edme light dried malt extract

Hops
28 g Northern Brewer pellet hops (aa 10%)
26 g Styrian Goldings pellet hops (aa 8. 5 %)
7 g Willimette leaf hops
7 g Cascade leaf hops

Other
2 oz 100% dextrine
1 tsp gypsum
3/8 tsp Irish moss

Yeast 10 g (2 pkgs) Nottingham English Ale dried yeast

Procedure Steep grains in 3 qts H2O at 150 deg F, 45 min, then sparge with 170 deg H2O boil (60 minutes) with extracts, dextrine, gypsum, Northern Brewer and Styrian Goldings. Add Willamette, Cascade, and Irish moss in last 12 minutes of boil. Pitch 10 g (2 pkgs) Nottingham English Ale dried yeast (hydrated warm H2O). Dry hop in secondary with 28 g Cascade pellet hops.

Primary fermentation 5 days at 20 deg C (68 F), secondary 20 days at 18 deg C. OG 1032, FG 1005 (3.75 % alc by wt), est bitterness 57 IBU, est color 15 SRM

Three Hour Tour Ginger Pale Ale

Category Pale Ale
Recipe Type Extract

Fermentables
8 lbs. Alexander's Pale Malt Extract
. 5 lb. crystal malt
.25 lb. toasted malt
1 1/4 cup pale dried malt extract (priming)

Hops
1 1/2 oz. Northern Brewer hops - 6.4%
. 5 oz. Cascade hops - 5.9% (finishing)
. 5 oz. Cascade hops - 5.9% (dry)

Other
.75 oz. fresh grated ginger
. 5 tsp. Irish moss

Yeast pkg. Wyeast 1056 - American Ale Yeast

Procedure Put on Axis: Bold as Love by Jimi Hendrix. Steep crushed grains in muslin bag. When water boils, add malt extract and Northern Brewer hops. After 45 minutes, add Irish moss and ginger. Add Cascade hops during final two minutes of boil. Allow to steep for a few minutes, cool wort in Scottie's Patented Wort Chilling' Device. Sparge into fermenter. Pitch yeast when cool. Ferment for about 1 week in primary and rack to secondary fermenter. Dry hop with 1/2 oz. allow Cascades to sit for 1-2 weeks. Prime with DME dissolved in 1 pint of water. Bottle and enjoy!

Too Much Head

Category Pale Ale
Recipe Type All Grain

Fermentables

George Braun
8 lbs 2 row Klages malt
1 lb 20 L Crystal
. 5 lb Cara-pils
. 5 lb Malted Wheat

Hops
. 5 oz Perle hops (60 min)
. 5 oz Perle hops (30 min)
1. 5 oz Cascade hops (30 min)
1 oz Cascade hops (2 min)
1. 5 oz Cascade hops (dry)

Other
RO water with 2 tsp Gypsum/5 gal, 1/2 tsp Epsom salts/5 gal, 1/4 tsp NaCl/5 =
. 25 tsp powdered Irish Moss (10 min)

Yeast Yeast Labs American Ale Yeast (16 oz starter)

Procedure Protein rest 30 min @ 122=B0F
Mash 154=B0F to conversion
Mashout at 175=B0F and sparge at 170=B0F
Boil for 60 min.

Too Sweet Ale

Category Pale Ale
Recipe Type Extract

Fermentables
. 5 lbs crystal malt
3.3 lbs unhopped amber extract
3.3 lbs unhopped light extract

Hops
1. 5 oz Northern Brewers hops (boil)
. 25 oz Cascade hops (finish)

Yeast Whitbread ale yeast

Too Sweet Clone

Category Pale Ale
Recipe Type Extract

Fermentables
3.3 lbs M&F Unhopped Amber Extract (boil 30 mins)
3.3 lbs M&F Unhopped Light Extract (boil 30 mins)
. 5 lbs Crystal Malt 60L

Hops
1 oz Northern Brewers Plugs (boil 30 mins)
. 5 oz Northern Brewers Plugs (boil 20 mins)
. 25 oz Cascade Pellets (boil 10 mins)
.25 oz Cascade Pellets (boil 0 mins, let sit for 20 mins)

Other
. 25 tsp Irish Moss (boil 10 mins)

Yeast M&F Dry Ale yeast

Procedure Add Crystal malt to 1 1/2 gals of cold water and bring to a boil. Remove Crystal malt, add extract and 1 oz of Northern Brewers Hops. Boil for 30 mins adding 1/2 oz of Northern Brewers Hops at 20 mins, 1/4 oz of Cascade Hops at 10 minutes, Irish Moss at 10 minutes, and 1/4 oz of Cascade Hops at the end of the boil. Remove heat and let sit for 20 minutes. Strain into primary fermenter. Add 3 1/2 gals of cold water. Cola is using a submersion Wort Chiller to 70 degrees (f). Add yeast. Ferment at room temperature. After one week in primary, transfer to secondary fermenter and let sit at room temperature for one week. Transfer to bottling bucket, add 1 pint of boiled water with 3/4 cup of corn sugar for bottling. Bottle and wait.

George Braun

Three X Autumn Ale

Category Bitter Ale
Recipe Type All Grain

Fermentables
6.0 Lbs 2 Row (1lb toasted)
2.0 Lbs Munich
8.0 Oz Cara-Pils

Hops
2.0 Oz Nugget (aroma)
0. 5 Pints Northern Brewer (boil)

Other
0.25 Tsp Irish moss

Yeast White Labs WLP001 California Ale yeast

Procedure Toasted 1 lb of 2 row @ 450 for 15 minutes. Single step mash 155 for 2 hours. Sparge to collect 6 gallons. Boil to 5 gallons. Cool. Rack.

Trappist Ale 1

Category Belgian Ale
Recipe Type All Grain

Fermentables
8--1/2 lbs pale malt
1 lbs mild malt (or Munich malt)
. 5 lbs crystal malt
1 oz black patent malt
1 lbs dark brown sugar

Hops
2 oz Hallertauer hops (60 minute boil)

1 oz Kent Golding hops (60 minute boil)

Yeast Wyeast Belgian ale yeast (or culture Chimay)

Procedure Depending on your extract efficiency, this beer might come in at SG in the mid - 1060s or so. This is not intended to be a 1.100 beer! If you can find it, instead of using dark brown sugar, use 1 pound raw sugar crystals (seen in some gourmet food shops, but somewhat expensive). Note the mixture of continental and English hops. As the beer ought to have somebody, use a starch conversion temperature of 155-8 degrees F.

Trappist Ale 2

Category Belgian Ale
Recipe Type Partial Mash

Fermentables
1 lbs Biscuit malt
. 5 lbs Belgian Crystal (what is this 50L)
6 lbs Northwestern amber extract

Hops
35 IBUs hops (Tettnanger/Kent Golding plugs)

Other
. 5 lbs Special B (120L?)
. 5 lbs Roasted Chocolate

Yeast Wyeast Belgian ale

Procedure Mash grains for 45 minutes or so, then sparge. Add extract and boil. Add hops in at least 3 stages. Chill and pitch.

Trappist Ale 3

Category Belgian Ale
Recipe Type Extract

Fermentables
6.6 lbs M&F plain light extract
3.3 lbs M&F plain dark extract
1 lbs Clover honey

Hops
1 oz Fuggles leaf hops @ 3.3% alpha
1 oz Boullion leaf hops @ 7.1% alpha
1 oz Hallertauer leaf hops @ 5.4% alpha
1 oz Cascade leaf hops @ 6.4% alpha

Other
1 tsp Irish moss

Yeast, Yeast Lab Trappist Ale liquid yeast culture

Procedure Add 1 oz Fuggles + 1/2 oz Boullion hops to 8 pt cold H2O, bring to boil. Add malts and honey, bring back to boil for 60 min. At 30 min, add 1/2 oz Boullion + 1/2 oz Hallertauer + 1/2 oz Cascade hops + 1 tsp Irish moss. At 5 min add 1/2 oz Hallertauer + 1/2 oz Cascade hops. Sparge directly into 2 gal cold H2O in 5 gal carboy (note wort chiller *not* used...). Sparge water was previously boiled and allowed to cool to about 175 deg F. Stopper and cool overnight in the basement (which at this time of year is a nearly constant 60-62 deg F). Rack into clean, sanitized carboy, leaving the trub behind. Pitch yeast (about 18 fluid ounces of starter, just after high krausen), attach a blow off hose, cover to exclude light, and smile while having a homebrew.

Trappiste Ale 4

Category Belgian Ale
Recipe Type All Grain

Fermentables
7 lbs domestic 2-row pale malted barley
4 lbs Munich malt
8 oz wheat malt
1. 5 oz chocolate malt
1 lbs dark brown sugar (in boil)

Hops
1 oz Chinook (10.8% AA) (boil)
. 5 oz Tettnanger (4.7%)
. 5 oz Hallertauer (2.8%)
. 5 oz Kent Goldings (5.2%) (finish)

Other
Priming: 1

Yeast yeast cultured from a bottle of Chimay Rouge

Procedure Heat 14 quarts of mash water to 135 degrees. Mash-in for 3 minutes. Adjust pH to about 5.3. Let the protein rest for 30 minutes for 131-128 degrees. Conversion of about 2 hours at 150-141 degrees. Mash-out for 5 minutes at 168 degrees. Sparge with 5. 5 gallons at 168-165 degrees. Boil 2 hours. Add boiling hops at 60 mins and finish hops at end of boil. Chill. Pitch yeast.

Traquair House Ale

Category Scottish Ale
Recipe Type All Grain

Fermentables

George Braun

18 lbs British pale malt
4 lbs British crystal malt
2 lbs toasted malt (homemade in oven - 10 min. @350F)
4 oz roast barley - in mash out only
1 lbs chocolate malt - in mash out only

Hops

1.25 oz centennial hops - 11.3 alpha for 75 minutes
.75 oz tettnager hops - 4.8 alpha for 15 minutes

Other

1 tsp salt in boil
1 tsp gypsum in boil
Irish moss last 30 min.

Yeast Wyeast 1056 cultures

Procedure Mash at 155F for 1--1/2 hours. Collect first running with no sparge. Strike with 8 gallons at 170F. Mash out with 3 gallons at 200F with chocolate and roast grains. Collect about 8 gallons, boil down to 5 gallons.

Triple Double IPA

Category India Pale Ale
Recipe Type All Grain

Fermentables

8.0 Lbs American 2Row Pale Malt
10.0 Oz 75L Crystal Malt
8.0 Oz Willamette Hops

Yeast Whitelabs Irish Ale Pitchable Liquid Yeast

Procedure Mash: Single Step Infusion, bring 10 quarts water to 160 & add grain. Hold at 146-152 for 2 hours. Rest at 168 Degrees for 5 minutes. Sparge: 4. 5 Gallons of

168 Degree water for 45-90Minutes. Boil: Boil wort for 90 minutes. After 1st 30 minutes, add 6 oz Willamette hops. Add 2 oz Willamette hops in last 5 minutes of boil

Yeast Wyeast #1098

Potluck Ale

Category Pale Ale

Recipe Type Partial Mash

Fermentables

4. 5 lbs Klages

1.25 lbs 60lv Crystal Malt

5.25 lbs Rice

1. 5 lbs LME (all of my starter wort)

1 lb clover honey

Hops

3 oz Saaz (Only had finishing hops)

Other

1 Tbs Gypsum

. 5 tps Irish Moss

Yeast 2nd generation American Ale Yeast

Procedure I ground up the klages and rice in my grain mill. Used Gypsum in my mash water. Mashed according to standard

Procedures. Boiled until hot break finished. 1hr Added the 1. 5 lbs of LME (would have rather used grain, but this is potluck). Added 1oz Saaz (Why not, mild hop's taste). Put Irish Moss in hot tap water. 30 minutes Added 1oz Saaz 15 minutes Added Irish Moss Added Honey 5 minutes Added, 1 oz Saaz Let cool in the sink (with hops in wort) for about 45 minutes ~90F Poured in carboy with 2nd

George Braun
generation American Ale yeast. Fermented two weeks, Racked, in the new carboy Let sit two weeks, then bottled with standard 3/4's cup corn sugar (boiled in water).

Snail Trail Pale Ale

Category Pale Ale
Recipe Type All Grain

Fermentables
9 lbs Pale Malt
.75 lbs Crystal Malt
.5 lbs Carapils Malt

Hops
1.5 oz (4.9%) Kent Goldings (60 Minutes)
1.5 oz (4.9%) Kent Goldings (15 Minutes)
.25 oz Kent Goldings (dry)

Other
1 tsp Irish Moss (15 Minutes)
2 tsp Gypsum
2 oz Oak Chips

Yeast Wyeast 1059 American Ale

Procedure Mash Pale malt at 153 F for 30-60 minutes. Test after 30 minutes. Add Crystal and Carapils and mash-out at 168 F for 10 minutes. Sparge. Bring to boil. In a saucepan, boil the oak for no more than 10 minutes, then strain the liquid into your boiling kettle. Boil the wort, adding boiling hops after 30 minutes and the flavor hops and Irish Moss after 75 minutes. Chill and pitch a quart of 1059 starter.
Dry hop in the secondary fermenter. The beer will clear in the bottle

CHAPTER 5- LAGER

B.W. Lager

Category Lager, Amber
Recipe Type All Grain
Tastes great, but low alcohol, according to the measurements. Nice amber lager.

Fermentables
7 lbs cracked lager malt
5 lbs amber dry malt extract

Hops
2 oz Talisman leaf hops
. 5 oz Hallertauer leaf hops
1 oz Willamette hops pellets

Other
1 tsp gypsum
2500 mg ascorbic acid
1 tsp Irish moss

Yeast Red Star lager yeast

Procedure Add grain to 2-1/2 gallons of 170 degree water, giving an initial heat of 155 degrees and a pH of 5.3. Maintain temperature at 130-150 degrees for 2 hours. Sparge. Bring to boil. Add extract, and Talisman hops. In last 20 minutes, add Irish moss. In last 10 minutes add Hallertauer hops. Strain wort and cool. Add Willamette pellets for aroma. Pitch yeast

Baumerator

Category Lager, Bock

George Braun
Recipe Type All Grain

Fermentables
10 lbs s 2 row malt
3 lbs ds Munich malt
. 5 lbs toasted malt
. 5 lbs chocolate malt
. 25 lbs roasted barley
.25 lbs black patent malt
. 5 crystal malt 90L

Hops
4 oz Tettenger boiling hops (60 min)
. 5 oz Tettenger finishing hops (10 min)

Yeast, Yeast Labs Bavarian Lager Yeast

Procedure Protein rest 125 (30 min), Mash 154 (90 min), Mashout 168 (10 min).
Primary @ 50F for 18 days (racked after 3 days).
Diacital(sp?) reduction @ 64F for 2 days. Cold lagered @35-39F for 90 days.

Bock

Category Lager Bock
Recipe Type Extract

Fermentables
2 cans M&F dark malt extract (3.3 pound cans)
. 5 lbs pale malt
. 25 lbs chocolate malt
.25 lbs crystal malt
. 75 cup corn sugar

Hops
1 oz Hallertauer pellets

1 oz Tettnanger pellets

Yeast 1 pack Red Star lager yeast

Procedure Roast pale grain in 350 oven for 10 minutes. Bring grains boil in 2 cups water, 1/4 pound at a time. Strain the grain water into brew pot and add water to 1--1/2 gallons. Add extract and Hallertauer. Boil 45 minutes. Add Tettnang and boil 1 minute. Pour 3--1/3 gallons cold water into bucket. Siphon in wort. Pitch yeast. Ferment at 50-55. Rack to secondary after 2 weeks. Two weeks later, prime and bottle.

Boxing Day Bock

George's April's Fool Bock
Category Lager Bock
Recipe Type Extract

Fermentables
3.3 lb Beirkeller Dark Malt Extract
4 lb Laaglander Dutch Bock Hopped Malt Extract

Hops
0. 5 oz Tettnanger Hops (4.3%AA) --flavor, 15 minutes
0. 5 oz Tettnanger Hops aroma--added at end of boil

Yeast Wyeast 1007 German Ale Yeast

Procedure Dissolved malts in 3 gallons of warm water. Boil for 30 mins. Added flavor hops and boiled an additional 15 minutes. Removed from heat and stirred in aroma hops. Ice bathed for 20 minutes to 90*F. Added to *new* carboy (which I have nicknamed "Bertha") that had 2. 5 gallons of cold tap water. Add more tap water to yield 5 gallons. Shook the hell out of the carboy (I did not roll it around the floor this time). Shook some more. Pitched yeast and shook some more. Popped an airlock onto the carboy and went to bed at 1:00 AM. This morning I am happy to report I have a krausen starting.

Brewhaus Golden Lager

Category Lager Pale
Recipe Type All Grain

Fermentables
8 lbs 2-row Klages malt
.5 lbs 2-row German Munich malt
2/3 cup corn sugar (priming)

Hops
1.5 oz Perle hop pellets (6.2% Alpha - boil)
1 oz Hallertau hop pellets (finish)

Other
1 tsp Irish moss
1 tsp gelatin finings
1 tsp gypsum
Lactic Acid

Yeast Wyeast #2308

Procedure Mash grains at 152 degrees for two hours, or until conversion is complete. Sparge with 170 degree water to collect 6 gallons. Bring wort to a boil and let boil for 15 minutes before adding the boiling hops. Boil for one hour. Add Irish moss. Boil 30 minutes. (1 hour, 45 minutes total boiling time). Cut heat, add aromatic hops and let rest for 15 minutes. Force cool wort to yeast pitching temperature. Transfer cooled wort to primary fermenter and pitch yeast starter. Fine with gelatin when fermentation is complete. Bottle with corn sugar boiled in one cup water.

Brierley'S Lager

Category Lager Amber
Recipe Type Extract

Fermentables
2.0 Can 1.7 Kg Cans of Lager Malt or Unhopped light Malt extract

Hops
12.0 Grams Hallertau
12.0 Grams Saaz

Other
1.0 Tsp Gelatin

Yeast Lager

Procedure Boil the Hallertau Hops for at least 10 minutes then remove from heat and add the Saaz Hops and cover and leave for a further 10 minutes. Add to fermenter with 2 cans of lager malt extract. I have found that even "No Name" brands of extract work well in this recipe due to the fact that the hops are up front and in your face. (If you use the unhopped light malt extract then increase the amount of hops you add by 50%) This recipe works nice in bottles but I prefer it kegged.

Burst Bubbles, No Troubles Munich Dunkel

Category Lager Dark
Recipe Type All Grain

Fermentables
6 lbs Klages
1. 5 lb Vienna

George Braun
1 lbs light Munich
1 lbs dark Munich
1. 5 lbs dark crystal
1/5 lbs chocolate malt

Hops
. 5 oz Hersbrucker plugs (2.9% alpha)
. 5 oz Northern Brewer plugs (7. 5 %)
1 oz Hersbrucker plugs
. 5 oz Hersbrucker plugs
. 5 oz Tettnanger leaf hops

Other
. 5 tsp Irish Moss at 30 min

Yeast WYeast #2308 Munich Lager

Procedure Dough in at 90 degrees and raise temperature to 155 degrees over 60 minutes. Saccharification rest of 1 hour at 155 degrees. Heat to mash out over 10 min and hold for 5 minutes. Mashout temperature: 164 degrees. Sparge with water acidified to pH 6.0 with lactic acid. Bring to a boil and add 1/2 ounce each of Herbrucker and Northern Brewer hops. Add 1 ounce of Hersbrucker at 30 minutes. Add 1/2 ounce Hersbrucker for the final fifteen minutes of boil. Dry hop (during lagering stage) with 1/2 ounce of Tettnanger hops. Cool. Pitch yeast.

Chuckweiser

Category Lager, Pale
Recipe Type All Grain

Fermentables
5 lbs lager malt
1 lbs flaked maize
. 5 lbs rice syrup/solids

Hops
1 oz Hallertauer leaf (alpha 4.0) (1 hour boil)
1 oz Saaz leaf (alpha 3.0) (1 hour boil)
. 25 oz Tettnanger leaf (alpha 4.0) (5 minute boil

Yeast Wyeast #2124

Procedure Mash schedule: 30 min - Protein Rest @132F, 90 min - Slowly raise temp to 155F, 15 min - @155F, 15 min - Mash-out @170.
Bring mash liquid to a boil, add bittering hops (no hop bag for this one), boil 1hr. Add finishing hops, boil 5 minutes, steep 10 minutes, pour into primary, cool to 75F, and pitch yeast starter.

Den's Bock

Category Lager, Bock
Recipe Type Extract

Fermentables
9.0 Lbs Muntons Dark Malt Extract
8.0 Oz Pale Malt
4.0 Oz Chocolate Malt
4.0 Oz Crystal Malt
1.0 Lbs C&H Light Brown Sugar

Hops
1.0 Oz Hallertauer

Other
0.75 Cup Corn Sugar

Yeast 1 pack Superior Lager Yeast

George Braun

Procedure Spread pale malt out on a large cookie sheet, roast at 350 deg. for 10 min. Simmer grain in 1/2 gal. of water at 150 deg.(in a grain bag) for 30 min. Strain into brew pot. Add 1 gal. Water, Malt extract and Hallertauer, bring to a rolling boil for 60 min. Cool and transfer to fermenting container, add water to 5 gal. mark. Activate your yeast in 2 Oz. 80 deg. water for 30 min., pitch yeast. Wort and yeast culture should be the same temperature when added together. Do not add yeast until the temperature of wort is below 84 deg. f.. Ferment at 50 to 55 deg., the closer the ferment temp. is at 50 deg. the more complete the ferment process will be. The fermentation process will take about 21 to 28 days depending on the temp. The result of this will be higher alcohol levels, and smoother flavor. When the airlock activity stops for 24 hrs. it is ready to prime and bottle. Enjoy!!!!

Dopplebock

Category Lager, Bock
Recipe Type Partial Mash

Fermentables
6 lbs Dutch dry extract
4 lbs pilsener malt
2 lbs Munich malt
1 lbs German crystal malt
1 lbs chocolate malt

Hops
1. 5 oz Hallertauer (60 minute boil)
. 75 oz Hallertauer (30 minute boil)
. 5 oz Hallertauer (15 minute boil)
. 25 oz Hallertauer (5 minute boil)

Yeast Wyeast Bavarian lager yeast

Procedure Eight quarts water to strike heat of 140 F. Protein rest at 122 for 30 minutes. Starch conversion 1/2 hour at 153, then 1/2 hour at 149. Mash out at 169. Sparge with 4 gallons. Boil 60 minutes.

Ersatz Baderbrau

Category Lager, Pale
Recipe Type All Grain

Fermentables
8--1/2 lbs pilsner malt
1 lbs light Munich malt
. 5 lbs crystal malt (40L)

Hops
2 oz Saaz (3.1% alpha)
1 oz Saaz
1 oz Saaz

Yeast Wyeast Bavarian lager yeast

Procedure Conduct step infusion mash with starch conversion temperature around 152--153 F.
Primary ferment at about 50 and cold condition the beer in secondary.

Fakin' Gammel Brygd

Category Lager Dark
Recipe Type Extract

Fermentables
6-7 lbs German dark malt extract syrup
1 lbs crystal malt
. 5 lbs chocolate malt
. 5 cups brown sugar (just guessing)

Hops
1 oz Hallertaur hops (boiling)
.5 oz Goldings hops (finishing)

Yeast lager yeast

German Malz Bier

Category Lager
Recipe Type Extract

Fermentables
7 lbs light unhopped syrup
2 lbs Cara-pils malt
2 lbs light crystal malt
1 lbs extra rich crystal malt

Hops
.5 oz Hallertauer (5.0% alpha)
1 oz Willamette (4.5 alpha)

Other
1 tsp salt
1 tsp citric acid
1 tbsp Irish moss

Yeast Edme ale yeast

Procedure Mash cara-pils and crystal malt for 2 hours in 140 degree water. Sparge to make 4 gallons. Add syrup and Hallertauer hops. Boil 60 minutes, adding Irish moss in last 30 minutes. Decant to primary, adding enough water to make 5 gallons. Add salt, citric acid, yeast nutrient, and dry hop with Willamette hops.

High-Gravity Bock

Category Lager, Bock
Recipe Type All Grain

Fermentables
8 lbs pale malt
1 lbs Vienna malt
. 5 lbs chocolate malt
2. 5 lbs dark extract syrup
2. 5 lbs light DME

Hops
1 oz Chinook 12. 5 % alpha boil
1 oz Hallertau finish

Yeast yeast

Procedure Grains mashed in a RIMS. Extracts added to boil. Forgot my Irish moss. I used Wyeast London Ale because it's what I had.

Honey Amber

Category Lager
Recipe Type Partial Mash

Fermentables
6. 5 lbs Amber extracts (2 cans if using canned)
2 cups honey
1 lbs crystal malt
5/8 cup honey (priming)

Hops
1. 5 oz Hallertauer hops (boil
0. 5 oz Hallertauer hops (finishing)

Yeast Wyeast #1056 (American)

George Braun

Procedure Heat water to 160 degrees and steep malt for 30 minutes. Remove grains and heat to boiling. Add extract and honey and return to boil. Add boiling hops and boil for 45 minutes. Add finishing hops and boil for 15 minutes. Cool and pitch yeast (I used a starter). When active fermentation subsides rack to secondary. Leave in secondary for 4 weeks. When ready to bottle boil honey with a pint of water for 10 minutes and prime

Honey Ginger Lager 1

Category Lager
Recipe Type All Grain

Fermentables
8.75 lbs German 2-row Pils malt
. 5 lbs Wheat Malt
. 5 Lbs Crystal Malt - 20L
2 lbs. honey

Hops
1 oz. Perle hops (boil)
1 oz. Tettnang hops (finish)

Other
. 5 lbs Dextrine
4 oz. grated Ginger root

Yeast lager yeast

Procedure Mash with no protein Rest... Single 155F infusion until conversion is complete.
Boil with 4 oz. grated Ginger root, 2 lbs. honey and 1 oz. Perle hops.

Finish with 1 oz. Tettnang hops

Honey Ginger Lager 2

Category Lager
Recipe Type All Grain

Fermentables
8 lbs German 2-row pils malt
. 5 lbs wheat malt
. 5 lbs dextrine malt
. 5 lbs crystal malt (10L)
2 lbs light clover honey (boil)

Hops
1 oz perle (8% alpha, 50 minute boil)
1 oz Willamette (4% alpha, 2 minutes)

Yeast lager yeast

Procedure I am adding the wheat malt, dextrine and crystal for the body and head retention. I was planning a two temp mash (152F & 158F) unless someone can tell me why a protein rest would be needed. I will add two pounds light clover honey to the boil. I will also boil in 4 oz. grated ginger root. I know it sounds like a lot, but I have used it in an extract beer with excellent results. It's sort of toxicity for the first 4 months, but after six it becomes a dry, snappy, excellent refreshing beer.

Maibock 1

Category Lager, Bock
Recipe Type All Grain

Fermentables
10 lbs Klages malt
3 lbs Munich malt

Hops
1 oz Mt. Hood loose hops (60 minute boil)
. 5 oz Mt. Hood loose (30 minutes)
. 5 oz Mt. Hood loose (5 minutes)

Other
1 tsp Irish Moss

Yeast Wyeast 2308 (Munich) in 1 pint 1.022 starter (1/10)

Procedure 30-minute protein rest at 125 degrees Fmaibock 60-minute mash at 159 degrees F 15-minute mash out at 170 degrees F Primary and secondary fermentation insulated glass carboys at about 50 degrees F

Maibock 2

Category Lager, Bock
Recipe Type All Grain

Fermentables
7 lbs Lager malt
2 lbs Munich malt
1. 5 lbs German light Crystal Malt
. 5 lb home toasted lager malt

Hops
1. 5 oz Hallertau pellets- boil (4.0% aa)
. 5 oz Tettnang pellets- boil (3.4%aa)
. 5 oz Hallertau pellets-flavor (4.0%aa)
. 5 oz Tettnang pellets-finishing (3.4%aa)

Yeast Wyeast 2308 Munich Lager Yeast- 1.0 L starter

Procedure Add 2.25 gallons of 54degC water to crushed grains, stabilize temp at 50degC. Add 1.25 gallons boiling

water to bring temp to 68-70degC. Hold for 90 minutes. Sparge with 4 gallons of 77degC water.
Bring wort to a boil and add boiling hops. After 30 minutes, add flavor hops. 10 minutes before end of boil, add finishing hops. Chill, etc., pitch yeast.

My o.g. was a little low (1.050)...I am still trying to improve my extraction efficiency :). If I were to do this again, I would have definitely used more grain; my impression is that for a Maibock, you want to target an o.g of around 1.060 or so.

Mikes Maple Hammer

Category Lager Amber
Recipe Type Extract
Rich, full bodied beer. Excellent heat retention. Definitely one to share with only your closest friends.
Yeast Muntons ale dry

Procedure 3. 5 lbs Muntons extra light malt extract (hopped, red label.) 1/2 gallon maple syrup (PURE) 1. 5 oz cascade hops 1/2 tsp Irish moss 1 pkg dry yeast (follow instructions on package.) 3/4 cup corn sugar (priming) boil 2 gallons water with syrup and 1 oz hops for 30 mins. add 1 oz hops and moss boil 15mns. sparge w/4 gals. cold water. Pitch yeast at 80'F. primary for 1 week. rack to secondary for as long as it takes to stop fermenting (depends on the sugar content of the syrup.) bottle and age at least 2 weeks.

Moretti Amber Lager

Category Lager, Amber
Recipe Type Extract
If anyone does this brew I would like to compare notes.

Fermentables

George Braun
. 75 lbs crystal malt
. 75 lbs Munich malt
6. 5 lbs Ireks Munich amber extract

Hops
1. 5 oz Cascade hops (60 minute boil)
1 oz Hallertauer hops (steep 5 minutes)

Other
1 tsp gypsum
1 tsp Irish moss

Yeast Wyeast #2206 Bavarian

Procedure All malt boiled for an hour. I started a yeast culture in 22oz champagne bottle to kick start the brew. Pitched at 83 degrees F and by morning it was at 50 degrees in the garage. It is now sitting in a spare refer at 40 degrees. Unfortunately, I left the brew on the its trub for 3 weeks before becoming enlightened about the nastiness that can introduce. I must admit it has a bit of off-odor. No idea if this is normal or not.

Legin Lager 2

Category Lager, Pale
Recipe Type Partial Mash

Fermentables
7 lbs cracked lager malt
3.3 lbs light unhopped John Bull malt extract

Hops
1. 5 oz Northern Brewer hops pellets
1 oz Talisman leaf hops
1 oz Willamette hops pellets

Other
1250 mg ascorbic acid
1 tsp Irish moss

Yeast Red Star lager yeast

Procedure Add grain to 2-1/2 gallons 170 degree water, giving an initial heat of 155 degrees. Maintain temperature for two hours. Sparge and add malt extract. Bring to boil. Add Northern Brewer hops, Talisman hops, and Irish moss in last 20 minutes of boil. Dry hop with Willamette pellets and cool. Add water to make 5 gallons and pitch yeast.

Legin Lager 1

Category Lager, Pale
Recipe Type Extract

Fermentables
3.3 lbs Northwest malt extract
1 lbs light dry malt
. 5 lbs Munich malt
2 lbs Klages malt

Hops
1 oz Hallertauer hops (5.1 alpha)
. 25 oz Nugget hops (11.0 alpha)
1 oz Hallertauer hops (finish)

Yeast Wyeast #2042: Danish

Procedure Start yeast ahead of time. Mash Munich and Klages malts together. Sparge. Add extract and boiling hops. Boil one hour. Add finishing hops. Chill to 75-80 degrees. Pitch yeast. When the airlock shows signs of activity (about 6 hours) put fermenter in the refrigerator at 42 degrees. After one week, rack to secondary and ferment at 38 degrees for two more weeks. Bottle or keg.

Light Wheat Lager

Category Lager, Pale
Recipe Type Extract

Fermentables
3.3 lbs M&F light extract
1 lbs Malted wheat

Hops
. 75 oz Hallertauer (boiling)
. 25 oz Hallertauer (finishing)
.25 tsp Alpha Amylase

Other
2 tsp Gypsum
1 tsp Irish Moss
. 75 cup Dextrose (for priming)

Yeast Wyeast Pilsner Culture

Procedure Mash the wheat with Alpha Amylase at 135 degrees for 1-3 hours in 1 quart of water. Test with Iodine. Sparge with 3 quarts of water and boil before adding the extract to avoid enzymatic changes to the barley malt. Irish Moss for the last 10 minutes of the boil and the finishing hops for the last 2 minutes. Ferment at 40-45 degrees for 6 weeks to 3 months. I found that all the starch completed conversion at the end of one hour. I held the mash temp at 130-135 in about 1 quart of water by mashing in a microwave oven with a temperature probe. The dissolved sugars were fairly low. SG was 1.027.

Munich Beer

Category Lager, Pale
Recipe Type All Grain

Fermentables
10 lbs pale alt malt
5 lbs Munich malt
. 5 lbs dextrin malt
1. 5 lbs amber crystal malt

Hops
5-1/2 grams Hallertauer
1. 5 oz Cascade 60 min
. 25 oz Cascade 30 min
.25 oz Cascade 15 min
. 25 oz Hallertau (dry hop)

Other
1 oz gypsum
1/3 oz Burton H2O salts

Yeast Wyeast Munich beer yeast

Procedure Use standard mashing

Procedure. Sparge. Boil 90 minutes. Add Hallertauer at beginning of boil. Add 1-1/2 ounces Cascades 30 minutes into boil. Add 1/4 oz Cascades at 60 minutes. Add final 1/4 ounces Cascades for the last 15 minutes. Cool. Pitch yeast. Ferment at 40 degrees for 2 months. Add polyclar, rack to secondary and dry hop with 1/4 oz Hallertau pellets two days later. After a week move to room temperature and let sit for another week. Bottle.

Munich Fest

Category Lager, Amber

George Braun
Recipe Type All Grain

Fermentables
6 lbs pilsner malt
3 lbs Munich malt
. 75 lbs cara-pils malt
.25 lbs 40L crystal malt
. 25 oz black malt (for color)

Hops
6--7 AAUs Hallertauer

Yeast

Procedure For the hop schedule, follow the suggestions in Fix's recipe (above), with multiple additions and the last addition 15 minutes before the end of the boil.

Munich Lager

Category Lager
Recipe Type All Grain

Fermentables
2 Kg Canadian 2-row malt grain
1 Kg Munich Lager grain
. 75 cups light DME

Hops
2 oz Hallertauer hops

Yeast 1 Yeast Lab - Munich Lager yeast

Procedure I used the decoction mashing procedure found at sierra.stanford.edu in the allgrain.faq. I tested the gravity before boiling and was just shy of 1.050 (what I was aiming for) so I added the 3 cups of DME to bump it up. I added 1oz of the hops at hot break and the rest just 5 minutes before the end of the boil. I did make a starter for the yeast and fermentation was done on the 5th day. I racked it to secondary and lagered for 2 weeks. Filtered, carbonated, relaxed and enjoyed!

Munich Style Lager

Category Lager
Recipe Type All Grain

Fermentables
7 lbs Klages malt
3 lbs Vienna malt
6 oz pearl barley

Hops
1. 5 oz Hallertauer leaf hops
. 5 oz Hallertauer hops (finish)

Yeast Wyeast #2206

Procedure Soak the pearl barley overnight in the refrigerator, mix it into a starchy glue using a blender. Mash the pearl barley with the grains. Boil 1-1/2 ounces of Hallertauer with the wort. Add 1/4 ounce of finishing hops in last 10 minutes and steep 1/4 ounce after boil is complete. Pitch yeast at about 76 degrees.
I put the fermenter in fridge for 23 days, then racked to secondary for another 49 days before bottling.

Nice Larger With Flavor And Some Bite

Category Lager
Recipe Type All Grain

Fermentables

George Braun
3. 5 kg Larger Grain
0. 5 kg Munich Larger Grain

Hops
35.0 Grams Northern Brewer
15.0 Grams Hersbrucker Hops

Yeast saflarger

Procedure Start Protein 57 Deg Celsius For Half an Hour. Raise Temp To 65 Deg Celsius For 90 min, Mash Out At 85 Deg For 10 Min. Add 22 Liters through Grian In Lauter Tun Boil Wort 90 Min Add Northern Brewer Hops At 60 min Mark. Ferment At 20 Deg Celsius, Rack Brew, Then Dry Hop, Hersbrucker Hops. Let Meture Bottle Or Keg.

Number 17

Category Lager Pale
Recipe Type Extract

Fermentables
3.3 lbs plain light malt extract
2.2 lbs maltose

Hops
. 75 oz Cascade hops (boil)
. 75 oz Cascade hops (finish)

Yeast yeast cultured from a Sierra Nevada bottle

Procedure The maltose is a cheap rice-malt mix obtainable from oriental markets. Boil malt, hops, and maltose in 2-1/2 gallons of cold water. In last 2 minutes, add the finishing hops. The yeast was cultured from a bottle of Sierra Nevada pale ale. By the next day, the yeast did not seem to start, so I added a packet of Vierrka lager yeast. Rack to secondary after one week. After another week, prime with 3/4 cup corn sugar and bottle.

Oktoberfest

Category Lager, Amber
Recipe Type All Grain

Fermentables
5. 5 lbs DWC Pilsner Malt
4 lbs. Great Western Munich (8L)
0. 5 lbs. DWC Belgium Aromatic
0. 5 lbs Hugh Baird Carastan (30L)
0.25 lbs Cara-Pils
0.25 lbs. Hugh Baird Crystal (50L)

Hops
1. 5 oz Tetnanger for 60 min (3. 5 %)
1.0 oz Styrian Goldings 30 min (5%)
1.0 oz Saaz 15 min (3.9%)

Yeast Wyeast 2206: Bavarian

Procedure Mash schedule is a 50-60-70 (Celsius) step mash.
Primary 8 days at 50 deg. F.
secondary 20 days at 45 deg. F.
Lagered at 33 deg F. for 6 weeks

Oktoberfest

Category Lager, Amber
Recipe Type All Grain

Fermentables
9. 5 lb German Vienna malt
1 lbs German Munich malt
. 75 lb Belgian Aromatic malt

George Braun
.75 lb German Caramel malt (10L)
. 75 lb German Wheat malt
. 5 lb Flaked Oats

Hops
1 oz. Hallertau Herrsbrucker (3.8% A) --45 mins.
. 6 oz. Northern Brewer (8.8% A)--15 mins.

Yeast Wyeast Bavarian Lager (#2206)

Procedure, Double decoction mash
45 min. boil
Primary Fermentation: 7 days at 48 F
Secondary Fermentation: 14 days at 48 F
Lagering: 63 days at 34 F
OG--1.055 FG--1.016
Carbonated at 2.6 vols.

Pilsner Pigs

Category Lager, Pilsner
Recipe Type Extract

Fermentables
6.75 lbs Laaglander extra-pale malt (extract)

Hops
1 oz. Tettnang (boil, 60 mins, 4. 5 AAU)
1 oz. Saaz (finish, 15 min, 3.1 AAU
. 5 oz. Saaz (finish, 1 min)

Yeast pitched Wyeast Bohemian

Pilsner Pups

Category Lager Pilsner
Recipe Type Extract

Fermentables
4 lbs Mountmellick hopped light malt extract
3 oz crystal malt

Hops
. 25 oz Saaz hops (boil)
. 5 oz Saaz hops (finish)

Other
2 tsp gypsum

Yeast Wyeast #2007

Procedure This recipe makes 5-1/2 gallons. Make 2-quart starter for yeast. Steep crystal malt at 170 degrees for 20 minutes in brew water. Remove grains. Boil extract and boiling hops for 75 minutes. Add finishing hops in last 10 minutes. Conduct primary fermentation at 47-49 degrees for 3 weeks. Lager for 4 weeks at 30 degrees

Pilsner Urquell

Category Lager, Pilsner
Recipe Type Extract

The yeast I used to produce a very clean, clear beer and I'd recommend it highly. If you haven't gotten into liquid yeast cultures yet, do it for this batch. The difference is tremendous. Also, I feel the key to success here are:
The lightest extract you can find.
Fresh hops or pellets packed in Nitrogen (only Saaz will do).
Liquid yeast fermented at a steady low temp.

Fermentables
4 lbs Alexander's Pale malt extract syrup
2-1/3 lbs light dry malt extract

George Braun

Hops
15 AAU's Saaz hops

Yeast Wyeast 2007 Bohemian Pilsner yeast

Procedure Bring extracts and 2 gallons of water to boil. Add 5 AAU's of Saaz hops at beginning of boil. Add 5 AAU's again at 30 minutes and at 10 minutes. Pitch yeast when cool.

Red Bock

Category Lager, Bock
Recipe Type Partial Mash

Fermentables
5 lbs American 2 row
1 lb 10L crystal
1 lb carapils
2 ea 3.3lb bags NW gold LME

Hops
1 oz eroica boil
. 5 oz Tettnang boil
. 5 oz Tettnang +20
. 5 oz Tettnang +40
. 5 oz Tettnang steep 10mins

Yeast Bavarian pils yeast slurry temp in garage 40-50F

Procedure 3 step mash, added LME to hot sweet wort, brought to boil, added the boiling hops. Wort tasted great before pitching, was pale red in color. I'm expecting great things from this brew. The hop schedule may not be in style, but it was all I had.

Red Hickory Lager

Category Lager, Amber
Recipe Type Extract

Fermentables
3.3 lbs M & F amber malt extract
3.3 lbs M & F light malt extract

Hops
1 oz Saaz hops (60 minute boil)
1 oz Bullion pellets (boil 1 minute)
1 oz Fuggles hops (boil 1 minute)
1 oz Willamette hops (boil 1 minute)

Other
2--3 pinches Irish moss
. 75 cup corn sugar (to prime)

Yeast Whitbread lager yeast

Sam Adams

Category Lager
Recipe Type Extract

Fermentables
2 cans Unhopped Light extract

Hops
1 oz. Cascade hop
2 oz. Hallertau hops

Yeast Lager yeast

Procedure Bring gallon of cold water to a boil. Remove from heat and add 2 cans of Unhopped light, Bring back to

George Braun
a boil. Add 1 oz. of Cascade hops and simmer for 30 minutes. Then add 1/2 oz. Hallertau hops and simmer for 10 minutes; add another 1/2 oz. Hallertau and simmer for another 10 minutes; add another 1/2 oz. Hallertau and simmer for another 10 minutes; At the last minute of simmer, add 1/2 Hallertau.

Samuel Adams Taste-Alike Beer

Category Lager
Recipe Type Extract

Fermentables
1 can Munton & Fison Premium Kit
2 1 1 lb. packages Amber DME
1 cup corn sugar (for priming)

Hops
1 1 1 oz package Hallertauer hop pellets
1 1 1 oz package Tettnang hop pellets

Yeast 1 Packet yeast (under cap)

Procedure Remove labels from Kit and stand in warm water for 15-20 minutes. In a pot sufficient to boil 2 gallons of liquid, empty DME. Open can of malt and empty contents into pot onto DME. Using one gallon hot water, rinse out can and add to pot. Turn on heat and carefully bring to a boil. Ass package of
Hallertauer hops, Adjust heat and simmer for 20 minutes. Add Tettnang hops and simmer for 10 minutes. Meanwhile, put 4 gallons cold water into primary fermenter. When boil is complete, the empty hot wort into cold water. When temperature reaches 80 degrees Fahrenheit, open yeast and sprinkle onto surface of the wort and cover tightly.

Place fermentation lock with water in lid. Allow the beer to ferment for four days in primary fermenter,

Transfer to clean secondary fermenter and allow to ferment for an additional ten to fourteen days.

Syphon beer from secondary fermenter into the clean bottling bucket. Dissolve priming sugar in a small amount of beer and add to bottling bucket. Fill clean bottles and cap. Let stand for five days at room temperature and then move to a cool place.

Beer will be carbonated in three weeks and will improve for several months

Scotch Ale

Category Scottish Ale
Recipe Type All Grain

Fermentables
9 lbs pale ale malt
1 lbs crystal malt
1 lbs Munich malt
. 5 lbs chocolate malt

Hops
. 5 oz Bullion (60 minutes - 9% alpha)
2 oz Fuggles (30 minutes - 4. 5 % alpha)
. 75 oz Golding (10 minutes - 4.9% alpha)

Other
1 tsp Irish moss (30 minutes)

Yeast Whitbread or Wyeast 1007 ("German Ale")

George Braun

Procedure Heat 14 quarts for 140F strike heat. Mash in, starch conversion 1--1/2 hour at 154F. Mash out and sparge with 5 gallons at 168F. Boil 1--1/2 hour, adding hops and Irish moss as indicated above.

Scottish Ale

Category Scottish Ale
Recipe Type All Grain

Fermentables
10.00 lbs. British Pale Grain M&F
2.00 oz. Roast Barley

Hops
2/3 oz Kent Goldings hops (5.7% alpha, 60 minute boil)

Yeast Wyeast #1728 (Scottish ale)

Procedure Strike Water: 2. 5 3 gallons of water at 152F. First Mash Temperature: 152F. 1 1/4 hour mash. Mash-out 168 for 10 minutes. Pitched with 1/2 gal. starter. Fermentation had begun within ~2 hours Racked to secondary after 3 days - fined with Polyclar Bottled two weeks later.

Shiner

Category Lager
Recipe Type All Grain

Fermentables
5 lbs American pale malt (Briess)
1. 5 lbs Munich 10L
1 lb flaked Maize
1/8 lb black Patent

Hops

1 oz Centennial Hops (bittering)
. 5 oz Liberty hops (finishing)

Yeast Wyeast #2178 Lager blend

Procedure Mash all grains at 155 degrees for an hour boil for an hour adding Centennial a start of boil & Liberty after 50 minutes cool quickly and pitch yeast Since the lager blend is twice as much yeast as normal packs I rarely make a starter with this one Ferment 2 weeks @ 45 degrees rack & ferment for 1 more week @ 40 degrees rack into a keg & prime set for two more weeks @ 35 degrees enjoy!!

Snowbound Pils

Category Lager
Recipe Type Extract

Fermentables
2. 5 lb honey
. 75 cup corn sugar, for bottling
6. 5 lb M&F light ME
1 lb crystal malt grains

Hops
. 5 oz Saaz (aroma, boiled last 2 min)
2. 5 oz Saaz (boiling, entire 47 min)
. 5 oz Tettnanger (boiled last 12 min)

Other
1 tsp. Irish moss added at 25 min into boil

Yeast 1 14 gr. package Red Star lager yeast

Procedure Crystal malt added in 1. 5 gal cold water, brought to a boil, grains removed. Extracts and 2. 5 oz Saaz added, boiled 35 min. Added Tettnanger, boiled 10 more minutes. Added. 5 oz Saaz, boiled 2 minutes. Wort pot chilled in sink and transferred to fermenter with cold water. Carboy topped off to 5 gals. O.G. was 1.042 (may be a bit low, I later discovered that our water is 0.990!) F.G. was 1.010, bottled 34 days after pitching

Tessellator

Category Lager, Bock
Recipe Type Extract

Fermentables
8 lbs Heidelberg Bavarian Bock Malt Dark
1 lb M&F dry light
. 25 lb Chocolate Malt, crushed
1/8 lb Black Roasted Barley, crushed
. 5 lb German light crystal, crushed
1 1/2 inches licorice, crushed

Hops
2 oz Fresh Bullion Hops
. 5 oz Fresh Chinook Hops
1 oz Fresh Perl Hops
. 5 oz Compressed Kent Goldings Hops

Other
1 tsp Irish Moss

Yeast 2 packages Whitbred Ale yeast

Procedure Crush all grains, place in a muslin bag in 6 quarts water. Bring to a boil. Remove grains in bag and add all malts. Boil 20 minutes. Add Bullion Hops. Boil 30 minutes. Add Chinook Hops, Licorice, and Irish Moss. Boil 15 minutes. Add 1/4 oz Perl hops. Boil 10 minutes. Add 1/4 oz Perl hops. Boil 5 minutes. Chill wort and sparge into

primary fermenter. Add water to 5 1/2 gals. Dry hop 1/2 oz Kent Goldings in muslin bag. Pitch yeast.
Rack to secondary, removing hops after fermentation slows. Bottle with 1 1/4 cup M&F dry malt for priming.

The Grommator

Category Lager, Bock
Recipe Type Extract

Fermentables
. 5 lbs pale malt
. 5 lbs crystal malt
. 5 lbs chocolate malt
9.9 lbs dark malt extract syrup
1 lbs dry amber malt extract
. 75 cup corn sugar (priming)

Hops
3-1/2 oz Saaz hops (boil)
. 5 oz Hallertauer hops (finish)

Yeast lager yeast

Procedure Roast pale malt in 325 degree oven for 15 minutes or until golden brown. Crack grains and add to 1-1/2 gallons cold water. Bring to boil. Before serious boil starts, remove grains. Add extract and Saaz hops. Boil 60 minutes. Add Hallertauer hops and boil 5 more minutes. Remove from heat. Cover and let hops steep 15 minutes. Strain into 3-1/2 gallons cold water. (Be sure to strain out as much stuff as possible.) Pitch yeast and ferment one week at about 65 degrees, then rack to secondary. Secondary fermentation should last about 3 weeks at 45-50 degrees. Prime and bottle. Refrigerate bottles for about 1 month.

The Haircut Beer

Category Lager
Recipe Type Extract

Fermentables
3.3 lbs Australian lager malt extract (hopped)
3.3 lbs Australian plain light malt extract (unhopped)
3/4cup Corn Sugar for bottling

Hops
1 oz. Fuggles hops (boiling)
0. 5 oz Cascade hops (boiling)
0. 5 oz Cascade hops (finishing)

Yeast 1pkg. Superbrau yeast

Twelfth Lager

Category Lager, Pale
Recipe Type All Grain

Fermentables
10 lbs lager grain
1 lbs light dry malt extract
9 oz Chinese yellow lump sugar

Hops
1 oz Talisman hops (leaf)
1 oz Hallertauer hops pellets
1 oz Cascade hops

Other
4000 mg ascorbic acid
1 tsp Irish moss

Yeast Red Star ale yeast

Procedure Add grain to 3 gallons of 170 degree water, giving an initial heat of 155 degrees. Mash at 130-155 degrees for 2 hours. Sparge and add extract and Chinese lump sugar. Boil. In last 20 minutes, add Talisman hops. In last 10 minutes add Hallertauer hops and Irish moss. Strain. Add Cascade hops and steep. Strain into fermenter when cool and pitch yeast.

Vespa

Category ESB
Recipe Type Extract

Fermentables
4.0 Lbs Light Dry Malt Extract
2.0 Lbs Clover Honey
0.25 Lbs Chocolate Malt
0.75 Lbs 20 L Crystal Malt
0. 5 Lbs Carapils Malt

Hops
1.0 Oz North Down (6.2% AA) 60 minute
1.0 Oz East Kent Goldings (5.6% AA) 20 minute
0. 5 Oz EK Golding (5.6% AA) 1 minute
0. 5 Oz Cascade (5.0% AA) 1 minute
0. 5 Oz EK Golding (5.6% AA) dry hop
0. 5 Oz Cascade (5.0% AA) dry hop

Other
1.0 Tbsp Gypsum
1.0 Tbsp Irish Moss (20 minute)

Yeast White Labs London Yeast (WLP013)

George Braun

Procedure 1. Crush Grains and steep them in 5 gallons of water in a muslin bag for 25 minutes at 150 F. Remove and drain bag. 2. Bring the water to a boil, and dissolve DME and honey. 3. Add boiling hops for 60 minutes 4. Add flavor hops and Irish Moss during the last 20 minutes of the boil 5. Shut off heat and steep aroma hops for about a minute. 6. Cool wort and pitch yeast in a fermenter Kept in primary fermenter (plastic) for 5 days Kept in secondary fermenter (and dry hopped) for 11 days.

CHAPTER 6- SPICE BEER

Sparky's After-Burner Brew

Category Spiced Beers
Recipe Type Extract

Fermentables
3.3 lbs John Bull amber malt extract
. 5 lbs crystal malt
. 5 lbs dark, dry malt
. 5 lbs corn sugar

Hops
2 oz Cascade hops

Other
10 ea fresh Jalapeno peppers

Yeast Munton & Fison ale yeast

Procedure Chop up Jalapeno peppers and boil them with the wort for 30 minutes or so. Strain them out when pouring wort into primary. Rack to secondary about 4 hours after pitching yeast.
Note: When handling jalapenos, be sure to wash hands thoroughly or wear rubber gloves. You'll find out why if you are a contact lens wearer. (I discovered this the hard way---making pickles, not beer.)

Spiced Brown Ale

Category Spiced Beers
Recipe Type Extract

Fermentables

George Braun
7 lbs dark Munton & Fison malt extract syrup (2 cans)
.5 lbs crystal malt
1 lbs chocolate malt

Hops
1 oz Fuggles pellet hops -- boil
1 oz Fuggles pellet hops -- 15 minutes before end of boil
1 oz Willamette pellet hops -- finish

Other
1 nutmeg, grated -- 15 minutes before end of boil
1 oz sliced ginger root -- 15 minutes before the end

Yeast Whitbread ale dry yeast in a 20 oz. starter

Procedure Grain steeped in a colander in 2 gallons of cold water and brought to boiling: grain removed when boiling began. Some hops and spices allowed to pour into carboy. My notes don't mention fermentation times, so I would guess 1 to 1--1/2 weeks in primary, 2 weeks in secondary as a rough estimate.

Spicy Xmas Beer

Category Spiced Beers
Recipe Type Extract

Fermentables
3.3 lbs Northwestern light malt extract
2 lbs dark malt extract
2 lbs wildflower honey

Hops
2 oz Hertsburger hops (boil)
.5 oz Goldings hops (finish)

Other

2 oz grated ginger (boil)
1 oz grated ginger (finish)

Yeast 2 packs Munton & Fison ale yeast

Procedure Start yeast. Boil malt extract, honey, boiling hops and boiling ginger for about 1 hour. Strain. Add finishing hops and ginger. Cool rapidly in tub. Pitch started yeast. Ferment. Prime and bottle.

Spruce Beer Butts 1

Category Spiced Beers
Recipe Type Extract

Fermentables
6.6 lbs Munton & Fison dark malt extract
3 lbs dry, dark extract

Hops
3 oz Cascade hops (4.3 alpha)
1 oz Cascade hops

Other
3 tsp gypsum
. 5 tsp Irish moss
. 5 oz spruce essence

Yeast Leigh & Williams Beer & Stout yeast

Procedure Boil malt and boiling hops for 1 hour. In last 10 minutes, add the 1 ounce of Cascade finishing hops and the Irish moss. In the last 2 minutes, add the spruce essence. Chill and pitch yeast.

Spruce Beer Butts 2

Category Spiced Beers

George Braun
Recipe Type All Grain

Fermentables
10 lbs American 2-row malt
. 5 lb crystal 40 Lovibond
1/3 lb chocolate malt

Hops
1 oz cascade hops (aa=7. 6%, 60 minutes)

Other
1 pint fresh spruce growths (30 min.)

Yeast German Ale Yeast

Procedure I mashed all grains together and did a protein rest at 122 degrees for 30 minutes and then mashed at 148-152 degrees for 1 hour.

Spruce Juice

Category Spiced Beers
Recipe Type Extract

Fermentables
5 lbs Premier Malt hopped light malt extract
1 lbs dried light plain malt extract
1/8 lbs roasted barley

Hops
2 oz Cascade hops

Other
20 oz cup loosely filled with blue spruce cuttings

Yeast Ale yeast

Procedure Bring extract and 1 1/2 gallons of water to boil. Add Cascade hops and boil for a total of 45 minutes. Rinse spruce cuttings, then toss into the wort for the final twelve minutes of the boil. Cool. Pitch yeast.

Vanilla Cream Ale

Category Spiced Beers
Recipe Type Extract

Fermentables
4.0 Lbs Alexander's Pale Malt Extract
0. 5 Lbs Crushed Caramunich Malt
1.0 Lbs Rice Solids
1.0 Lbs Lactose

Hops
1.25 Oz 4% AA Tettnanger (aroma)
0.75 Oz 4% AA Tettnanger (boiling)

Other
1. 5 Tbsp Vanilla Extract
1.0 Tsp Irish Moss

Yeast WLP001

Procedure Steep crush grains in a muslin bag in 6 gallons water for 30 minutes at 150 Fahrenheit. Remove grains and discard. Bring Water up to a boil. Dissolve rice solids, lactose, and LME. Let wort come to a boil again and add boiling hops. After 45 minutes, add Irish Moss. After an additional 10 minutes, add aroma hops and vanilla extract. Turn off the heat after a full 60 minutes of boiling, cool and pitch yeast.

Winterbrew

George Braun
Category Spiced Beers
Recipe Type Extract

Fermentables
7 lbs. dark malt extract
1 lbs. Crystal malt
. 5 lbs. Chocolate malt
. 25 lbs. Black Patent
1 lbs. Honey (clover)

Hops
1 1/2 oz. Helletaur hops (bittering)
. 5 oz. Helletauer hops (finishing)

Other
4 tsp. nutmeg
10 inch Cinnamon stick
1 lbs. bakers chocolate

Yeast 14 grams Australian ale yeast

Procedure The O.G. on my batch was a healthy 1.065, but as you probably have guessed...the final gravity wasn't anywhere near 0...which was good. It is the adjuncts and unfermentables in this batch that give it that special holiday/winter character. I will definitely try this batch again... but before next winter!

Winter's Tavern Winter Ale

Category Spiced Beers
Recipe Type Extract

Fermentables
7 lbs Alexanders Pale Malt Extract
20 oz Clover Honey
1 lbs British Cara-Pils

1 lbs Crystal (40L)
2 lbs klages 2-row (for partial mash of cara-pils)
. 25 lbs Chocolate Malt

Hops
. 5 oz Chinook Pellets (12%) (60 minute boil)
. 5 oz Cascade Leaf (7%) (30 minute boil)
1 oz Hersbrucker Plugs (2.9%) (30 minute boil)
. 5 oz Hersbrucker Plugs (10 minute steep)
. 5 oz Hersbrucker Plugs (2 minute steep)
. 5 ounces Cascade Leaf (7%) (Dry hopped in secondary)

Other
3 ea 3" cinnamon sticks
1 tsp whole cloves
1 tsp ground Allspice
2 oz grated fresh ginger
6 pods cardamom - slightly crushed

Yeast Wyeast American Ale

Procedure Performed partial mash of cara-pils, crystal and klages as described in CJOHB. Added all other **Fermentables** and brought to a rolling boil. Added hops as indicated as well as all spices for the last 10 minutes of the boil. Cooled in ice bath for approximately 30 minutes before moving to bucket with 2 gallons cold water to reduce oxidation. Let sit for 1 hour and then racked off trub into primary. (Spices, etc. included in the primary fermenter.) Pitched approximately 1 liter yeast starter, attached blow-off tube and had a cold one minute.

Xmas Saint Beer

Category Spiced Beers
Recipe Type Partial Mash

George Braun

Fermentables

2 lbs Munich malt
. 25 lbs dextrin malt
1 lbs crystal malt
1 lbs 2--row malt
. 75 cup roast barley
. 5 cups black patent malt
6 lbs Australian amber extract
2 lbs dark honey

Hops

1 oz Chinook hops

Other

3 bags Spicy Duck spices (cinnamon
4 sticks cinnamon
2 tsp crushed cardamom
1/4 tsp Irish Moss
zest of lemon
2 tsp cloves (end)
2 sticks cinnamon (end)
1. 5 tsp allspice (end)
1 dash nutmeg (end)
1. 5 oz grated ginger (end)

Yeast Wyeast ale

Procedure Low temperature mash, 145F for 4 hours in 2 gallons of water treated with 2 teaspoons of gypsum. Sparge to 7 gallons. Bring to boil, adding extract, 1 ounce of Chinook, and spices. After 45 minutes, add another ounce of Chinook and some Irish moss. After 1 hour, turn off heat at add honey, orange zest, and spices denoted "(end)". Secondary had 2 more ounces of hops (did not write down the kind).

Xmas Spice Ale

Category Spiced Beers
Recipe Type All Grain

Fermentables
8 lbs Klages malt
2 lbs Munich malt
8 oz chocolate malt
12 oz honey (added to the boil

Hops
. 5 oz Willamette hops (5.4%) for 45 min
. 5 oz Willamette hops (5.4%) for 30 min

Other
6 oz fresh ginger (peeled
1 tsp whole cloves
1 tsp ground allspice

Yeast Ale yeast

Procedure Use Papazian's Step mash technique: 30 minutes at 130 degrees. 30 minutes at 155 degrees. Sparge with 175 degree sparge water. Collect about 6 gallons. Boil wort for one hour. Add 1/2 ounce. of Williamatte at 15 minutes. At 30 minutes, add: 1/2 ounce Williamette, ginger, orange zest, cloves, allspice, and cinnamon. Cool. Pitch yeast.

Xmas Merry Ale

Category Spiced Beers
Recipe Type Extract

Fermentables
4 1/4 Australian light extract, malt (liquid)

George Braun

. 5 lbs crystal malt
. 25 lbs chocolate malt
1/8 lbs flaked barley
. 5 cups brown sugar

Hops

2 1/2 Northern brewer hops
1 oz cascade (finishing)

Other

. 5 tsp cinnamon
1 tsp whole clove

Yeast Ale yeast

Procedure Add all the grain and malt into the water and boil. After it starts to boil, add Northern brewer and spices. After about 45 minutes, turn off heat, add the Cascade. After 20 minutes, filter into carboy. Pitch yeast when cool. Clarify and bottle in a week.

CHAPTER 7- ESB & STEAM BEER

Boonesburger Winterale

Category ESB
Recipe Type Extract

Twelve days in the bottle were sufficient. I prefer this over Widmer Festbier, after which it was patterned. It's also a lot cheaper.

Fermentables
5 lbs light, dry extract
3 lbs 2-row pale malt
. 5 lbs crystal malt (40L)
2 oz roasted barley
4 oz wheat malt
2 oz dextrin malt

Hops
2 oz Cascade hops (5.2% alpha)
. 5 oz Tettnanger hops (4.9% alpha)
. 5 oz Perle hops (7.2% alpha)
. 5 oz Kent Goldings hops (5.2% alpha)

Other
1 tsp Irish moss

Yeast 1 pack Wyeast Irish

Procedure I used Papazian's partial mash method, except used 2 gallons of sparge water. I got 18 pints of sparge and added two pints of water to the boil, along with the dry extract. Boil 60 minutes. Add 1 ounce Cascade, 1/4 ounce Perle, and 1/4 ounce Tettnanger at 40 minutes. Add 1/2 ounce Cascade, 1/4 ounce Perle, and 1/4 ounce Tettnanger

George Braun

at 30 minutes. Add 1/2 ounce Cascade, and 1/2 ounce Kent Goldings in hop bag for 3 minutes. Strain into primary fermenter. Transfer hops bag to primary.

Fullers ESB

Category ESB

Recipe Type All Grain

Fermentables

. 5 lb Crystal 60L - 90L

1 lb brown sugar, 60 minutes

Hops

. 5 oz Kent Golding, 30 minutes

. 5 oz Kent Golding, 5 minutes

1. 5 oz Kent Golding, dry hopped in secondary

2 oz Fuggles, 60 minutes

Yeast Wyeast London Ale (1028) yeast

Procedure There is no Fuggles in ESB or any of the Fullers beers. They use English Target, Challenger and North Down. EKG is in the finish & cask hopping of both Chiswick Bitter (very good bitter) and ESB. BTW the kettle hops are Lupofresh (challenger, 91) pellets from Kent and Worcester. They "Burtonize" the brewing water using mineral salts. A single temp infusion is employed. The ESB is 1.052 OG (apparently this was reduced for the US market, according to a brewer I was drinking within the Pub next door). I was told they used to use sugar, but this is no longer required with the new mash tuns. I missed out on the Maize part so I do not know, but I assume George has this correct. Try 5- 10 % in the mash. Skip the sugar, use caramel malts to get the color and sweetness.

Red Hook ESB

Category ESB

Recipe Type Extract

Fermentables
6 lbs light malt extract syrup
4 oz crystal malt (40L)
4 oz chocolate malt
4 oz roasted barley

Hops
1. 5 oz Northern Brewer Hops for Bittering
1 oz Cascade Hops for Finishing

Yeast ale yeast

Procedure I have also modified this as of late to increase the 'redness' in the ale by increasing the roasted barley and crystal malt to 6 oz and 10 oz respectively, while keeping the chocolate the same. I did the usual batch by adding the specialty grains in a grain bag until 170F and then adding half the bittering hops at 60 minutes and the other half at 30 minutes with the finishing at the end with a simmer/steep for 10 minutes without heat and covered

Sour Mash

Category Sour Mash
Recipe Type All Grain

Fermentables
5 lbs 2--row Klages (mash @ 158 for 14 hours)
10 lbs wheat malt
10 lbs 2--row Klages (infusion mash @155 for 1--1/2 hours)
2 lbs wheat malt

Hops
2 oz Centennial hops (12% alpha)

George Braun

Other
. 5 oz coriander (freshly crushed, added to fermenter)

Yeast yeast

Procedure Notes: I sour 1/2 (one half) of the mash, the high % wheat half, the other is straight infusion. I do however make an effort to minimize heat loss by using an ice chest and sealing the lid with duct tape. If it smells rotten, it is OK. The bacteria at work are for the most part aerobic. If it looks bad, it's OK. After 14 hours no matter how bad you think you screwed up, it's OK, just see the thing through, it is worth it. Combine mashes for mash out @ 170F for 15 min. Sparge @ 170F. Boil for 75 minutes, then cool and split into two carboys. Pitch a Chimay culture into one and a Chico ale yeast into the other. Add 1/4 ounce freshly crushed coriander to each. After 7 days fermentation, blend the two batches together in a larger vessel. Ferment 7 days longer. Keg with 1/4 cup corn sugar per 5 gallons. Counter pressure bottled after 2 weeks.

Sourdough Beer

Category Sour Mash
Recipe Type Extract

Fermentables
2.75 lbs hopped light extract
. 5 lbs pale malt
2 oz crystal malt (40 L.)
2 oz wheat malt
1. 5 cups sourdough starter (wheat flour

Hops
. 5 oz Hallertauer hops

Yeast ale yeast

Procedure Dissolved extract in hot water, cooled and added starter. Let rest covered for 24 hours. Crushed and mashed grains. Poured liquid off sourdough sediment and strained into the wort. Boiled 1 hour and added hops at 40 minute mark. (Foul smelling boil!). Cooled and added ale yeast. Ferment as usual Desert Storm American Steam Beer
Category Steam Beer
Recipe Type All Grain

Fermentables
5 lbs Klages lager malt
4 lbs Pale Ale malt
1 lbs crystal malt (40 or 60 deg Lovibond)

Hops
1. 5 oz Northern Brewer (alpha 8.0)
1. 5 oz Hallertauer (alpha 4.1)

Other
. 5 tsp Irish moss

Yeast MeV High Temp Lager liquid yeast

Procedure Mash grains for 25 minutes at 125 degrees and 90 minutes at 150 degrees. Mash-out for 10 minutes at 168 degrees. Sparge. Bring to boil and add Northern Brewer hops. Boil 60 minutes. At the last minute toss in Hallertauer. Cool. Pitch yeast.

Frahnkensteam

Category Steam Beer
Recipe Type Extract

George Braun

Fermentables
1 cup English 2-row pale malt
1 cup Crystal Malt, 60L
1 cup Crystal Malt, 120L
6 lbs light M&F dried malt extract
. 75 cup corn sugar for priming

Hops
1. 5 oz Northern Brewer hop pellets (alpha = 6. 5 ; 50
1 oz Northern Brewer hops pellets (1 min.)

Other
. 5 tsp Irish Moss (15 min.)

Yeast Wyeast #2035 American Lager yeast (cultured from a previous

Procedure Toasted pale malt in a 375 degree oven for 20 minutes. Cracked it along with the crystal and steeped in 2 quarts of 150-175 degree water for 20 minutes. Sparged with approx. 1 gallon of water. Dissolved DME in sparge water plus cold water to make 3 and 1/2 gallons. Boiled for 60 min., adding hops and Irish Moss for indicating times. Chilled with a 2-gallon ice block and 20 degree outdoor temps. Racked off hot/cold break, topped up to 5 gallons, pitching a 2-3 cup starter at about 90 degrees. IBUs approximately 37. Single-stage fermentation for 14 days; bottled with 3/4 cup priming sugar. F.G. = 1.022, a little high, but fermentation was definitely done.

Ginger Steamer

Category Steam Beer
Recipe Type Extract

Fermentables

6 lb unhopped Amber liquid extract
1 lb 120L Carmel Malt
1/2 lb Victory Malt (25L) (Oven Toasted at 350F for 15 min)
1/2 lb Double Malt (45L)

Hops
. 5 oz Cascade (15 min left)
. 5 oz Cascade (7 min left)
1 oz Chinook 13.6 % (Boil)
. 5 oz Cascade (2 min steep)
. 5 ounce Cascade (dry hop in secondary)

Other
1 oz fresh Ginger indiscriminately put in the last few minutes of the boil (15 min left)

Yeast Wyeast's California yeast

Not-So-Sweet Beer (Steam)

Category Steam Beer
Recipe Type Extract

Fermentables
6.6 lbs M&F amber extract
. 25 lbs toasted barley
.25 lbs crystal malt

Hops
1-3/4 oz Northern Brewer hops

Yeast Vierka lager yeast

George Braun

Procedure Steep toasted and crystal malts. Boil wort with hops for 45 minutes. Chill and pitch. Age in carboy for 2 weeks

Ole Bottle Rocket (Steam)

Category Steam Beer
Recipe Type Extract

Fermentables
6 lbs light dry malt extract
. 5 lbs toasted malt

Hops
. 75 oz Northern Brewer hops pellets (boil)
. 25 oz Northern Brewer hops pellets (finish)

Yeast 1 pack lager yeast

Procedure Toast grains on a cookie sheet in 350 degree oven for about 10 minutes. Crush malt as you would grain. Put in 1-1/2 gallons water and bring to boil. Strain out grain. Add extract and boiling hops. In last 2 minutes of boil, add finishing hops. Add in enough water to make 5 gallons and pitch yeast.

Southside Steam Beer
Category Steam Beer
Recipe Type All Grain

Fermentables
8 lbs Klages malt
1 lbs light Munich malt
. 5 lbs 10L Crystal malt
. 25 lbs 40L Crystal
.25 lbs 80L Crystal

Hops
2 oz Northern Brewer Hops (Whole) (7. 5 % a)

Other
1 tbsp Irish Moss

Yeast Wyeast #2112 California Lager yeast in 1/2 gallon starter

Procedure Mash in at 130F.
Protein rest at 122. (30 minutes)

Starch conversion at 150. (1 hour)

Mash-out at 166 F. (30 minutes)

Sparge at 170.

Add 1/2 ounce of Northern Brewer for boil, another 3/4 ounce and Irish moss after 30 minutes. In last 5 minutes of boil, add 3/4 ounce of Northern Brewer. Chill and pitch yeast.

Steam Beer

Category Steam Beer
Recipe Type All Grain

Fermentables
9. 5 lbs Klages malt
1. 5 lbs Crystal malt 40L
. 5 lbs Cara Pils malt

Hops
2. 5 oz Northern Brewer whole hops

George Braun

Yeast Wyeast #2007

Procedure Using a standard mash

Procedure: Protein rest of 30 minutes at 125 degrees. Raise temperature to 155 degrees and hold for 90 minutes or until starch is converted. Sparge to collect enough that a 1 hour boil will still leave you 5 gallons of beer (brewing -- art or science?). Bring wort to boil. Add 1-1/2 ounces of Northern Brewer at beginning, 1/2 ounce at 30 minutes and 1/2 ounce for the last ten minutes.

Chapter 8- Porter

Anchor Porter Clone

Category Porter
Recipe Type Partial Mash
I made a porter last year that was loosely based on Miller's partial mash

Fermentables
4 lb British pale ale 2-row malt
1 lb black patent malt
. 5 lb dark crystal malt
3.3 lbs M&F extra light syrup

Hops
12.8 AAU Northern Brewer (boil)

Yeast Wyeast #1084 the Fighting Irish

Procedure Mash all grains together in a single infusion at 150F using 1-1/3 quarts water per pound of grain. Sparge with 11 quarts water, dissolve syrup, and add water to make 6-1/2 or 7 gallons. Boil 1 hour, using all the hops. Chill, aerate, pitch, etc. Gravities were 1.055 and 1.016. I used a two-step starter on the Wyeast, and did a secondary on the beer. 18 days from boil to bottle (this was in November).

Brewhaus Porter

Category Porter
Recipe Type All Grain

Fermentables
8 lbs 2-row Klage malt

George Braun
1 lbs crystal malt (90 Lovibond)
1 lbs dextrin malt
. 5 lbs chocolate malt
. 5 lbs, black malt
. 75 cup corn sugar (priming)

Hops
1-1/3 oz Northern Brewer hop pellets (8. 5 % pellets)
. 5 oz Fuggle hop pellets (3.7% alpha)

Other
. 5 tsp gypsum
Lactic acid to adjust the mash water to pH 5.2
1 tsp Irish Moss
1 tsp gelatin finings

Yeast Ale yeast (High Temp. Ale Yeast)

Procedure Mash grains in 11 quarts of mash water at 152 degrees for two hours, or until conversion is complete. Sparge with 170 degree water to collect 6 gallons. Bring wort to a boil and let boil for 15 minutes before adding the 1-1/3 ounces Northern Brewer hops. Boil for one hour. Add Irish moss. Boil 30 minutes. (1 hour, 45 minutes total boiling time). Cut heat, add aromatic hops and let rest for 15 minutes. Force cool wort to yeast pitching temperature. Transfer cooled wort to primary fermenter and pitch yeast starter. Fine with gelatin when fermentation is complete. Bottle with 3/4 cup corn sugar boiled in one cup water.

Chocolate Point Porter

Category Porter
Recipe Type Extract

Fermentables

7 lbs unhopped extract syrup
1 lbs chocolate malt
. 5 lbs black patent malt
. 5 lbs crystal malt (90 degrees L.)

Hops
1. 5 oz Cascade hops (boil)
. 5 oz Cascade hops (finish)

Other
. 5 lbs Sumatra decaf coffee

Yeast yeast

Procedure Place chocolate, patent, and crystal malts in about 2 gallons of water and bring to almost boil, Sparge into boiling pot. Add 2 more gallons of water. Bring to boil and add bittering hops. 30 minutes into the boil, add 1/2 teaspoon Irish moss. Boil one more hour. Add finishing hops in last 2 minutes of boil. Pour into fermenter and add coffee. Pitch yeast.
Submitted by: Doug Roberts

Clean Out The Closet Porter

Category Porter
Recipe Type Extract

Fermentables
1 can Ironmaster Scottish Mild Ale extract
1 can Bierkeller light lager extract
1 lbs crushed crystal malt
1 lbs Munton & Fison Light DME

Hops
1 oz Brewer's Gold hop pellets
1 oz Cascade hop pellets

Other
. 5 cup Lactose

Yeast 1 package Whitbread dry ale yeast

Procedure Standard

Procedure---put crystal malt in cold water, heat to just shy of boil and sparge into brew pot. Add malt extracts and water, bring to boil. Add Brewer's Gold hops, boil a little over 1 hour. Stop boil, add Cascade hops and chill on the way into fermenter. I tossed the dry yeast directly into the fermenter atop the cooled wort.

David Smith's Porter

Category Porter
Recipe Type Extract

Fermentables
3.3 lbs John Bull dark extract
3.6 lbs light Australian dry malt
1 lbs, black patent malt (coarsely crushed)
. 75 cup corn sugar (priming)

Hops
2 oz Cascade hops
. 5 oz Tettnanger hops
1 oz Tettnanger hops (finish)

Yeast 1 pack Edme ale yeast

Procedure Add crushed black patent malt to 1-1/2 gallons cold water. Bring to boil. (This recipe was made by boiling malt for 10 minutes, however, conventional wisdom is to avoid boiling whole grains). Strain out the malt. Add extract and dry malt and Cascade and 1/2 ounce Tettnanger hops. Boil 60 minutes. Add finishing hops and boil 1 minute. Remove from heat and steep 1-2 minutes. Sparge into 3-1/2 gallons cold water. Cool and pitch yeast.

Dextrinous Porter

Category Porter
Recipe Type All Grain

Fermentables
8 lbs Munton & Fison 2-row pale malt
1. 5 lbs crystal malt
. 25 lbs chocolate malt
.25 lbs black patent malt
. 5 lbs flaked barley

Hops
1 oz Willamette hops (boil)
. 5 oz Cascade hops (boil)
. 5 oz Cascade hops (finish)

Yeast yeast

Procedure Mash grains. Add boiling hops and boil 90 minutes. Dry hop with 1/2 ounce Cascade

Extract Porter

Category Porter
Recipe Type Extract

Fermentables
3.3 lb M&F Dark Extract
4 lbs Alexander's Pale Extract
. 5 lb M&F Dark DME
1 lb Crystal Malt (90L)
. 5 lb Black Patent

George Braun
. 5 lb Dark Roast

Hops
1 oz. Willamette (Alpha=4. 2) 60 min Boil
1 oz. Willamette (Alpha=4. 2) 2 min Boil/Steep

Yeast Wyeast 1028

Procedure Steep specialty grains separately.

Fissuring' Porter

Category Porter
Recipe Type Extract

Fermentables
3 1/3 lb Northwestern Gold Extract Syrup
3 1/3 lb Northwestern Amber Extract Syrup
1 lbs. lb. DARK brown sugar
. 75 lbs. b. Crystal Malt (approx 60 deg.)
. 5 lbs. b. Chocolate Malt

Hops
9 HBU Bittering hops. boiled 60 minutes. I used:
. 5 oz 4.8% Tettnang pellets
. 5 oz 7.7% N. Brewer pellets
. 5 oz 5.8% Kent Golding pellets

Foggy Day Jumpin' Java

Category Porter
Recipe Type Extract

Fermentables
6.00 lbs. lb. Dark Dry Malt Extract
1.00 lbs. lb. Crystal 40L
0. 5 0 lb. lb. Roast Barley
0.25 lbs. lb. Black Patent

1.00 lbs. lb. Honey

Hops
1. 5 0 oz. Northern Brewer 7. 5 % 40 min
2.00 oz. Hersbrucker 2.9% 10 min
2. 5 0 oz. Cascade 6.1% 10 min steep

Other
2-3 CUP fresh-brewed espresso (yes, that's right!)
2 tsp gypsum
1 tsp Brewer's Salts
. 25 tsp Irish Moss, 20 min. boil

Yeast ale yeast

Procedure Crack the specialty grains; Partial mash with grain bag in 2 gal cold water; raises the temp. to 155 F for 45 min.; sparge into brew pot with 1 gal 170 water; bring to boil & add malt; bring to boil again and add Northern Brewer hops; boil for 30 min.; add Hersbrucker hops and boil 10 min.; add Cascade hops, honey and espresso, steep for 10 min. and chill. Strain to fermenter; add water to make 1 gal., pitch started yeast at 78; ferment @ 64-68. Transfer to secondary fermenter after 7 days; let sit in secondary to clarify at least 3 weeks. Bottle with 1/4 cup honey. Age at least *2* months. Patience, they say, *is* a virtue!

Gak & Gerry's #23: Anteater Porter

Category Porter
Recipe Type All Grain
Deep red color. Looks almost black in the fermenter.

Fermentables
7. 5 lbs pale malted barley
1 lbs crystal malt (10 Lovibond)

George Braun
. 5 lbs chocolate malt
2 oz black patent malt

Hops
11.4 grams Cascade - 10 min.
13.7 grams Cascade - finish

Other
41.3 grams Cluster - boil

Yeast Wyeast British

Procedure Add grains to 3. 5 gallons cold water. Heat to 150 degrees and maintain for 90 minutes, stirring constantly. Used 4. 5 gallons 170 degree sparge water. Collected 6 gallons wort. Boiled 60 minutes. Add Cluster at beginning of boil. Add 11.4 grams Cascade at 50 minutes. Turn off heat after 1 hour boil, and let the last of Cascade hops steep. Cooled to about 75 degrees and pitched.

Hell Gate Porter

Category Porter
Recipe Type Extract

Fermentables
6 lb Dark LME
1 lb Amber or Dark DME
1 lb 80-90L Crystal
. 5 cups Black Patent
1 c. Blackstrap Molasses
. 5 c. Honey

Hops
1 oz Cascade (60 min)
1 oz Northern Brewer (30 Min)
. 5 oz Cascade (30 min)

.5 oz Cascade (15 min)
.5 oz Tettnanger (2 min)
.5 oz Tettnanger (steep w/out boil)

Yeast Wyeast London Ale #1028

Procedure Steep grains.
60 min. boil.
hops to above schedule
misc. ingredients added at 45 min
Cool
pitched about a 20 oz. starter
Primary @ room temp (68 F) 10 days
Secondary @ same 8 days
Bottled with 1 c. corn sugar.
Drank after 1 week. YUM!

Historic Porter

Category Porter
Recipe Type All Grain

Fermentables
9.7 lb EDME pale malt
0.75 lb British crystals (~60L)
4 lb California concentrates light extract

Hops
1.6 oz Nuggett (14. 5 %) @ 60 minutes
1 oz Goldings (5.7%) @ 5 minutes
0.2 oz Willamette (? %) @ 5 minutes

Yeast Wyeast #1007 European

Procedure The high kilned malts were selected as what I had left over from a previous experimental series of beers, not by any deductive process.

George Braun

This was fermented rather warm for 5 days with WYeast 1007 (European). It was then transferred to a 5 and a 1 gallon fermenter with the following dry hops proportioned up: .4 oz Goldings (5.7%).2 oz Willamette (4.8%). The 1 gallon fermenter also received some of Yeast Lab's Brettanomyces lambicus.

The 5 gallon was bottled after 16 more days, the 1 gallon after 45 days, at which time it had some odd, hard-looking white colonies on top. FG's were 27 and 26 (+/-2) respectively.

Shelley's Honey Porter

Category Porter

Recipe Type Extract

This was posted in response to a request for a Sam Adams Honey Porter clone.

Fermentables

. 5 lbs. black patent malt crushed

. 5 lbs. chocolate malt crushed

1 lb. medium crystal malt crushed

6 lbs. amber malt syrup

3 lbs. light honey

Hops

1 oz. Perles - boiling (60 minutes)

. 5 oz. Fuggles - boiling (30 minutes)

. 5 oz. Fuggles - finishing (5 minutes)

Yeast Wyeast 1084 "Irish Ale"

Procedure Steep the crushed specialty grains from cold up to 160-170F and remove. Bring water to boil, turn off the heat before adding the malt extract to avoid scorching. Bring back to a boil and add boiling hops, after 30 minutes add the flavor hops, and at 55 minutes the finishing hops. Optionally add 1 tsp. Irish Moss at 45 minutes into the boil to help the break. Remove from heat, cool to 70F, transfer to carboy topping up to 5 gallons, and pitch yeast.

Barb's Honey Porter

Category Porter
Recipe Type All Grain

Fermentables
2 lbs Aroma Malt
5 lbs. British Pale
5 lbs. Vienna
2 cups Cara-Pils 40L
1 2/3 cup Chocolate Malt
8 oz. Malto-Dextrin
6 lbs. Honey

Hops
2 oz. Hallertaur Hops (Boil- 3.9% AAU)
2 oz. Brewers Gold (Finish- 8.9% AAU)

Other
1 tbsp. gypsum

Yeast AMERICAN WYEAST 1056

Procedure Single Infusion Mash, with treated water stabilized at 150 degrees for 1 hour. Mash out at 168 degrees. Sparge, SLOWLY, collect 6 gallons of wort. Bring to boil. Boil wort, and Malto-Dextrin. Every 15 minutes, add Hallertaur hops, for 1 hour, last 15 minutes, add honey, and all of the Brewers Gold hops. Cool wort to 75-90 degrees. Aerate wort adds Wyeast

Maple Porter

Category Porter
Recipe Type Extract

Fermentables
7 lbs. of liquid amber extract
0. 5 lbs. of chocolate malt
0. 5 lbs. of black patent malt
24 oz of grade A maple syrup (amber)
1-1/4 cups dry malt extract (priming)

Hops
1 oz of Northern Brewer hops (boiling)
0. 5 oz of Fuggles hops (boiling)
1 oz of Tettnanger hops (finishing)

Yeast Wyeast British ale yeast

Procedure Start warming 2 gal of water and add grains - "stew" them for 20 min or so.
Remove grains and bring water to a boil, adding extract and boiling hops. Add finishing hops for last 5 minutes of boil.
Add water to 5 gals. total (after cooling) and pitch yeast. I used a Wyeast British ale.
Transfer to secondary and add maple syrup. Ferment to completion, prime with 1 1/4 cups of dry malt extract, and bottle.
I am not sure if there will be enough maple taste with only 24 oz of syrup, so I may add addition syrup after testing it before bottling.

Maple Porter

Category Porter

Recipe Type Extract

Fermentables
6.6 lbs. unhopped light malt extract syrup
2 lbs. light dry malt extract
0.25 lbs. black malt
0. 5 lbs. roasted malt
10 oz. chocolate malt
0.75 lb. Caramel (crystal) malt, (50-60L)
16 oz. maple syrup

Hops
1. 5 oz. Northern Brewer hops

Yeast Wyeast 1098

Procedure Add the crushed grain in a grain bag to 1. 5 gallons of water in the kettle. Bring to a boil. Remove the grain just before boil begins. Add the extract and bring to a rolling boil. Add hops, and boil for one hour. Pour in maple syrup two minutes before the end of boil. Strain the wort into a fermenter containing 3. 5 gallons of cold water. Top up the fermenter to 5 gallons. Pitch the yeast and wait for the goodness

March Hare Honey Porter

Category Porter
Recipe Type Extract

Fermentables
6.6 lbs Premiere Light Malt Extract (hopped)
1 lb 40L crystal malt
1 lb chocolate malt
3 lbs honey
. 75 cup corn sugar

George Braun

Hops
1 oz cascade hops

Other
1 table gypsum

Yeast WYeast American Ale #1056

Procedure I brought 1 gal of water to 170 degrees F with both specialty grains in a muslin bag, removed from heat, and let it steep for 2 hrs. I then sparged the grain with 1. 5 gals hot water. Added all ingredients (except the yeast and hops), brought to a boil, and let it cook for 2 hrs. Removed from heat and added hops in a boil bag. Cooled, removed the hop bag, poured to primary, brought to 6 gal volume, and added yeast @ 80 degrees F.

Partial Mash Porter

Category Porter
Recipe Type Partial Mash

Fermentables
3 lbs 2-row pale lager malt
10 oz black patent malt
6 oz crystal malt
4 lbs Australian dark extract
. 5 cup corn sugar (priming)

Hops
11 AAUs Northern Brewer hops

Yeast Doric yeast

Procedure Mash-in (6 quarts water) at 131-122 degrees, stir 3 minutes. Adjust pH to 5.0-5. 5 (using calcium carbonate or gypsum). Protein rest 131-120 degrees for 30 minutes. Starch conversion 155 degrees for 60 minutes. Mash out at 168 degrees for 5 minutes. Sparge with 2 gallons of 168-160 degree water. Bring liquid to boil and add extract and hops. Boil 60 minutes.

Paul's Chocolate Porter

Category Porter
Recipe Type Extract

Fermentables
1 can dark John Bull malt extract syrup
1 can amber John Bull extract syrup
. 5 lbs. black patent malt
. 5 lbs. crystal malt
1 lbs. Dextrose (corn sugar)

Hops
1 oz. cascade hops (boiling)
1 oz. cascade hops (flavor)

Other
4 oz. cocoa

Yeast ale yeast

Procedure Add dextrose to 2 c. hot water. When dissolved, add cocoa. Bring this to a boil and stir while boiling for five minutes. Set aside.
Crack crystal malt and add to 1. 5 gallons water. Bring to a boil and remove crystal malt with strainer. Add malt extract syrups, cocoa syrup, and boiling hops. Boil for 45-60 min.

George Braun
During last 1-2 min. of boil, add finishing hops to wort. Pour hot wort into fermenter containing cold water. Add enough cold water to bring to five gallons. Pitch yeast when cool, ferment, and bottle as usual.

Deborah's Porter

Category Porter
Recipe Type Extract

Fermentables
1 can Munton & Fison dark hopped extract
.5 can Edme bitters kit
1 stick brewers licorice
.5 lbs toasted barley
1 lbs flaked barley

Hops
2 oz Cascade hops pellets
1 oz Northern Brewer hops pellets

Yeast Edme ale yeast

Procedure Make toasted barley into a tea. Bring flaked barley to boil. Sparge with kitchen strainer and boiling water. Boil extracts and Cascade hops. Add Northern Brewer. Cool and Pitch.

Porter? Porter?

Category Porter
Recipe Type Extract

Hops
1 oz Styrian Goldings plugs (alpha 5.3) (1 hour boil)
1 oz Hallertauer plugs (alpha 2.9) (10 minute boil)

Other

6.6 lbs Telford's porter (2 cans)

Yeast Wyeast #1056

Procedure Add the 2 cans of malt extract to 3 gallons boiling water, bring the mix back to a boil, then add Bittering Hops. I used a hop bag, so the utilization probably wasn't that terrific, but then again the malts are pre-hopped some, so I wasn't too concerned about that. Add finishing hops with 10 min left in the boil. Add tap water to 5 gallons, cool to 75F and pitch yeast starter (~12oz). Lag time is about 12 hours.

CHAPTER 9- SMOKED BEER

Brewhaus Golden Lager
Clubhouse Smoked Porter

Category Smoked Beer
Recipe Type All Grain

Fermentables
8 lbs M&F 2--row lager malt
2 lbs hickory smoked M&F 2--row pale malt
1 lbs Munich malt
1 lbs crystal malt
. 5 lbs chocolate malt
. 5 lbs black malt
. 5 lbs cara-pils malt

Hops
1 oz (about 30 IBU) Northern Brewer hop plugs (boil 60
1 oz Cascade leaf hops (finishing

Yeast Wyeast #1028 London Ale yeast

Procedure The smoked grain was done on a charcoal fired smoker with wet hickory chips. The total smoking time was close to 45 minutes. I would have cut the smoking time down, but I wet the grain first and it took that long for it to dry on the smoker. Struck mash at about 120F for protein rest. Pulled a single decoction, brought to a boil, held for about 10 minutes, and re-infused to raise temperature to about 155F which was held in a 5 gallon Igloo cooler until the conversion was complete. Sparged with 4--1/2 gallons of 170F water. Yielded about 7 gallons of wort. Total boil time was about 70 minutes. Chill and pitch starter. After 5 days in primary, I racked to a keg and refrigerated.

Peach Smoked Porter Recipe

Category Smoked Beer
Recipe Type All Grain

Fermentables
3 lbs smoked 2-row pale malt, using Peach Wood & smoked as described below
7 lbs 2-row malt
. 5 lb Black Patent Malt
. 5 lb Med Crystal
. 25 lb Chocolate Malt

Hops
. 25 oz Goldings 5% - 30 minutes
. 25 oz Goldings - Finish

Other
1 oz N. Brewer 7. 5 % - 60 minutes

Yeast Liquid Wyeast 1056 starter

Procedure Here is my smoking method with a backyard smoker. The smoker is similar to a grill, but has a higher level for the smoking items and a tray in between the heat source and smoking item, that holds water. The water produces steam that keeps the grain moist throughout the smoking. I cut 1/2" pieces of wood from 2" diameter branches, then soak the wood for 20 minutes. The wood pieces and then placed on top of hot charcoal, which produces smoke very quickly. Then the grains are placed on a stainless steel screen on the smoker rack & smoked for about 1 hour.

George Braun
(Low on hops for more smoke flavor character).

Single step Infusion Mash at 154 for 90 minutes.
Warning: This beer disappears very quickly when friends are around. For Extract batches, the smoked & specialty grains can be steeped up to 170 for 45 min.
This should produce a beer in the 1050's for starting gravity.

Rauchbier

Category Smoked Beer
Recipe Type Extract

Fermentables
6 lbs light malt syrup
1 lbs smoked pale malt
1 lbs smoked crystal malt
.5 lbs wheat malt
.5 lbs pale malt

Hops
.5 oz Hallertauer hops (10 minute boil)

Yeast Wyeast Pilsen lager yeast (#2007?)

Procedure The pale malt and crystal malt is soaked and then smoked over hickory for about 30 minutes. (See the 2nd version of Papazian's book for an all-grain recipe.

ABOUT THE AUTHOR

George Braun is an experienced and respected brewer. With his in-depth knowledge and years of experience in beer brewing, he loves to help other brewers make great beer and expand their knowledge while enjoying the adventure at the same time. He always speaks from personal experience , humbly including any mistakes he has made to help others avoid making them too. He is a real treat to read.

If you would like to have ALL of **George Braun's** secret recipes collection, go ahead and pick-up his other book:

189 Best Beer Brewing Recipes:
Brewing the World's Best Beer at Home
Book 2